CHAPTER 1

MEETING MY GIRLFRIEND

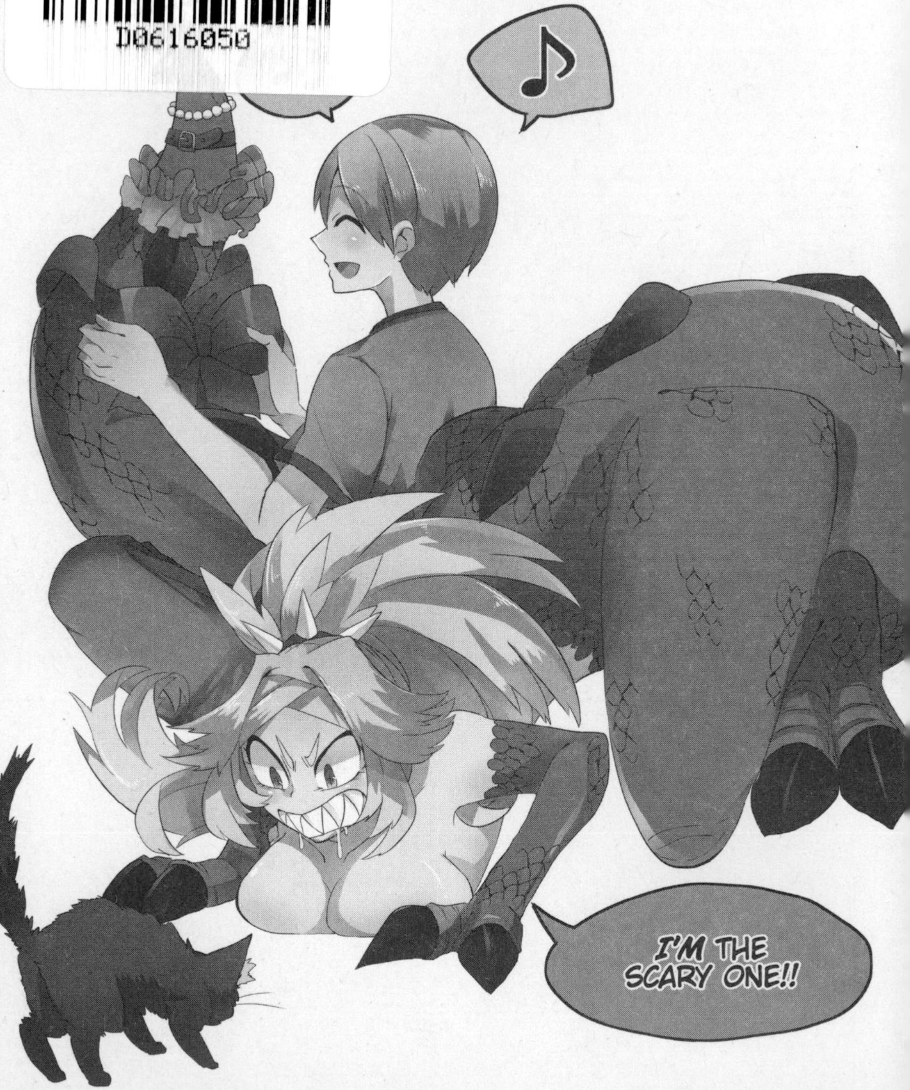
♪
I'M THE SCARY ONE!!

MODERN DINOSAUR'S CIRCUMSTANCES

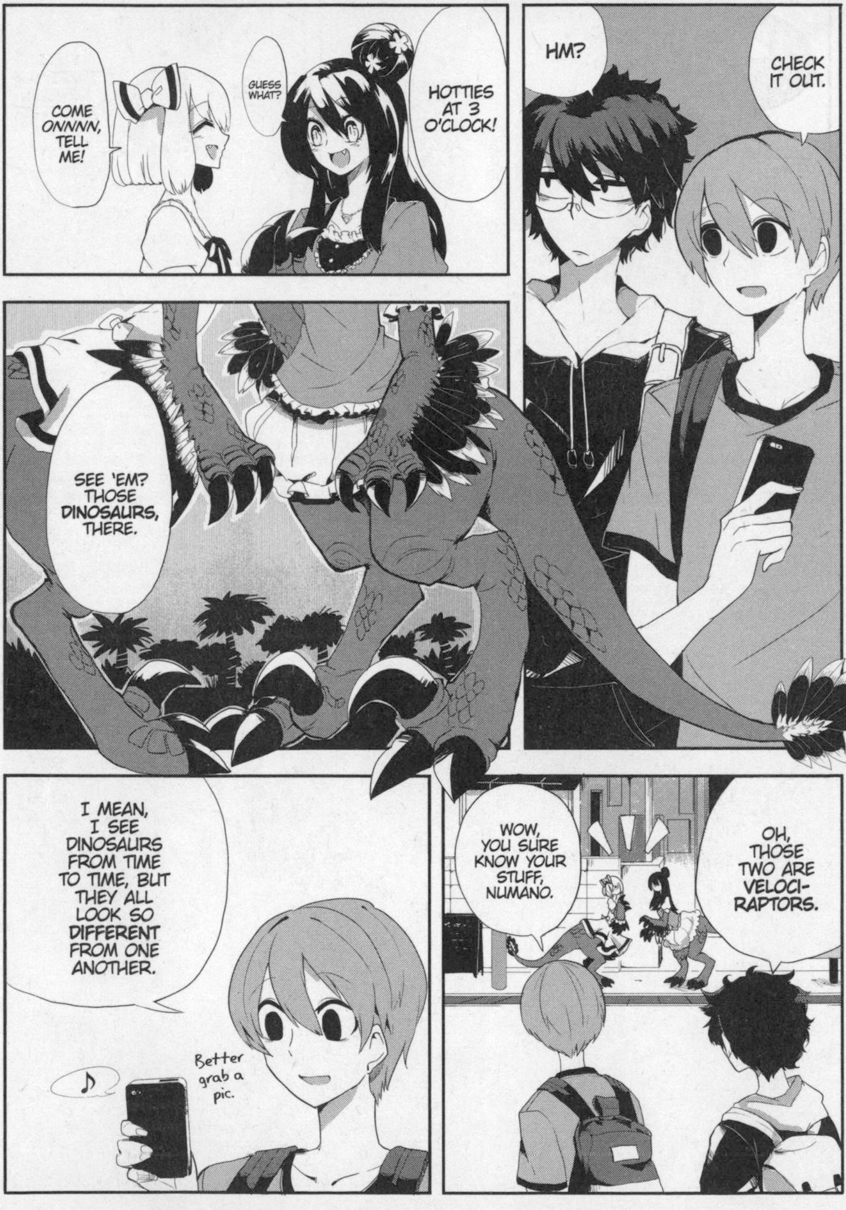

CHECK IT OUT.
HM?
HOTTIES AT 3 O'CLOCK!
GUESS WHAT?
COME ONNNN, TELL ME!
SEE 'EM? THOSE DINOSAURS, THERE.
OH, THOSE TWO ARE VELOCI-RAPTORS.
WOW, YOU SURE KNOW YOUR STUFF, NUMANO.
I MEAN, I SEE DINOSAURS FROM TIME TO TIME, BUT THEY ALL LOOK SO DIFFERENT FROM ONE ANOTHER.
Better grab a pic.
♪

My Girlfriend is a T-REX

Story & Art:
SANZO

1

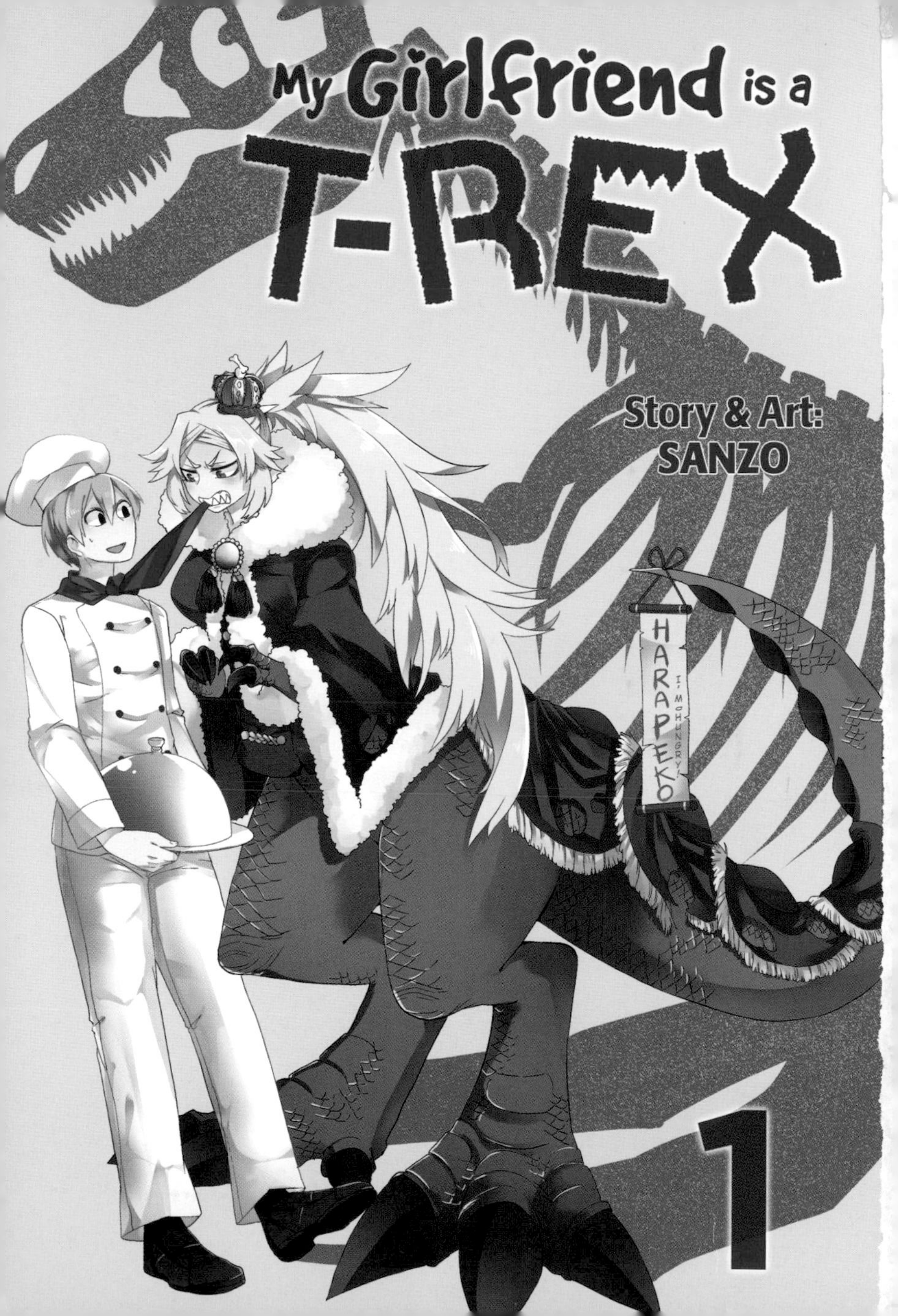
HARAPEKO
I'M HUNGRY!

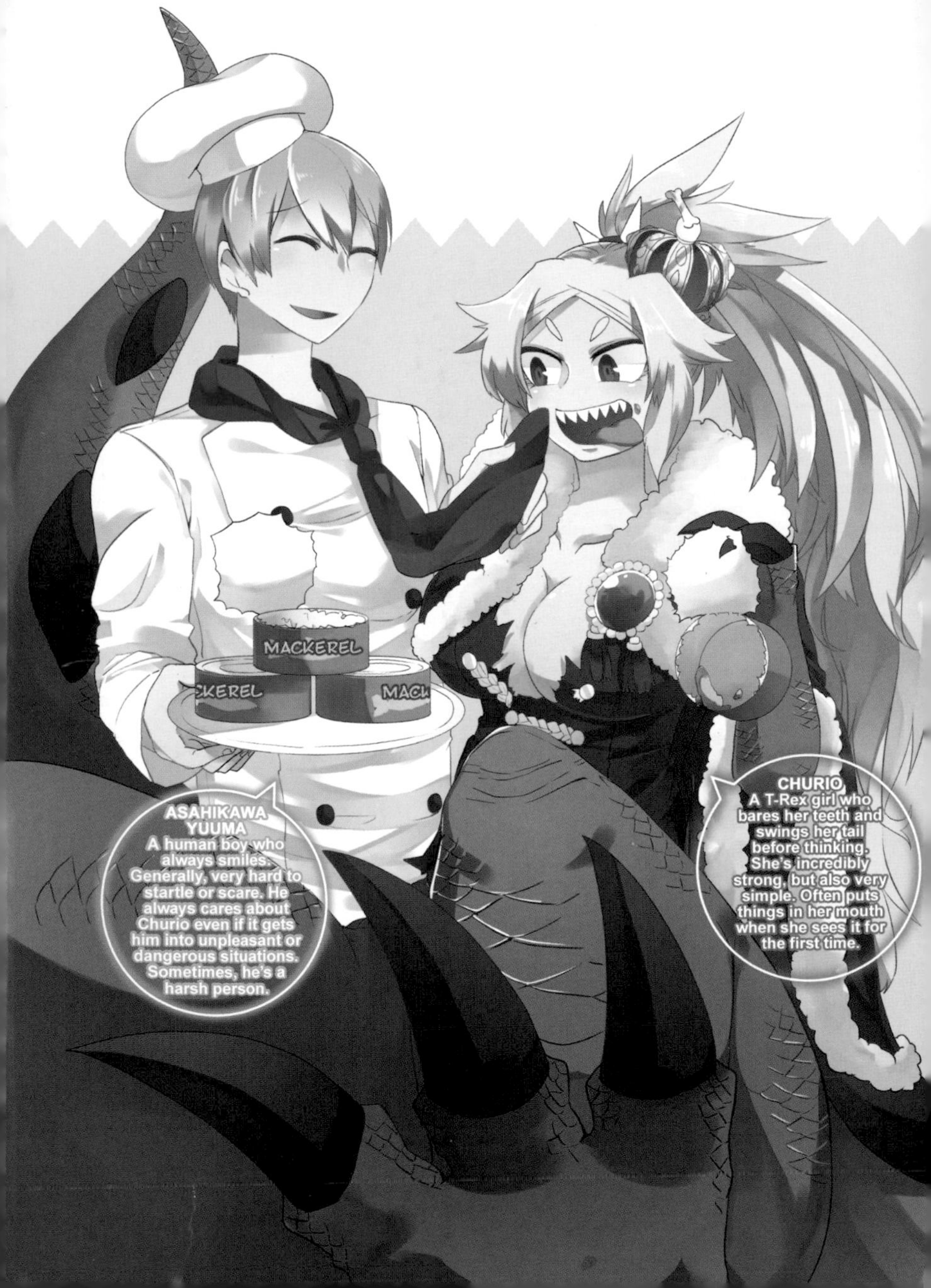
MACKEREL
MACKEREL
MACK
CHURIO
A T-Rex girl who bares her teeth and swings her tail before thinking. She's incredibly strong, but also very simple. Often puts things in her mouth when she sees it for the first time.
ASAHIKAWA YUUMA
A human boy who always smiles. Generally, very hard to startle or scare. He always cares about Churio even if it gets him into unpleasant or dangerous situations. Sometimes, he's a harsh person.

My Girlfriend is a

T-REX

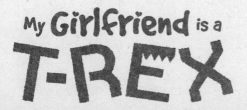

Snore...
Snoore...

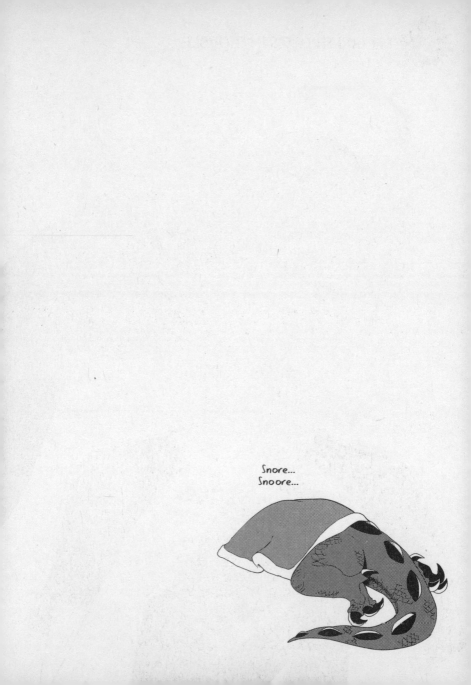

CHAPTER 3

MY GIRLFRIEND'S IN TROUBLE

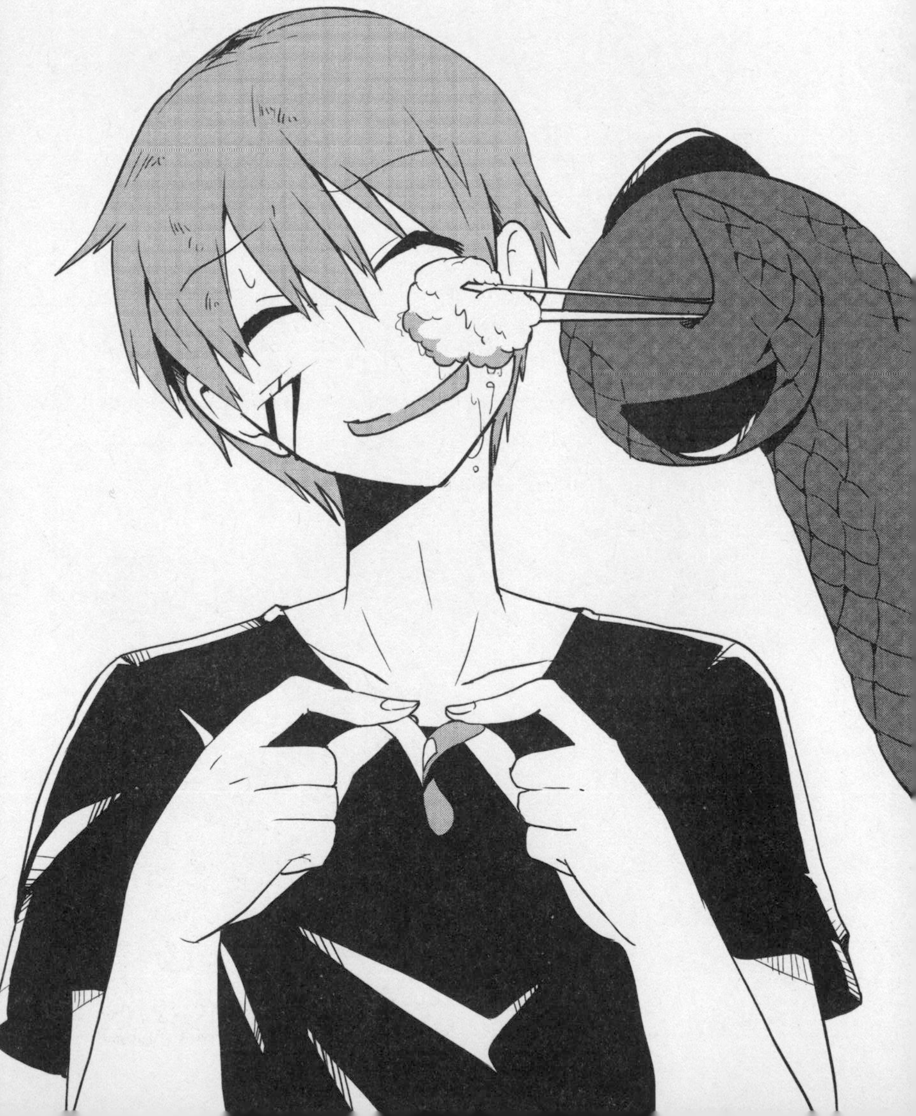

TROUBLE

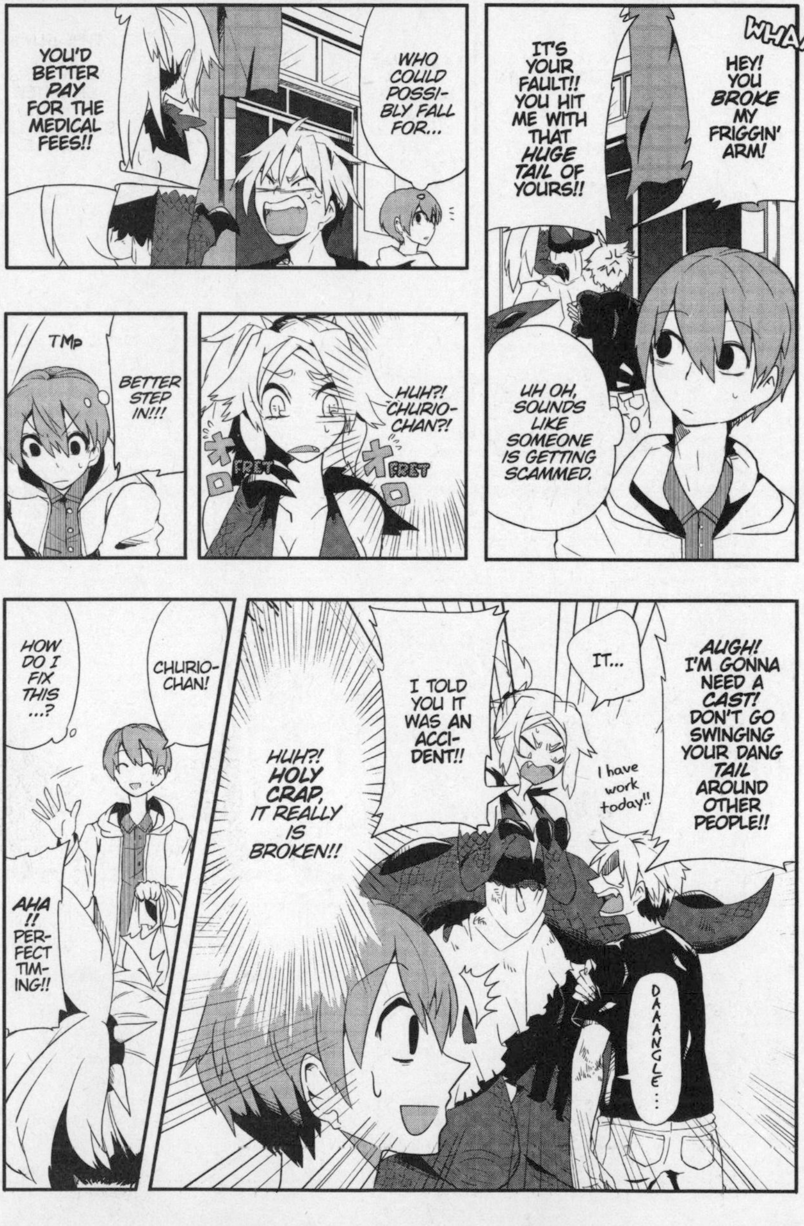
WHAM
HEY! YOU BROKE MY FRIGGIN' ARM!
IT'S YOUR FAULT!! YOU HIT ME WITH THAT HUGE TAIL OF YOURS!!
UH OH, SOUNDS LIKE SOMEONE IS GETTING SCAMMED.
WHO COULD POSSIBLY FALL FOR...
YOU'D BETTER PAY FOR THE MEDICAL FEES!!
HUH?! CHURIO-CHAN?!
FRET
FRET
BETTER STEP IN!!!
TMP
AUGH! I'M GONNA NEED A CAST! DON'T GO SWINGING YOUR DANG TAIL AROUND OTHER PEOPLE!!
IT...
I have work today!!
I TOLD YOU IT WAS AN ACCIDENT!!
HUH?! HOLY CRAP, IT REALLY IS BROKEN!!
DAAANGLE...
CHURIO-CHAN!
HOW DO I FIX THIS...?
AHA!! PERFECT TIMING!!

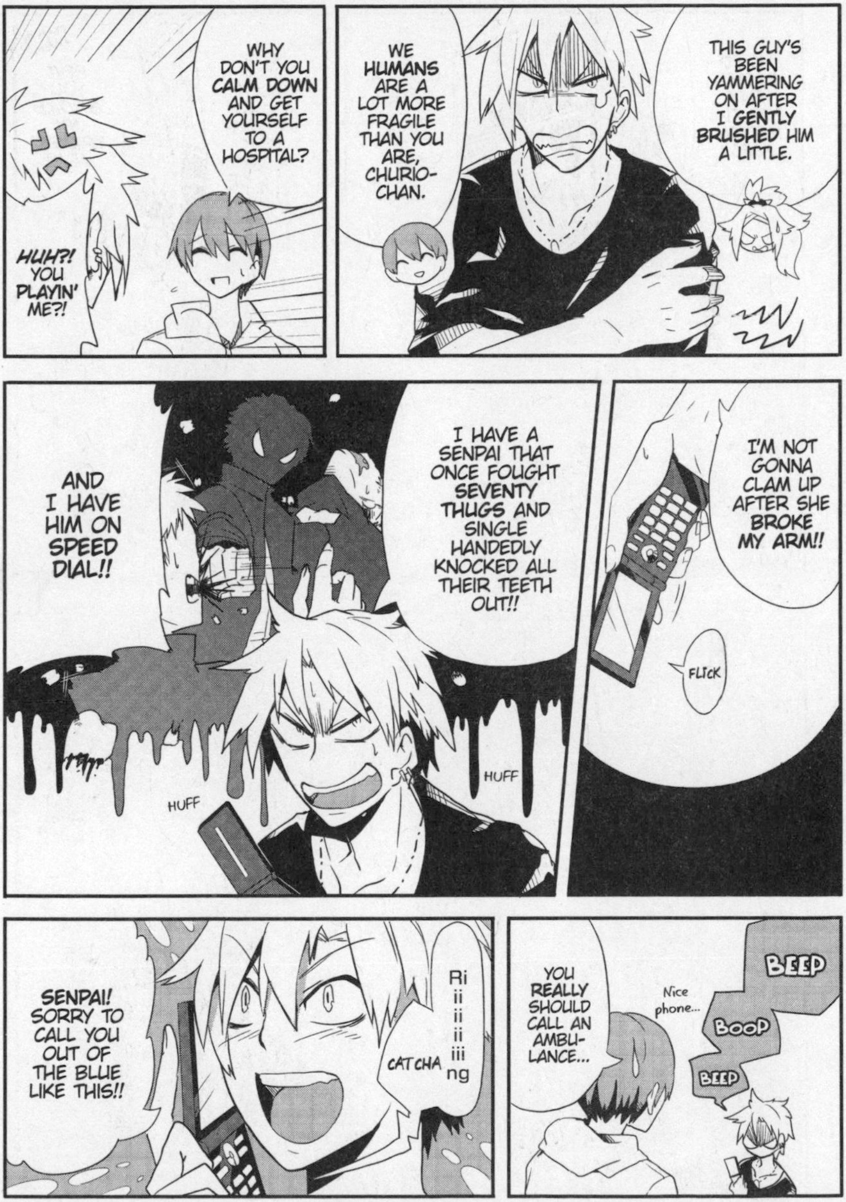
THIS GUY'S BEEN YAMMERING ON AFTER I GENTLY BRUSHED HIM A LITTLE.
WE HUMANS ARE A LOT MORE FRAGILE THAN YOU ARE, CHURIO-CHAN.
WHY DON'T YOU CALM DOWN AND GET YOURSELF TO A HOSPITAL?
HUH?! YOU PLAYIN' ME?!
I'M NOT GONNA CLAM UP AFTER SHE BROKE MY ARM!!
FLICK
I HAVE A SENPAI THAT ONCE FOUGHT SEVENTY THUGS AND SINGLE HANDEDLY KNOCKED ALL THEIR TEETH OUT!!
AND I HAVE HIM ON SPEED DIAL!!
HUFF
HUFF
BEEP
Nice phone...
BOOP
BEEP
YOU REALLY SHOULD CALL AN AMBULANCE...
Riiiiiiiing
CATCHA
SENPAI! SORRY TO CALL YOU OUT OF THE BLUE LIKE THIS!!

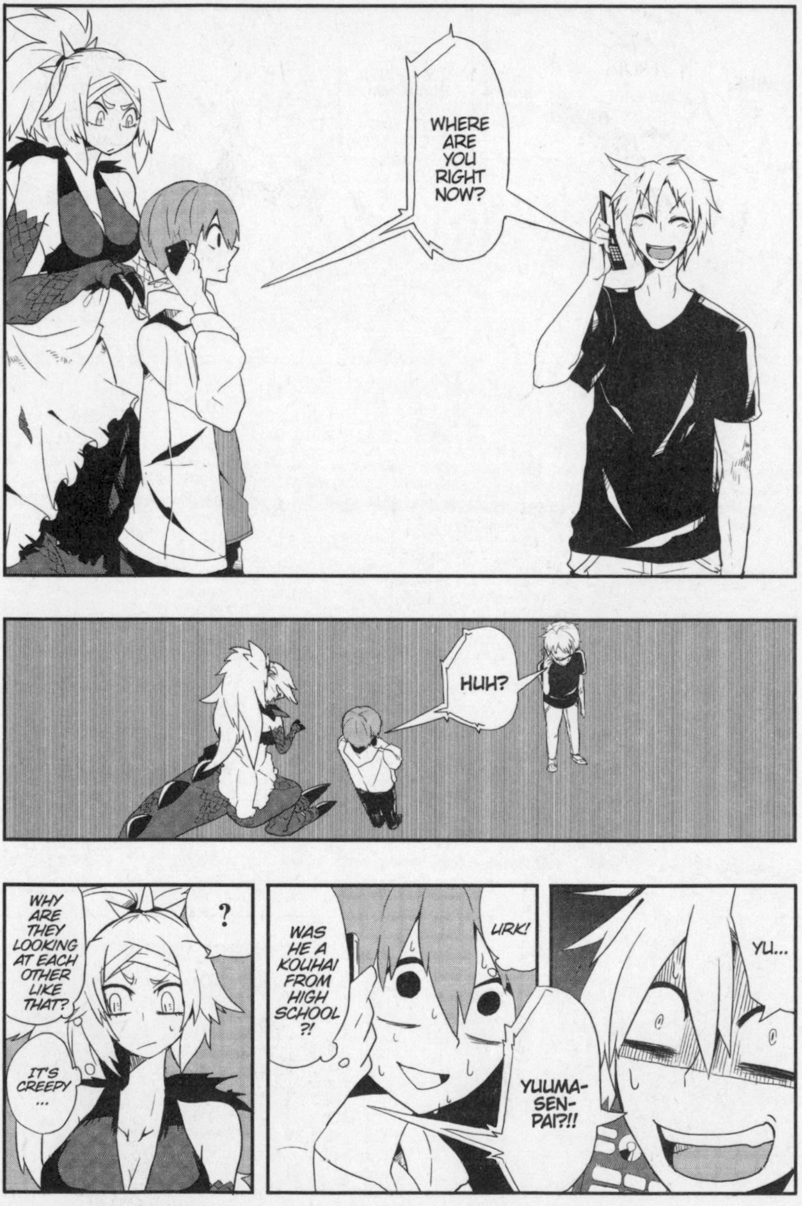
WHERE ARE YOU RIGHT NOW?
HUH?
YU...
YUUMA-SENPAI?!!
URK!
WAS HE A KOUHAI FROM HIGH SCHOOL?!
?
WHY ARE THEY LOOKING AT EACH OTHER LIKE THAT?
IT'S CREEPY...

QUELLING

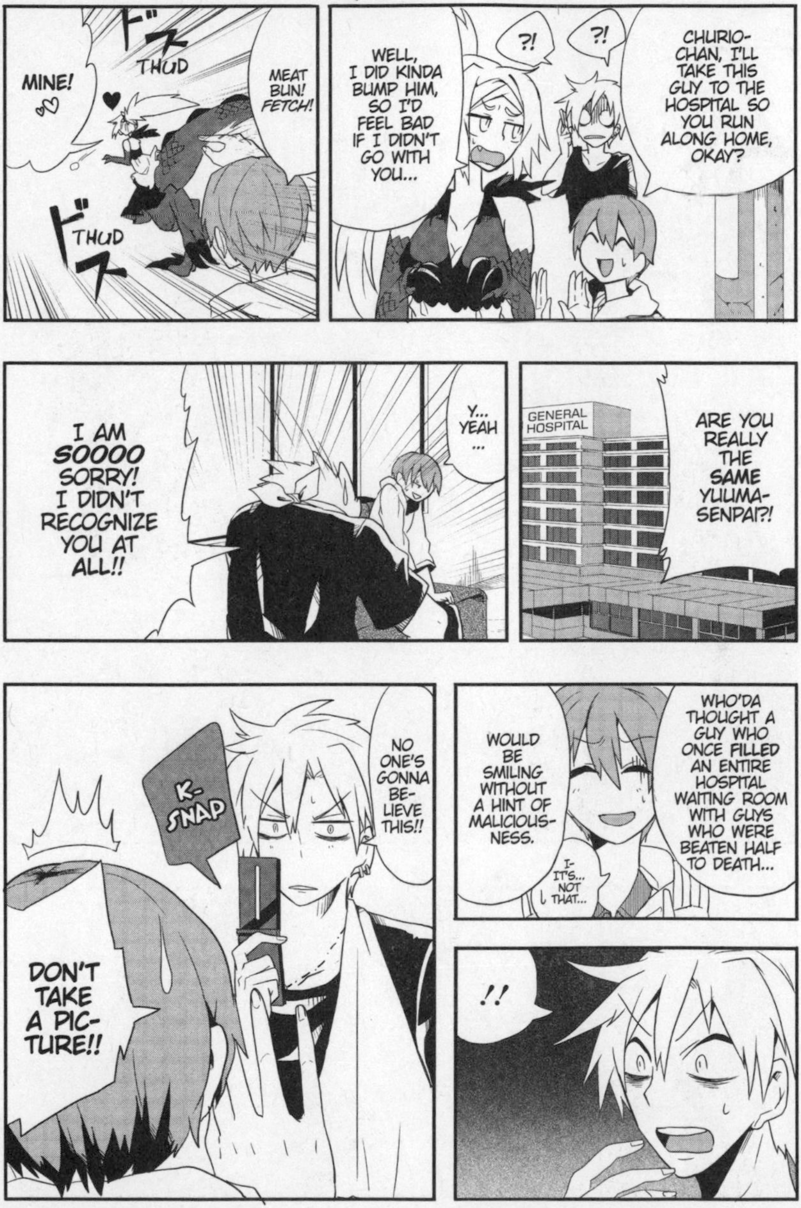
?!
?!
CHURIO-CHAN, I'LL TAKE THIS GUY TO THE HOSPITAL SO YOU RUN ALONG HOME, OKAY?
WELL, I DID KINDA BUMP HIM, SO I'D FEEL BAD IF I DIDN'T GO WITH YOU...
MEAT BUN! FETCH!
ドス
THUD
MINE! ♥
ドス
THUD
GENERAL HOSPITAL
ARE YOU REALLY THE SAME YUUMA-SENPAI?!
Y... YEAH...
I AM SOOOO SORRY! I DIDN'T RECOGNIZE YOU AT ALL!!
WHO'DA THOUGHT A GUY WHO ONCE FILLED AN ENTIRE HOSPITAL WAITING ROOM WITH GUYS WHO WERE BEATEN HALF TO DEATH...
WOULD BE SMILING WITHOUT A HINT OF MALICIOUS-NESS.
I-IT'S... NOT THAT...
!!
NO ONE'S GONNA BE-LIEVE THIS!!
K-SNAP
DON'T TAKE A PIC-TURE!!

UNREWARDED

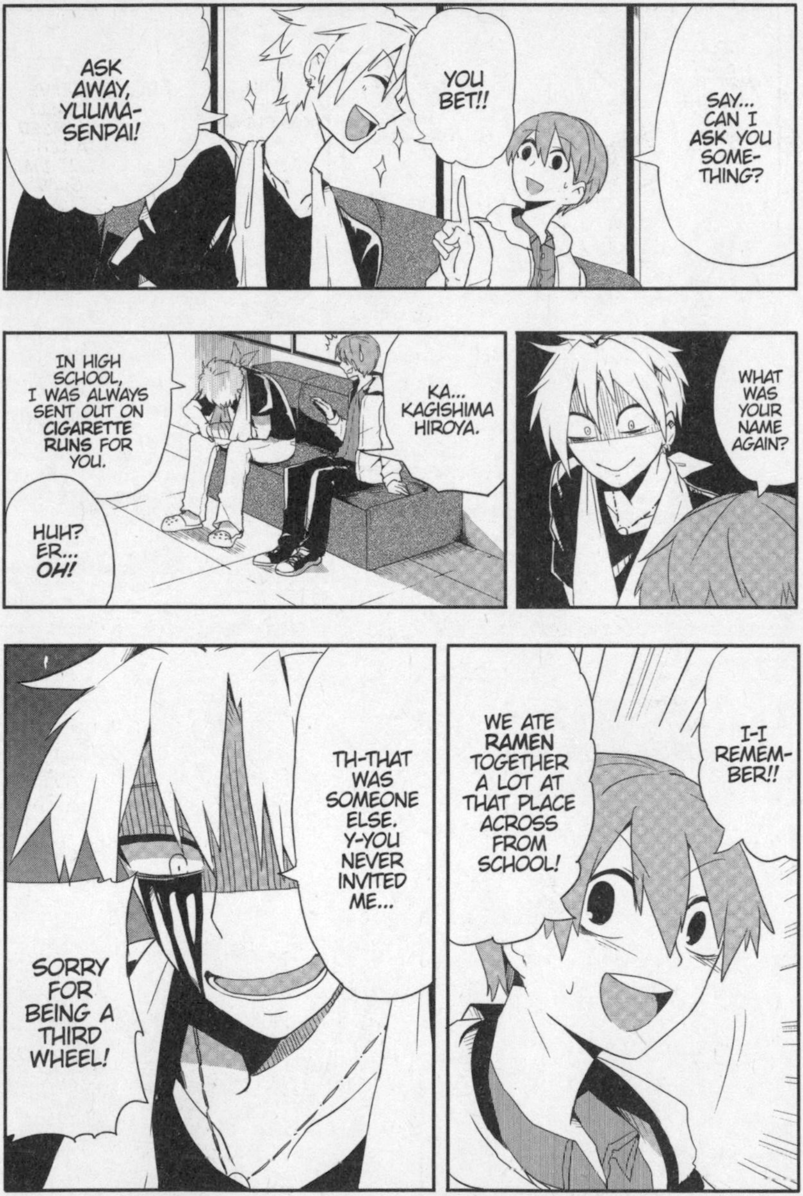
SAY... CAN I ASK YOU SOME-THING?
YOU BET!!
ASK AWAY, YUUMA-SENPAI!
WHAT WAS YOUR NAME AGAIN?
KA... KAGISHIMA HIROYA.
IN HIGH SCHOOL, I WAS ALWAYS SENT OUT ON CIGARETTE RUNS FOR YOU.
HUH? ER... OH!
I-I REMEM-BER!!
WE ATE RAMEN TOGETHER A LOT AT THAT PLACE ACROSS FROM SCHOOL!
TH-THAT WAS SOMEONE ELSE. Y-YOU NEVER INVITED ME...
SORRY FOR BEING A THIRD WHEEL!

SETTLEMENT

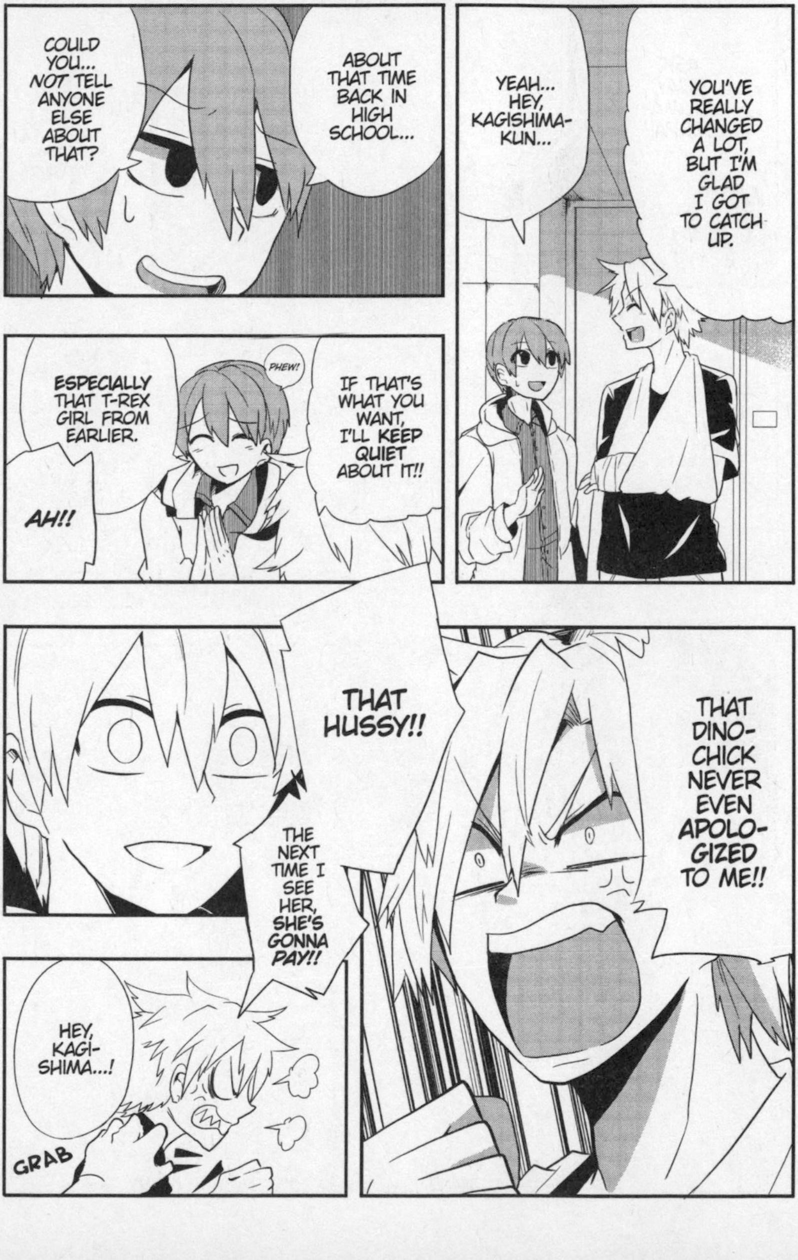
YOU'VE REALLY CHANGED A LOT, BUT I'M GLAD I GOT TO CATCH UP.
YEAH... HEY, KAGISHIMA-KUN...
ABOUT THAT TIME BACK IN HIGH SCHOOL...
COULD YOU... NOT TELL ANYONE ELSE ABOUT THAT?
IF THAT'S WHAT YOU WANT, I'LL KEEP QUIET ABOUT IT!!
PHEW!
ESPECIALLY THAT T-REX GIRL FROM EARLIER.
AH!!
THAT DINO-CHICK NEVER EVEN APOLOGIZED TO ME!!
THAT HUSSY!!
THE NEXT TIME I SEE HER, SHE'S GONNA PAY!!
HEY, KAGI-SHIMA...!
GRAB

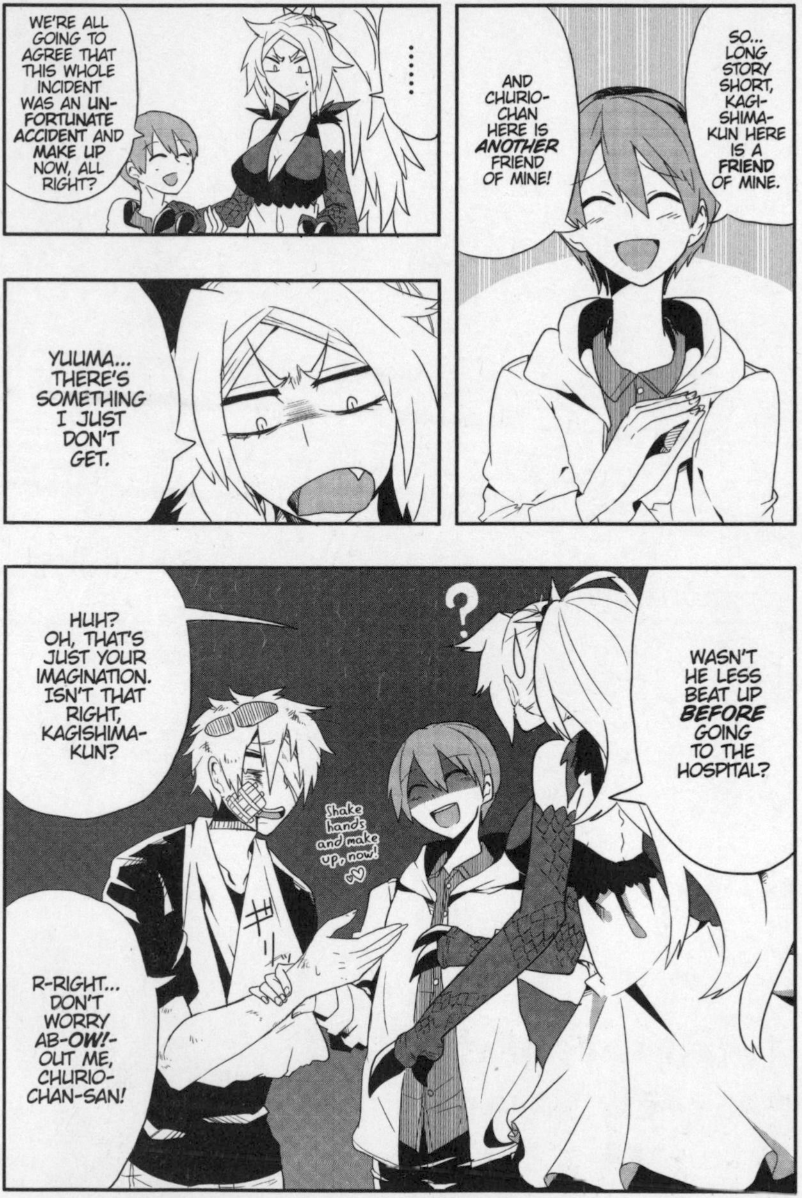
SO... LONG STORY SHORT, KAGISHIMA-KUN HERE IS A FRIEND OF MINE.
AND CHURIO-CHAN HERE IS ANOTHER FRIEND OF MINE!
......
WE'RE ALL GOING TO AGREE THAT THIS WHOLE INCIDENT WAS AN UNFORTUNATE ACCIDENT AND MAKE UP NOW, ALL RIGHT?
YUUMA... THERE'S SOMETHING I JUST DON'T GET.
WASN'T HE LESS BEAT UP BEFORE GOING TO THE HOSPITAL?
HUH? OH, THAT'S JUST YOUR IMAGINATION. ISN'T THAT RIGHT, KAGISHIMA-KUN?
Shake hands and make up, now!
R-RIGHT... DON'T WORRY AB-OW!-OUT ME, CHURIO-CHAN-SAN!

My Girlfriend is a

T-REX

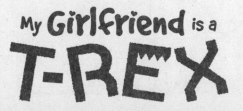

M'hungry!!

CHAPTER 4

MY GIRLFRIEND GIRL TALKS

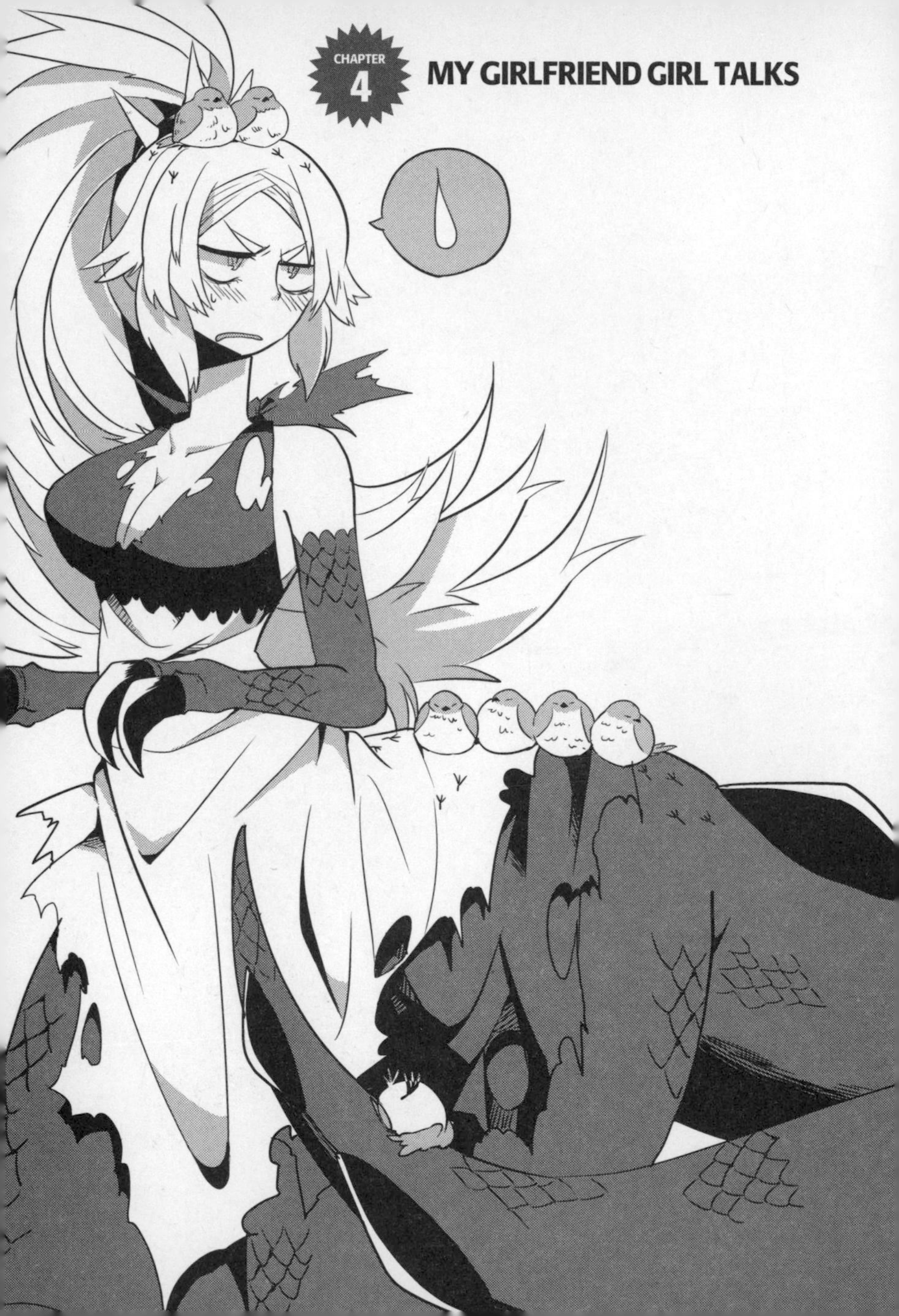

CHURIO AND TORIKA 1

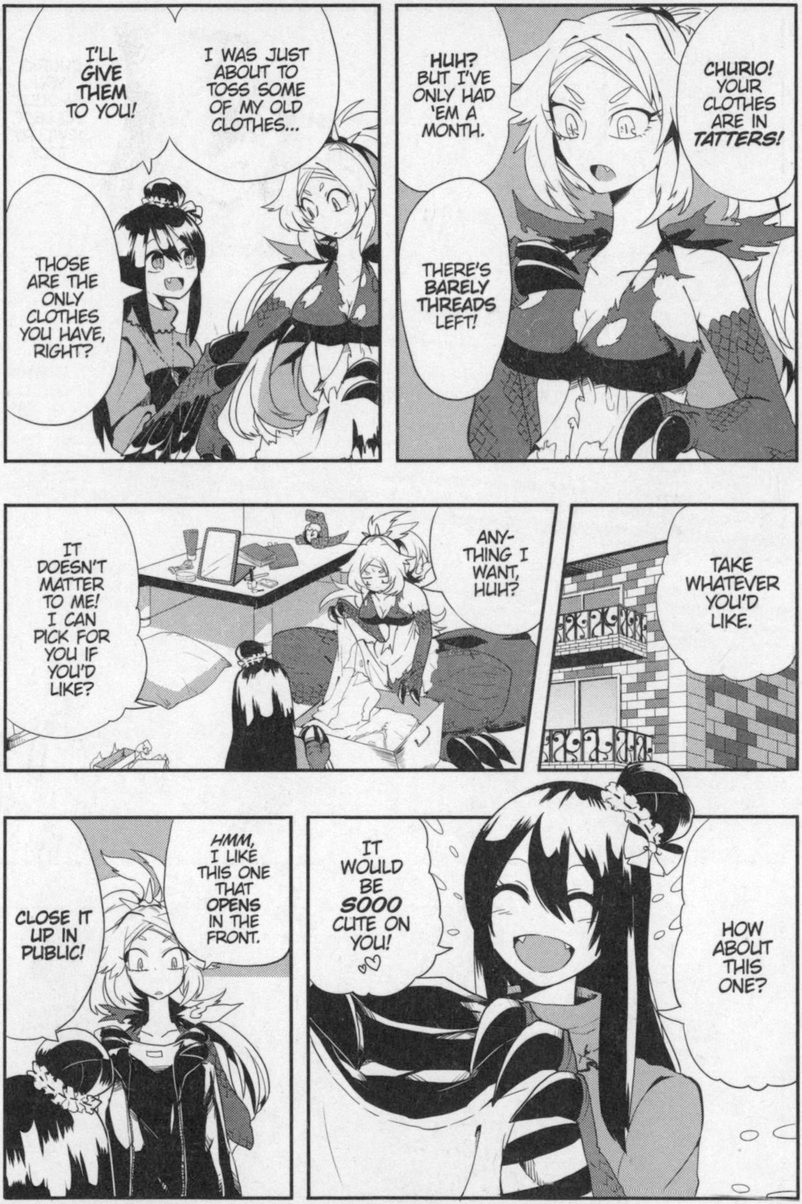
CHURIO! YOUR CLOTHES ARE IN TATTERS!
HUH? BUT I'VE ONLY HAD 'EM A MONTH.
THERE'S BARELY THREADS LEFT!
I WAS JUST ABOUT TO TOSS SOME OF MY OLD CLOTHES...
I'LL GIVE THEM TO YOU!
THOSE ARE THE ONLY CLOTHES YOU HAVE, RIGHT?
TAKE WHATEVER YOU'D LIKE.
ANY-THING I WANT, HUH?
IT DOESN'T MATTER TO ME! I CAN PICK FOR YOU IF YOU'D LIKE?
HOW ABOUT THIS ONE?
IT WOULD BE SOOO CUTE ON YOU! ♡
HMM, I LIKE THIS ONE THAT OPENS IN THE FRONT.
CLOSE IT UP IN PUBLIC!

CHURIO AND TORIKA 2

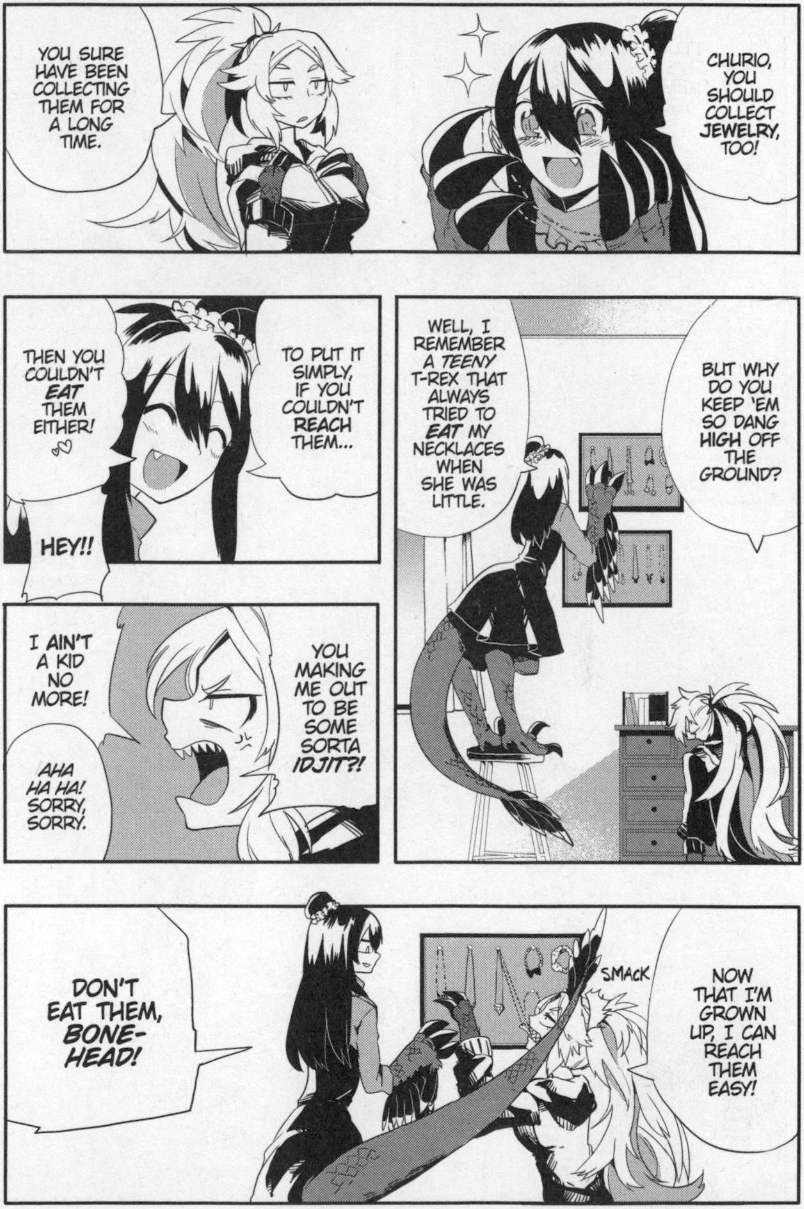

CHURIO, YOU SHOULD COLLECT JEWELRY, TOO!
YOU SURE HAVE BEEN COLLECTING THEM FOR A LONG TIME.
BUT WHY DO YOU KEEP 'EM SO DANG HIGH OFF THE GROUND?
WELL, I REMEMBER A *TEENY* T-REX THAT ALWAYS TRIED TO *EAT* MY NECKLACES WHEN SHE WAS LITTLE.
TO PUT IT SIMPLY, IF YOU COULDN'T REACH THEM...
THEN YOU COULDN'T *EAT* THEM EITHER! ♡
HEY!!
YOU MAKING ME OUT TO BE SOME SORTA *IDJIT?!*
I AIN'T A KID NO MORE!
AHA HA HA! SORRY, SORRY.
NOW THAT I'M GROWN UP, I CAN REACH THEM EASY!
SMACK
DON'T EAT THEM, *BONE-HEAD!*

GIRL POWER

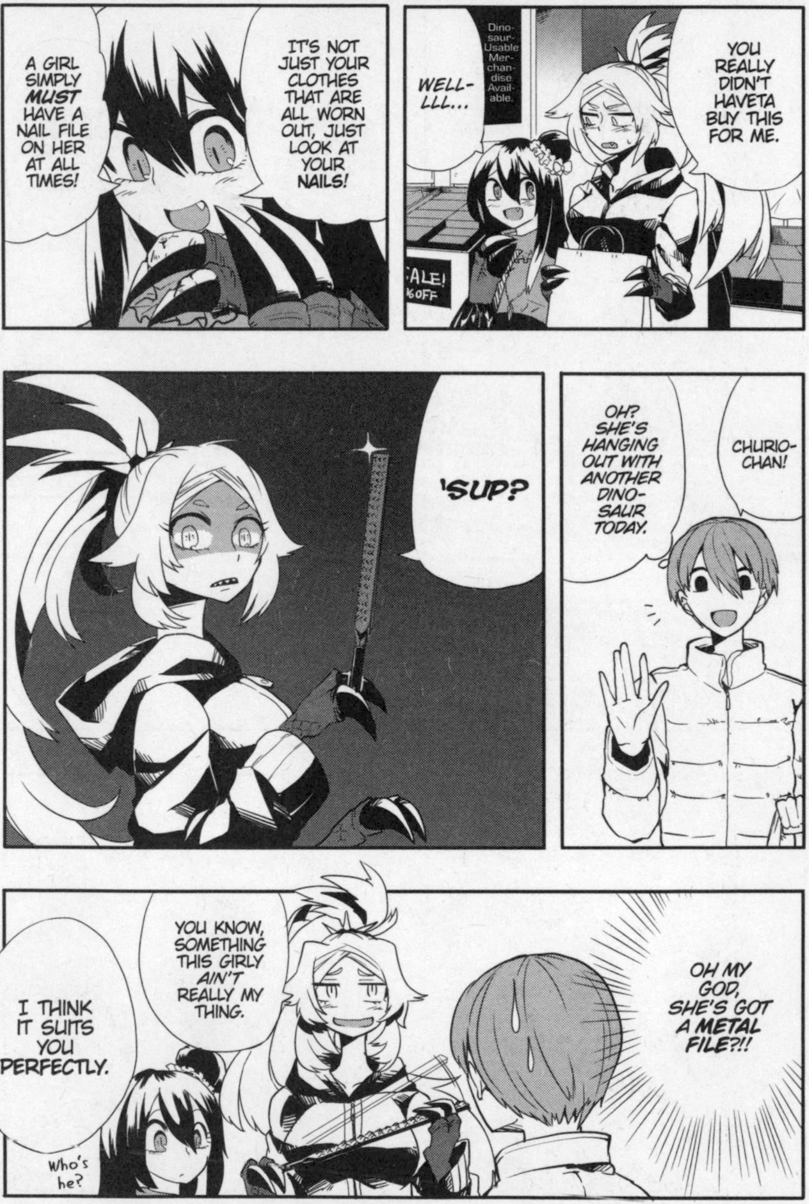
YOU REALLY DIDN'T HAVETA BUY THIS FOR ME.
Dinosaur-Usable Merchandise Available.
WELL-LLL...
IT'S NOT JUST YOUR CLOTHES THAT ARE ALL WORN OUT, JUST LOOK AT YOUR NAILS!
A GIRL SIMPLY *MUST* HAVE A NAIL FILE ON HER AT ALL TIMES!
CHURIO-CHAN!
OH? SHE'S HANGING OUT WITH ANOTHER DINOSAUR TODAY.
'SUP?
OH MY GOD, SHE'S GOT A *METAL* FILE?!!
YOU KNOW, SOMETHING THIS GIRLY *AIN'T* REALLY MY THING.
I THINK IT SUITS YOU PERFECTLY.
Who's he?

JEALOUSY

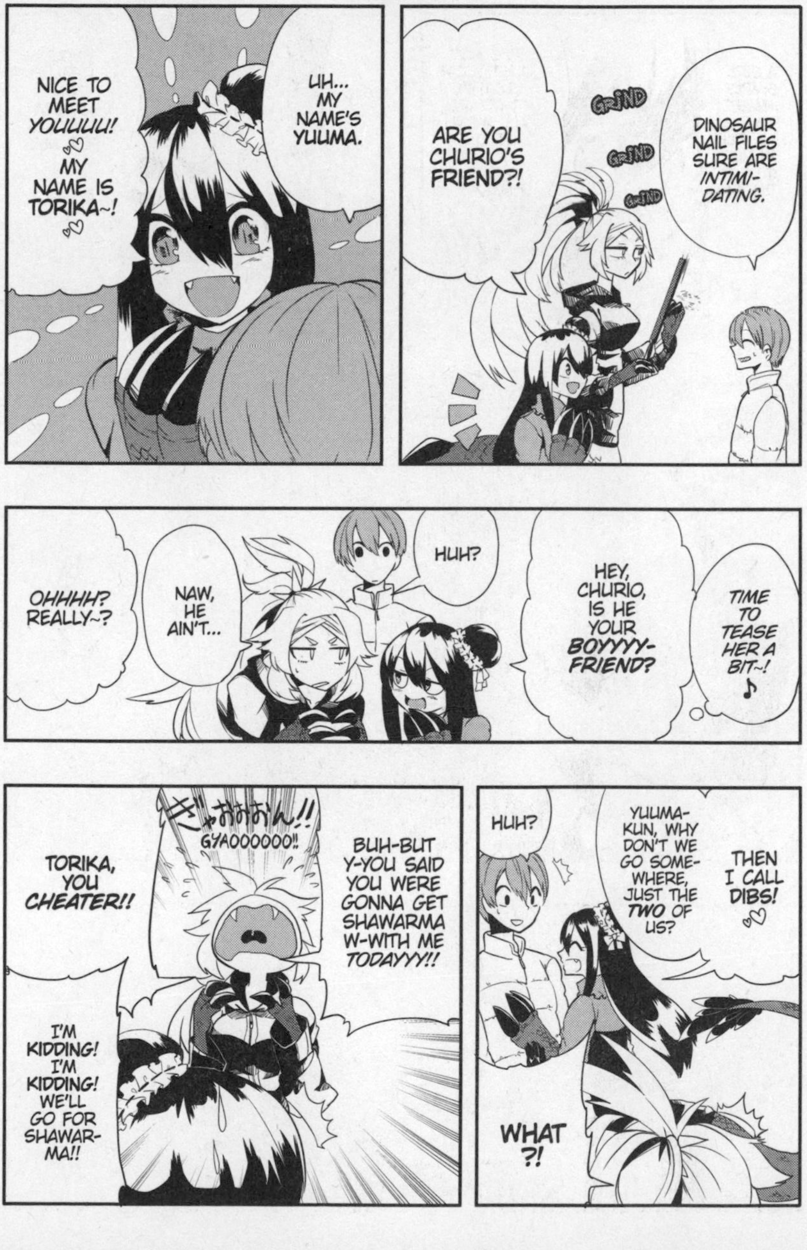

DINOSAUR NAIL FILES SURE ARE INTIMI-DATING.
GRIND
GRIND
GRIND
ARE YOU CHURIO'S FRIEND?!
UH... MY NAME'S YUUMA.
NICE TO MEET YOUUUU! ♡ MY NAME IS TORIKA~! ♡
TIME TO TEASE HER A BIT~! ♪
HEY, CHURIO, IS HE YOUR BOYYYY-FRIEND?
HUH?
NAW, HE AIN'T...
OHHHH? REALLY~?
THEN I CALL DIBS! ♡
YUUMA-KUN, WHY DON'T WE GO SOME-WHERE, JUST THE TWO OF US?
HUH?
WHAT?!
ぎゃおおおん!!
GYAOOOOOO!!
BUH-BUT Y-YOU SAID YOU WERE GONNA GET SHAWARMA W-WITH ME TODAYYY!!
TORIKA, YOU CHEATER!!
I'M KIDDING! I'M KIDDING! WE'LL GO FOR SHAWAR-MA!!

O.G. CUTE

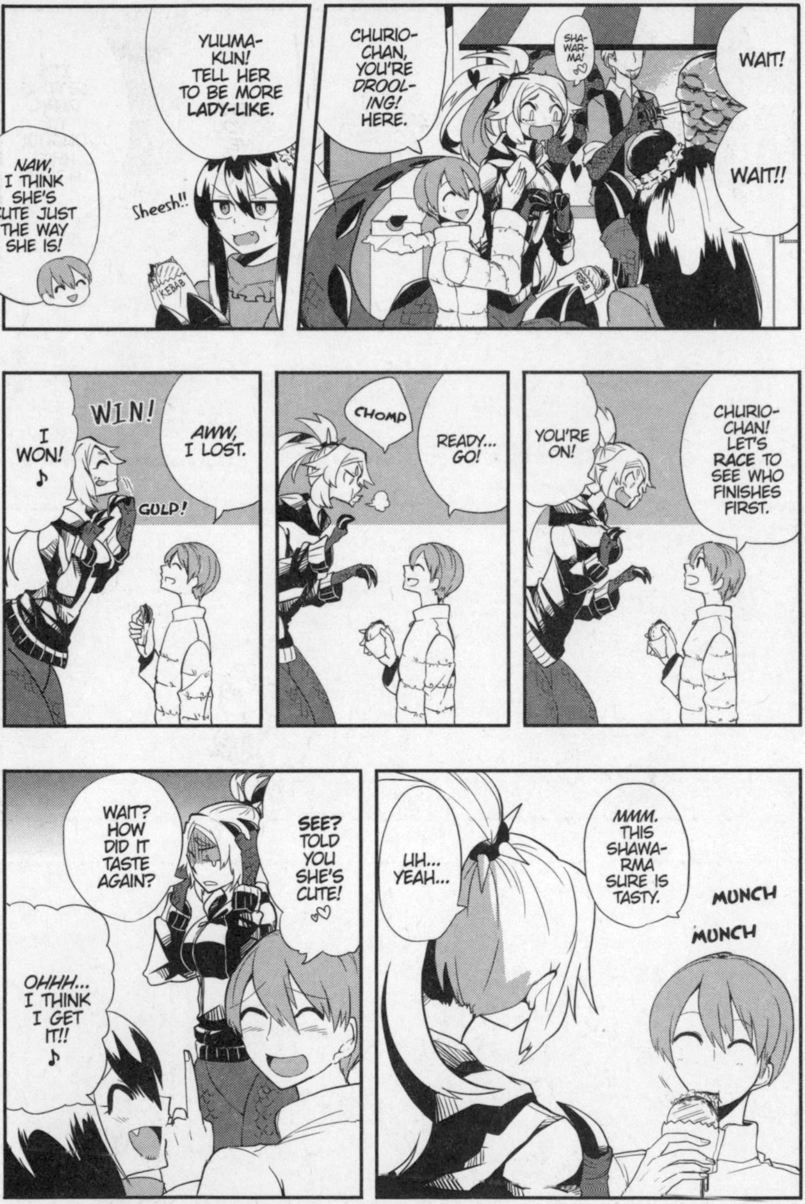
WAIT!
WAIT!!
SHA-WAR-MA! ♡
CHURIO-CHAN, YOU'RE DROOLING! HERE.
YUUMA-KUN! TELL HER TO BE MORE LADY-LIKE.
Sheesh!!
NAW, I THINK SHE'S CUTE JUST THE WAY SHE IS!
KEBAB
CHURIO-CHAN! LET'S RACE TO SEE WHO FINISHES FIRST.
YOU'RE ON!
READY... GO!
CHOMP
AWW, I LOST.
WIN!
I WON! ♪
GULP!
MUNCH
MUNCH
MMM. THIS SHAWARMA SURE IS TASTY.
UH... YEAH...
SEE? TOLD YOU SHE'S CUTE! ♡
WAIT? HOW DID IT TASTE AGAIN?
OHHH... I THINK I GET IT!! ♪

RESETTLEMENT PLAN 1

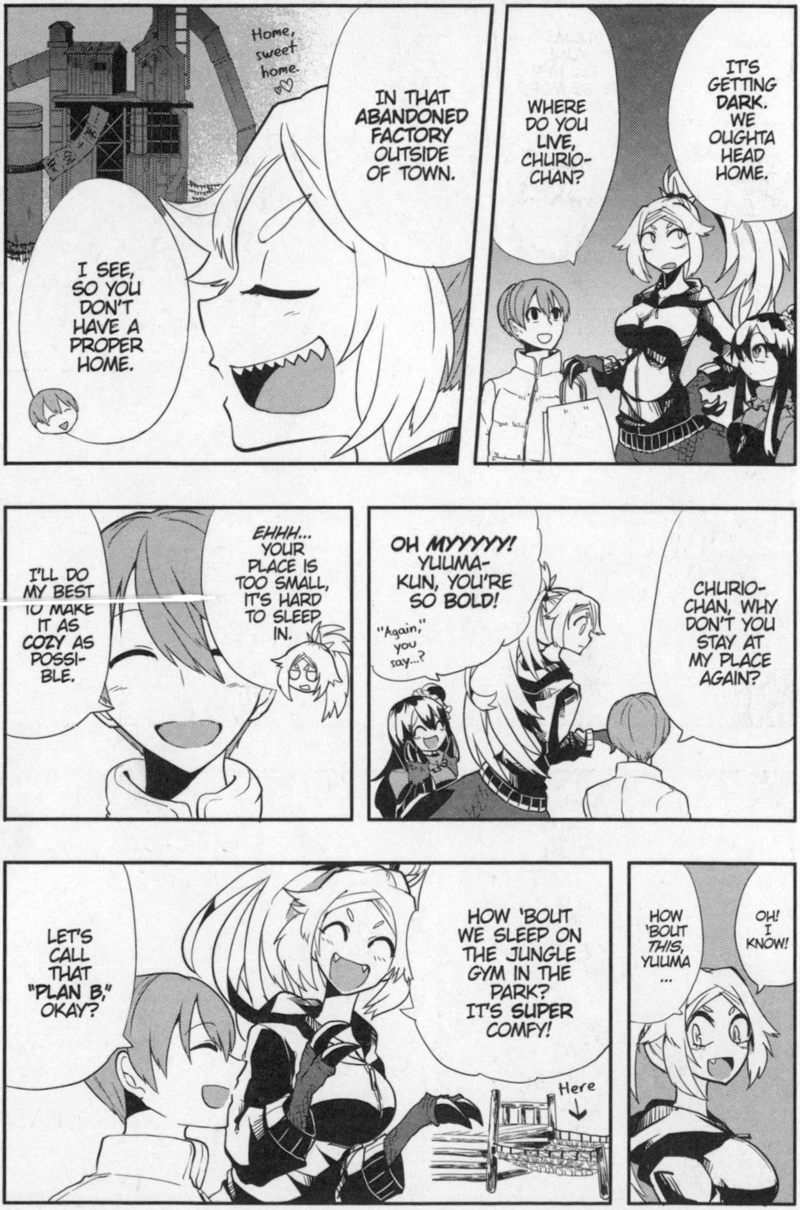
IT'S GETTING DARK. WE OUGHTA HEAD HOME.
WHERE DO YOU LIVE, CHURIO-CHAN?
IN THAT ABANDONED FACTORY OUTSIDE OF TOWN.
Home, sweet home. ♡
I SEE, SO YOU DON'T HAVE A PROPER HOME.
CHURIO-CHAN, WHY DON'T YOU STAY AT MY PLACE AGAIN?
OH *MYYYYY!* YUUMA-KUN, YOU'RE SO BOLD!
"Again," you say...?
EHHH... YOUR PLACE IS TOO SMALL, IT'S HARD TO SLEEP IN.
I'LL DO MY BEST TO MAKE IT AS COZY AS POSSI-BLE.
OH! I KNOW!
HOW 'BOUT *THIS,* YUUMA...
HOW 'BOUT WE SLEEP ON THE JUNGLE GYM IN THE PARK? IT'S SUPER COMFY!
Here
LET'S CALL THAT "PLAN B," OKAY?

RESETTLEMENT PLAN 2

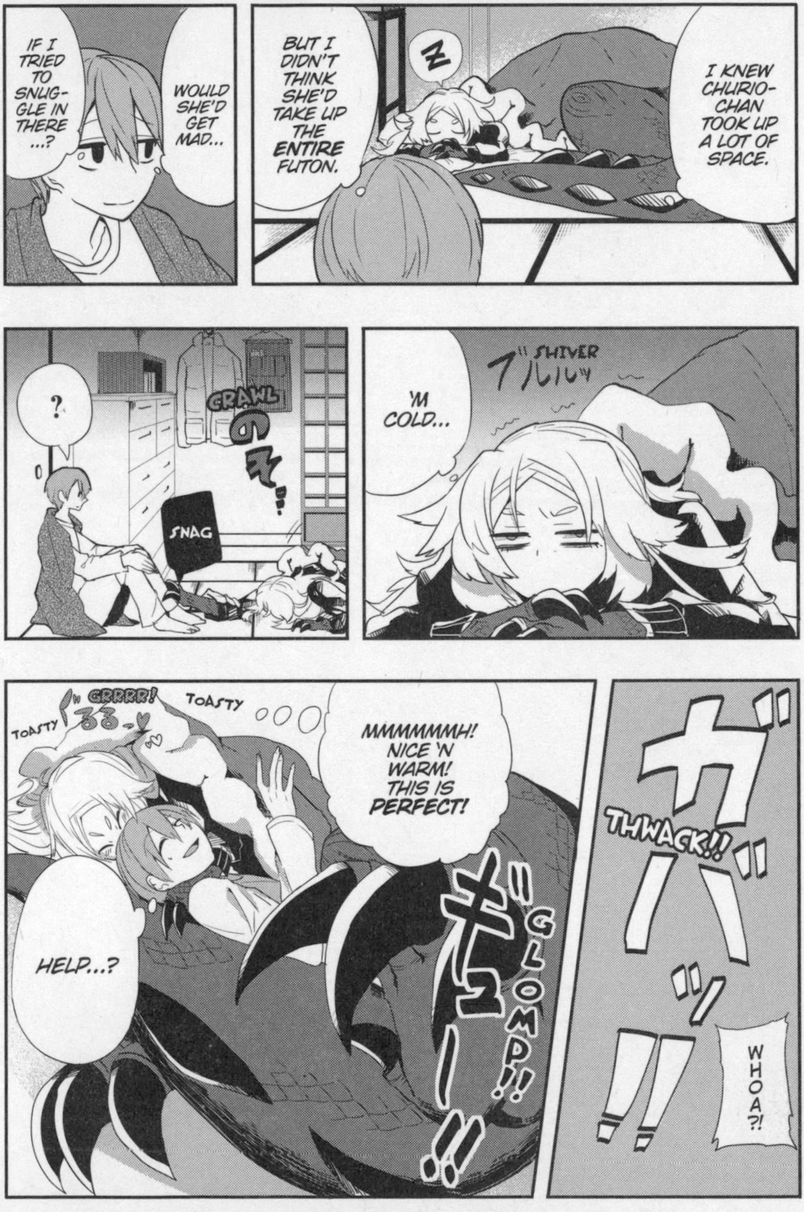
I KNEW CHURIO-CHAN TOOK UP A LOT OF SPACE.
Z
BUT I DIDN'T THINK SHE'D TAKE UP THE ENTIRE FUTON.
WOULD SHE'D GET MAD...
IF I TRIED TO SNUG-GLE IN THERE ...?
SHIVER
ブルルッ
'M COLD...
?
CRAWL
のそ…
SNAG
ガバッ!!
THWACK!!
WHOA?!
MMMMMMH! NICE 'N WARM! THIS IS PERFECT!
TOASTY
GRRRR!
ぐるる
TOASTY
HELP...?
ギュー!!
GLOMP!!

My Girlfriend is a

T-REX

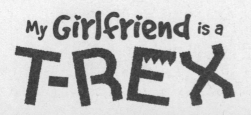

Don't throw this away...

CHAPTER 5 MY HELPFUL GIRLFRIEND

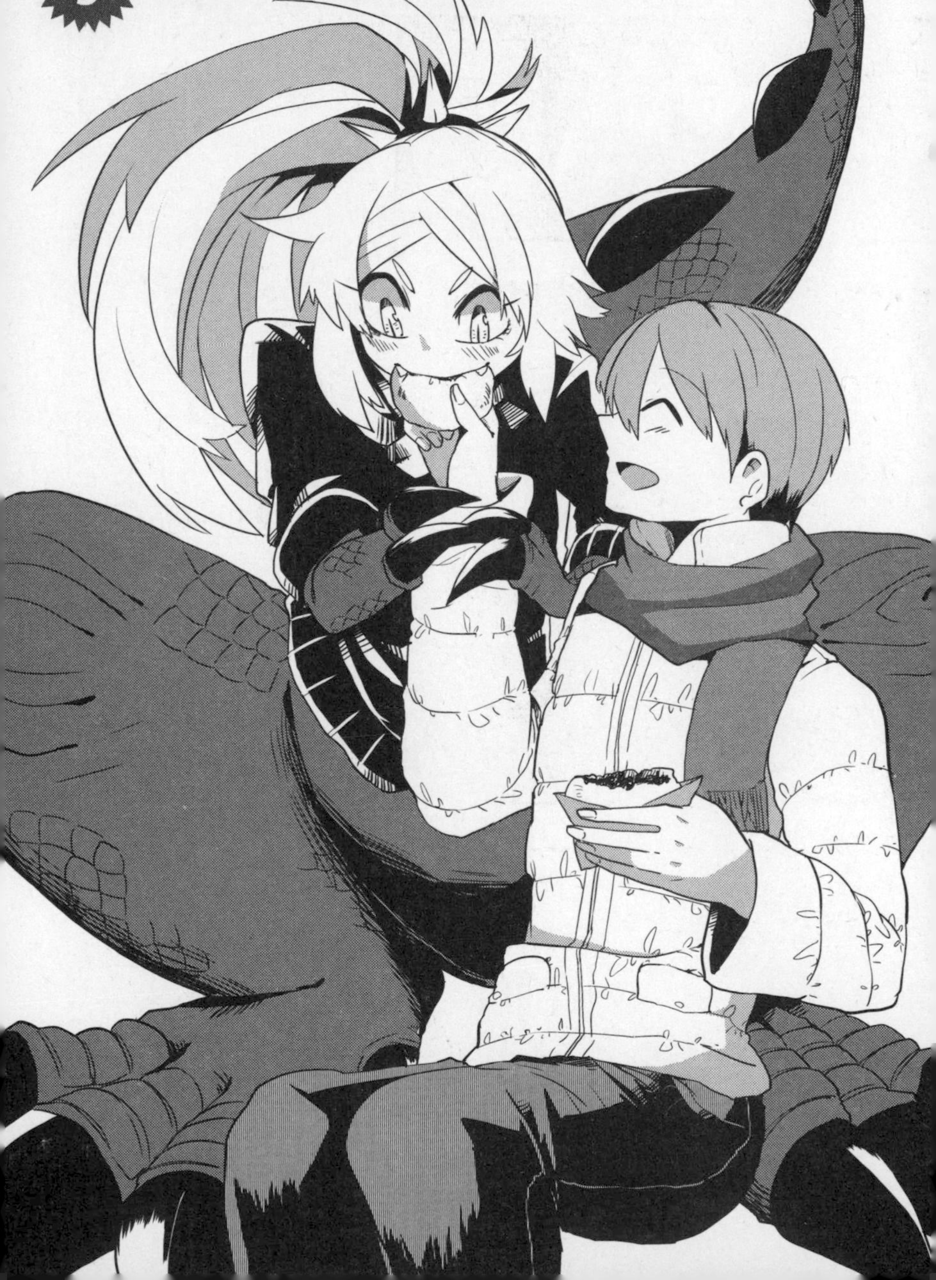

KAGISHIMA-KUN'S HARDSHIPS 1

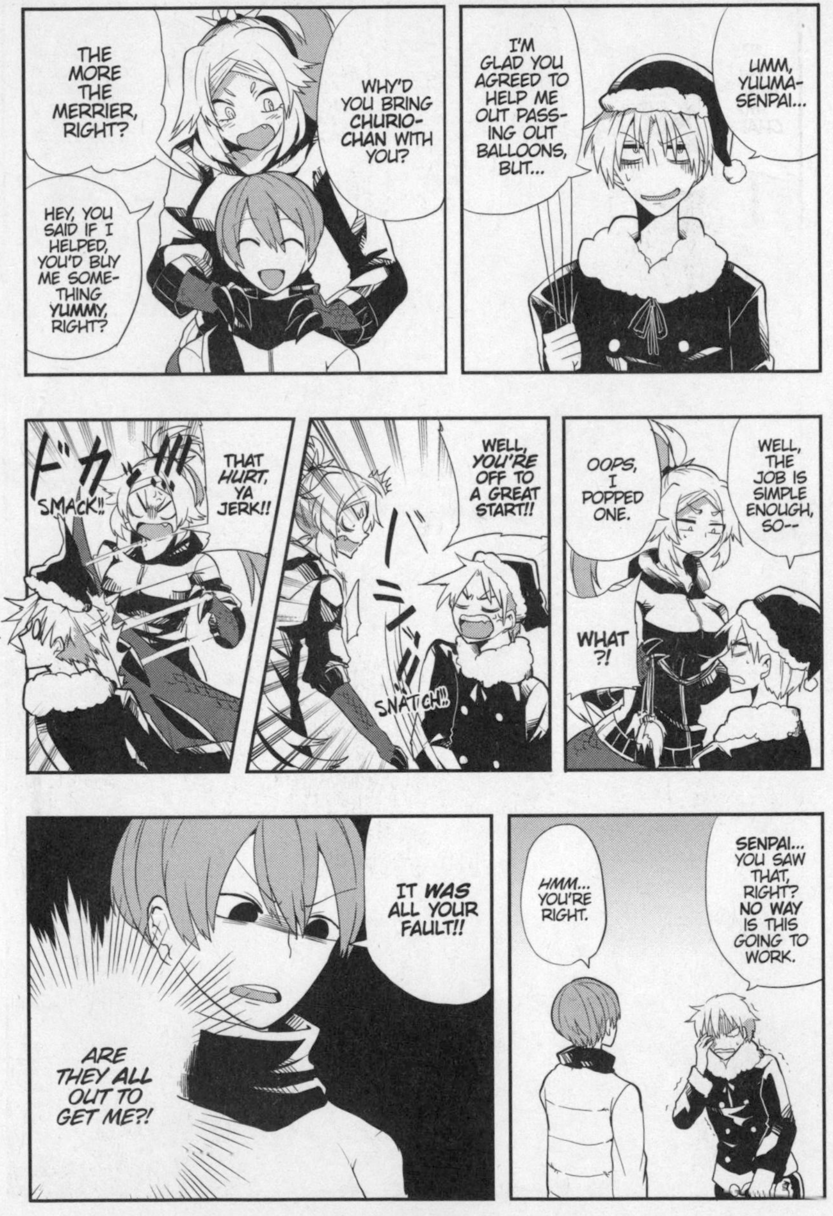
UMM, YUUMA-SENPAI...
I'M GLAD YOU AGREED TO HELP ME OUT PASSING OUT BALLOONS, BUT...
WHY'D YOU BRING CHURIO-CHAN WITH YOU?
THE MORE THE MERRIER, RIGHT?
HEY, YOU SAID IF I HELPED, YOU'D BUY ME SOMETHING YUMMY, RIGHT?
WELL, THE JOB IS SIMPLE ENOUGH, SO--
OOPS, I POPPED ONE.
WHAT?!
WELL, YOU'RE OFF TO A GREAT START!!
SNATCH!!
THAT HURT, YA JERK!!
ドカ
SMACK!!
SENPAI... YOU SAW THAT, RIGHT? NO WAY IS THIS GOING TO WORK.
HMM... YOU'RE RIGHT.
IT WAS ALL YOUR FAULT!!
ARE THEY ALL OUT TO GET ME?!

KAGISHIMA-KUN'S HARDSHIPS 2

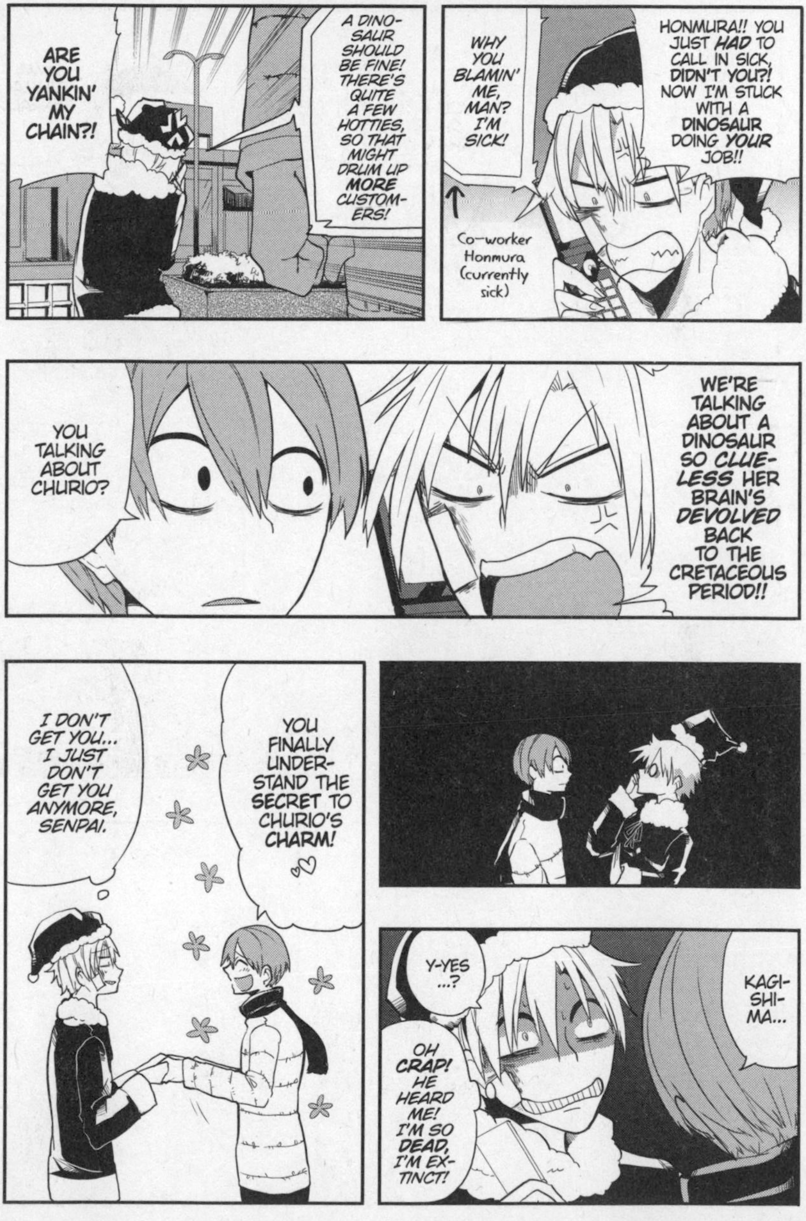
HONMURA!! YOU JUST HAD TO CALL IN SICK, DIDN'T YOU?! NOW I'M STUCK WITH A DINOSAUR DOING YOUR JOB!!
WHY YOU BLAMIN' ME, MAN? I'M SICK!
Co-worker Honmura (currently sick)
A DINO-SAUR SHOULD BE FINE! THERE'S QUITE A FEW HOTTIES, SO THAT MIGHT DRUM UP MORE CUSTOM-ERS!
ARE YOU YANKIN' MY CHAIN?!
WE'RE TALKING ABOUT A DINOSAUR SO CLUE-LESS HER BRAIN'S DEVOLVED BACK TO THE CRETACEOUS PERIOD!!
YOU TALKING ABOUT CHURIO?
KAGI-SHI-MA...
Y-YES ...?
OH CRAP! HE HEARD ME! I'M SO DEAD, I'M EX-TINCT!
YOU FINALLY UNDER-STAND THE SECRET TO CHURIO'S CHARM!
I DON'T GET YOU... I JUST DON'T GET YOU ANYMORE, SENPAI.

THE EXPERT

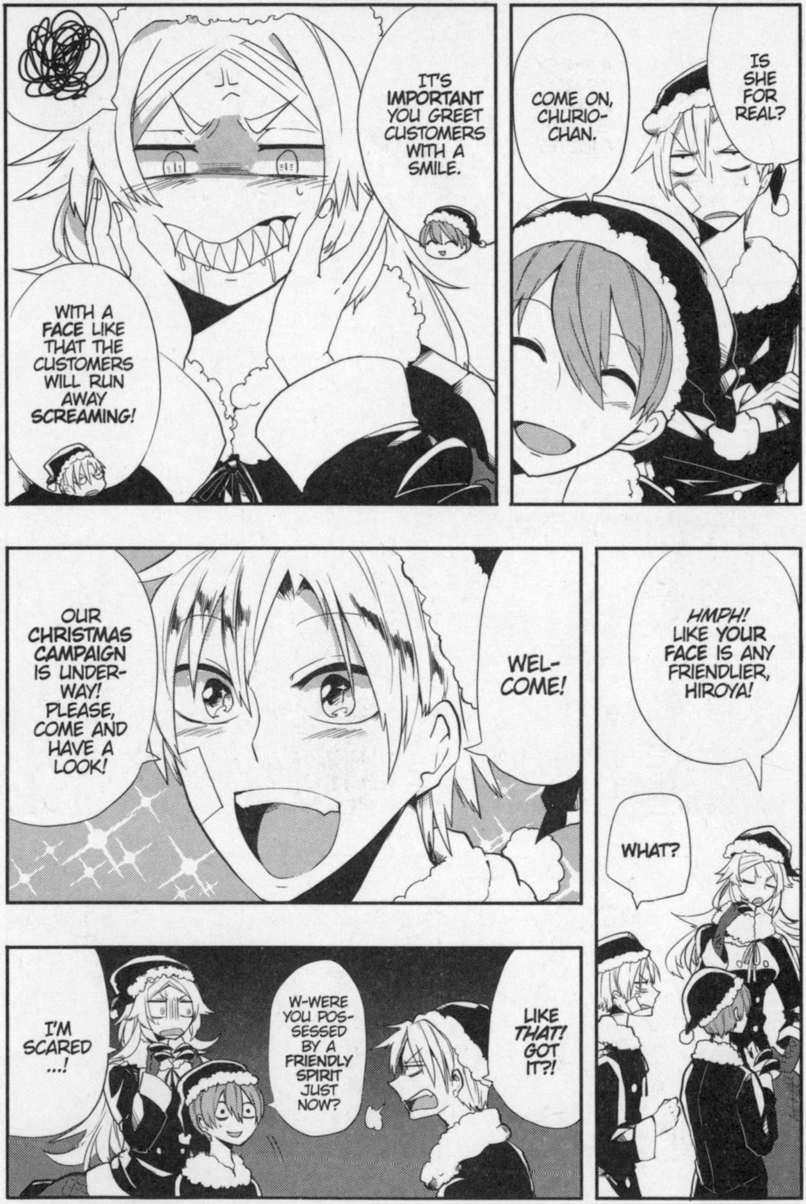
IS SHE FOR REAL?
COME ON, CHURIO-CHAN.
IT'S IMPORTANT YOU GREET CUSTOMERS WITH A SMILE.
WITH A FACE LIKE THAT THE CUSTOMERS WILL RUN AWAY SCREAMING!
HMPH! LIKE YOUR FACE IS ANY FRIENDLIER, HIROYA!
WHAT?
WEL-COME!
OUR CHRISTMAS CAMPAIGN IS UNDER-WAY! PLEASE, COME AND HAVE A LOOK!
LIKE *THAT!* GOT IT?!
W-WERE YOU POS-SESSED BY A FRIENDLY SPIRIT JUST NOW?
I'M SCARED ...!

THE TEST 1

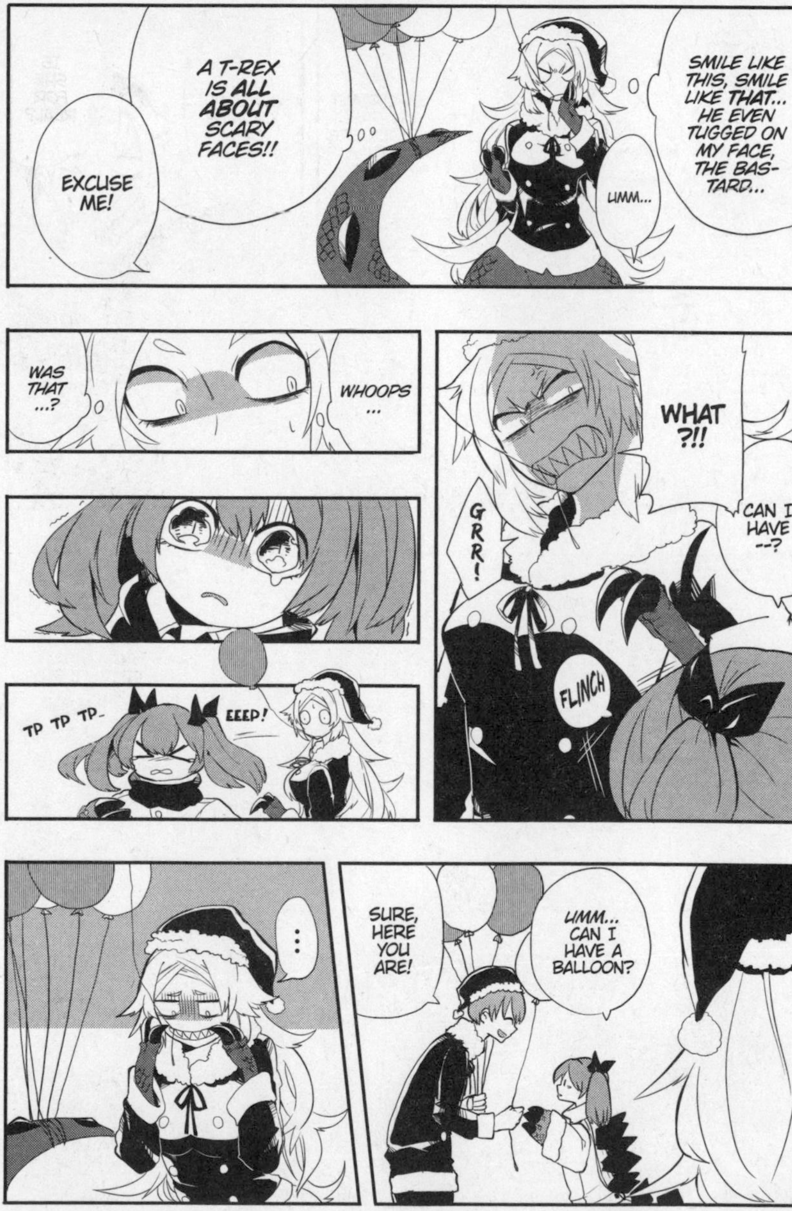
SMILE LIKE THIS, SMILE LIKE THAT... HE EVEN TUGGED ON MY FACE, THE BASTARD...
UMM...
A T-REX IS ALL ABOUT SCARY FACES!!
EXCUSE ME!
WHAT ?!!
CAN I HAVE --?
GRR!
FLINCH
WHOOPS ...
WAS THAT ...?
EEEP!
TP TP TP
UMM... CAN I HAVE A BALLOON?
SURE, HERE YOU ARE!
...

THE TEST 2

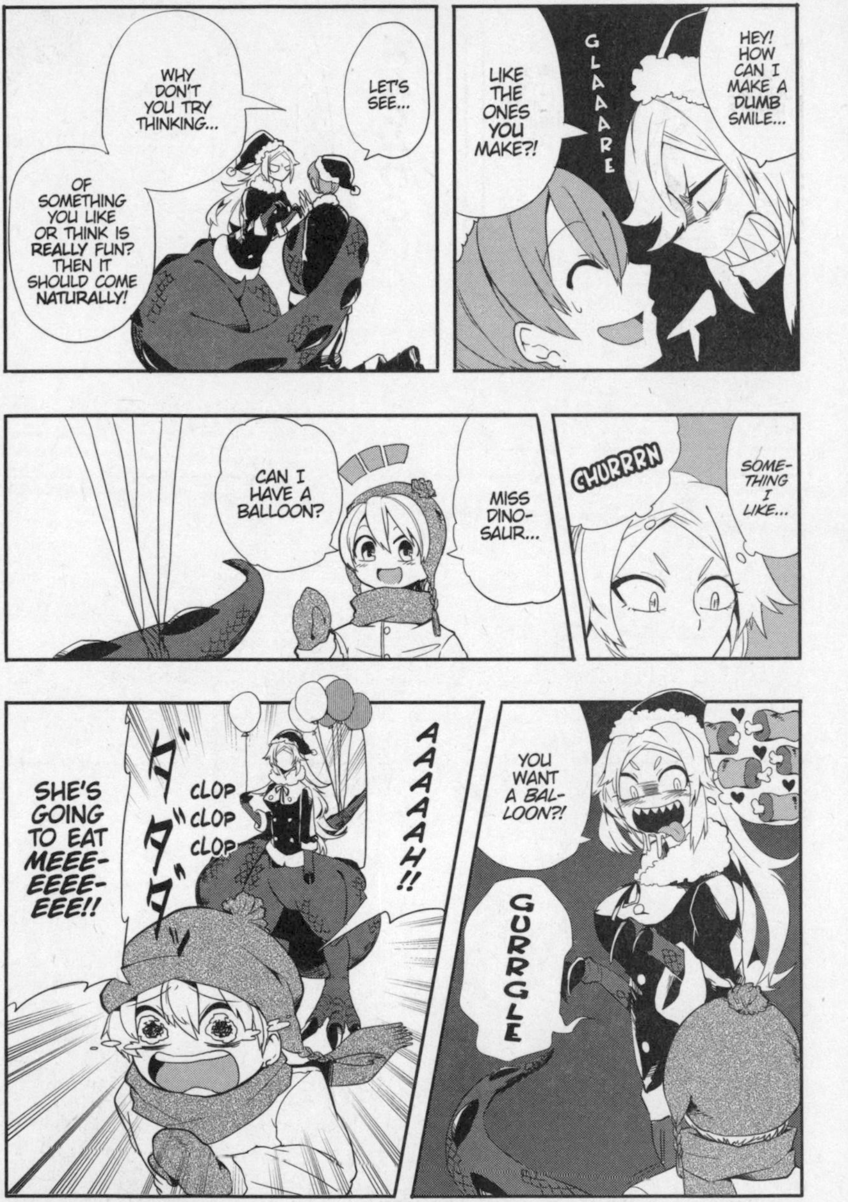
HEY! HOW CAN I MAKE A DUMB SMILE...
GLAAARE
LIKE THE ONES YOU MAKE?!
LET'S SEE...
WHY DON'T YOU TRY THINKING...
OF SOMETHING YOU LIKE OR THINK IS REALLY FUN? THEN IT SHOULD COME NATURALLY!
SOME-THING I LIKE...
CHURRRN
MISS DINO-SAUR...
CAN I HAVE A BALLOON?
YOU WANT A BAL-LOON?!
GURRGLE
AAAAAAH!!
CLOP CLOP CLOP
ダダダ
SHE'S GOING TO EAT MEEEE-EEEE-EEE!!

DINOSAUR SKILLS

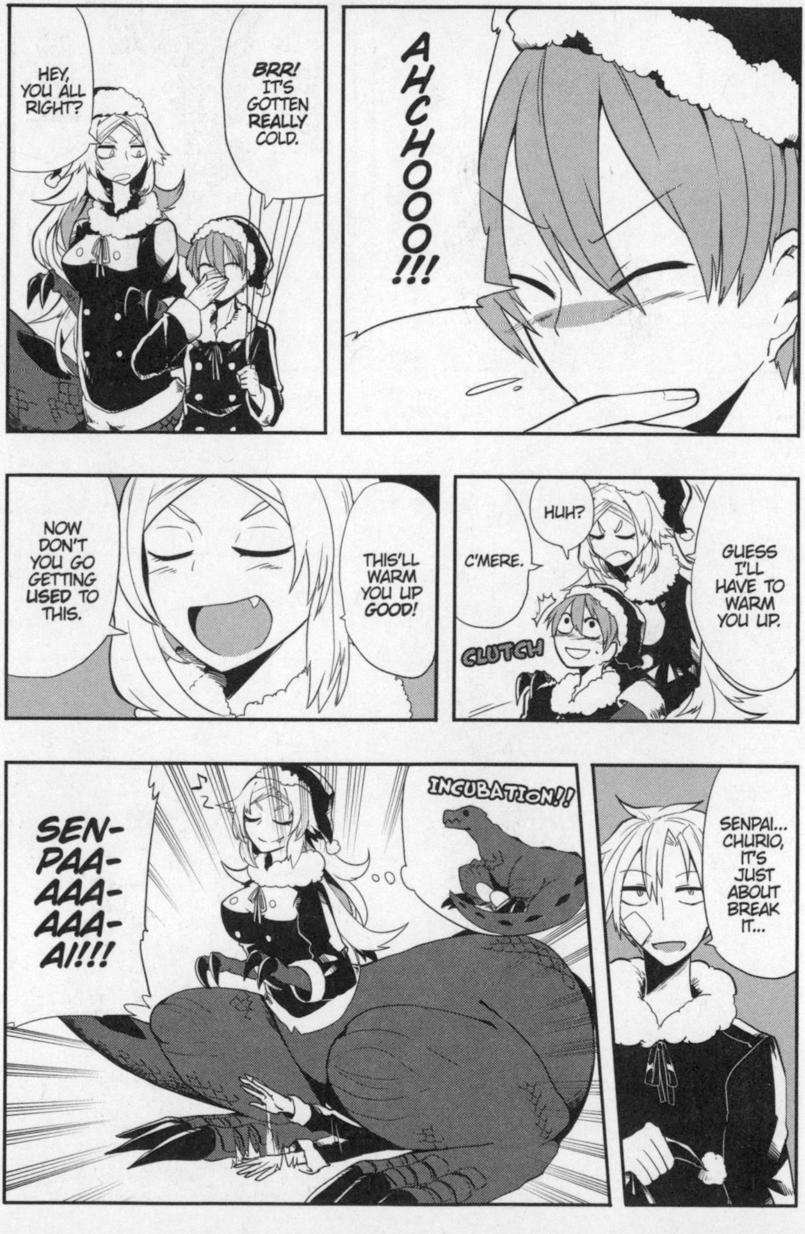
AHCHOOOO!!!
BRR! IT'S GOTTEN REALLY COLD.
HEY, YOU ALL RIGHT?
GUESS I'LL HAVE TO WARM YOU UP.
HUH?
C'MERE.
CLUTCH
THIS'LL WARM YOU UP GOOD!
NOW DON'T YOU GO GETTING USED TO THIS.
SENPAI... CHURIO, IT'S JUST ABOUT BREAK IT...
INCUBATION!!
SEN-PAA-AAA-AAA-AI!!!

KAGISHIMA-KUN VS. DINOSAUR

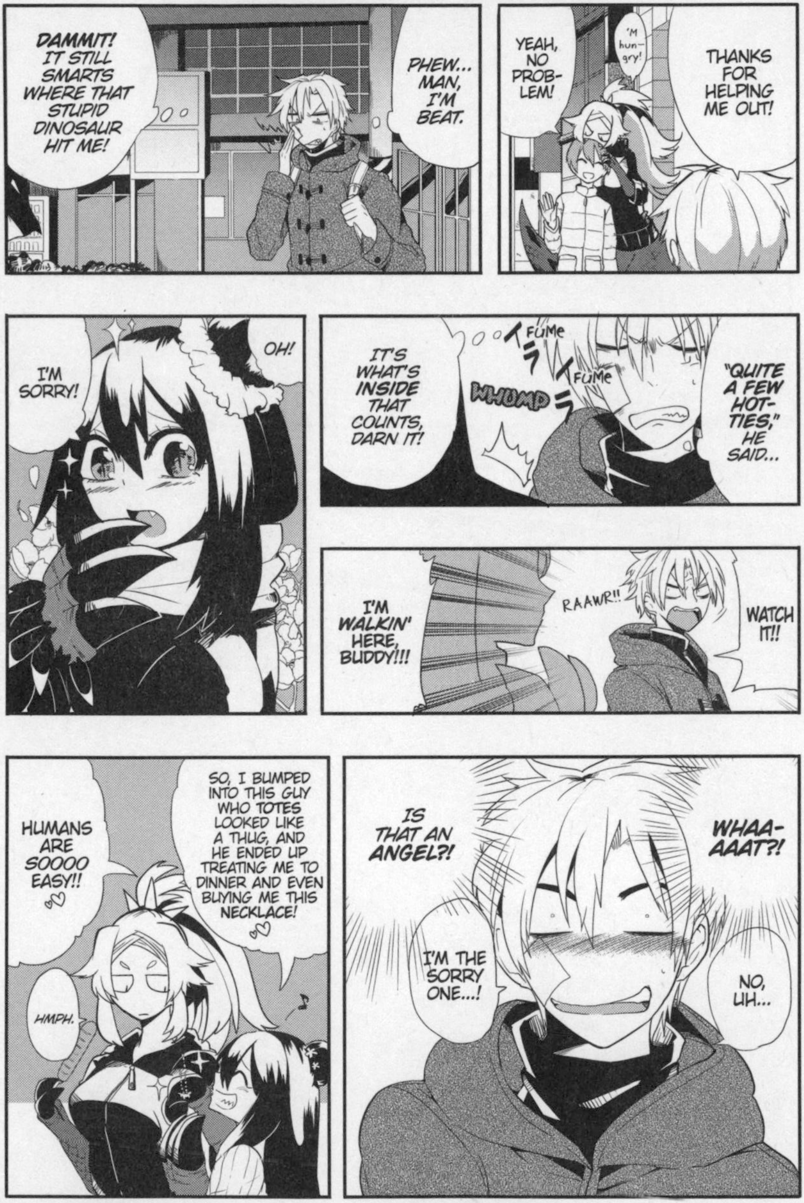
THANKS FOR HELPING ME OUT!
'M hun-gry!
YEAH, NO PROB-LEM!
PHEW... MAN, I'M BEAT.
DAMMIT! IT STILL SMARTS WHERE THAT STUPID DINOSAUR HIT ME!
"QUITE A FEW HOT-TIES," HE SAID...
FUME
FUME
WHUMP
IT'S WHAT'S INSIDE THAT COUNTS, DARN IT!
WATCH IT!!
RAAWR!!
I'M WALKIN' HERE, BUDDY!!!
OH!
I'M SORRY!
WHAA-AAAT?!
IS THAT AN ANGEL?!
NO, UH...
I'M THE SORRY ONE...!
SO, I BUMPED INTO THIS GUY WHO TOTES LOOKED LIKE A THUG, AND HE ENDED UP TREATING ME TO DINNER AND EVEN BUYING ME THIS NECKLACE!
HUMANS ARE SOOOO EASY!!
HMPH.

My Girlfriend is a
T-REX

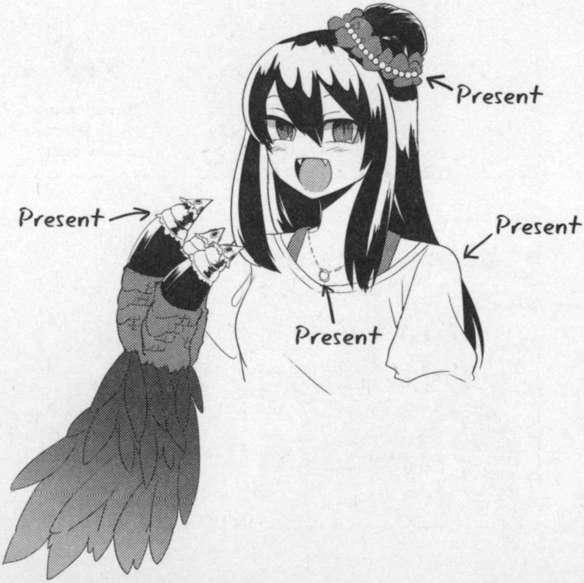
Present
Present
Present
Present

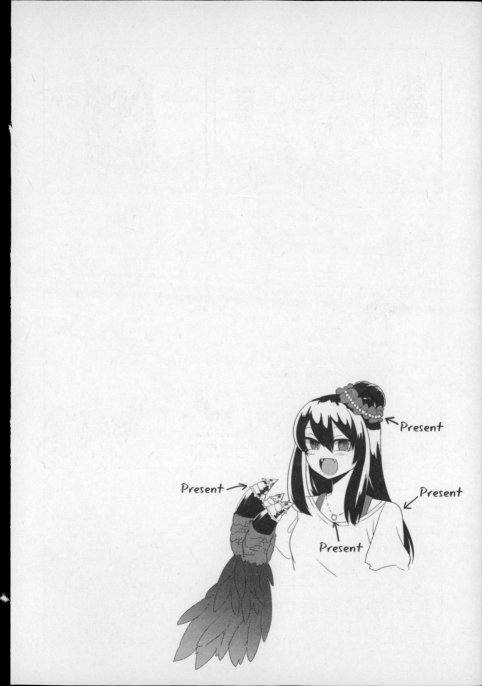

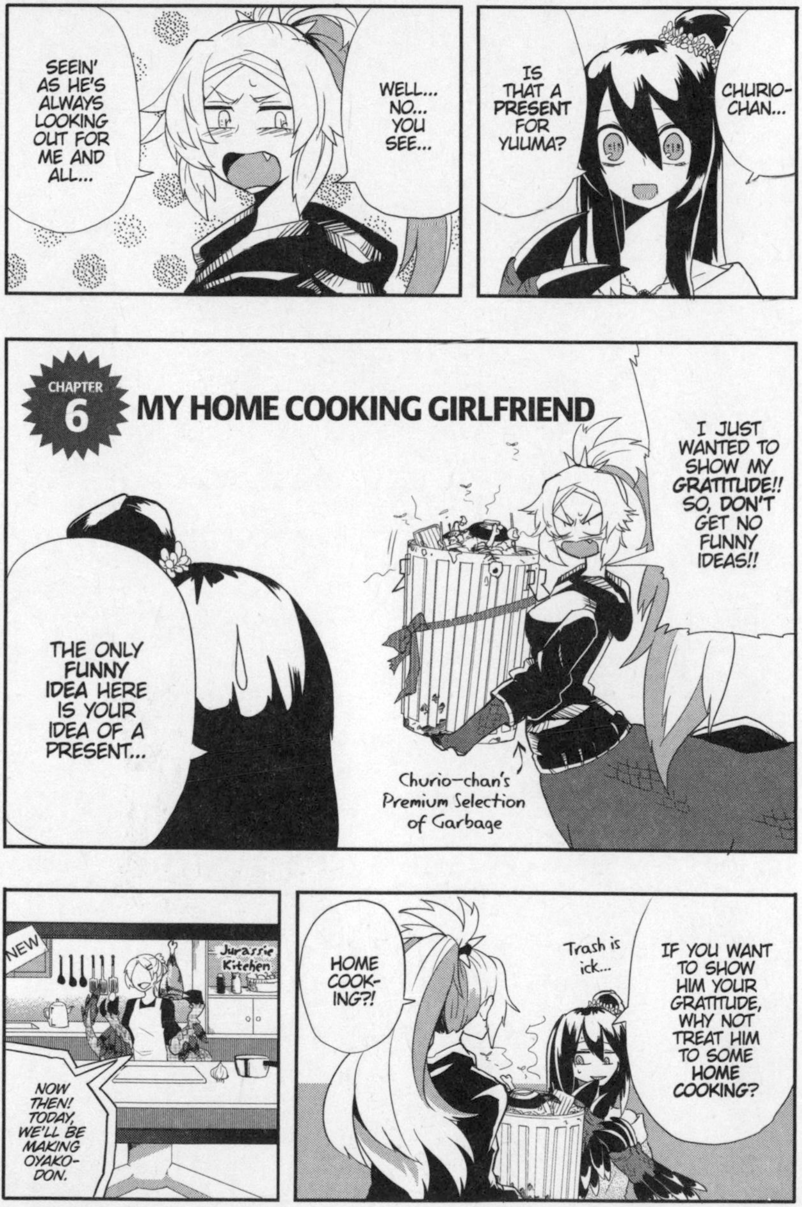
CHURIO-CHAN...
IS THAT A PRESENT FOR YUUMA?
WELL... NO... YOU SEE...
SEEIN' AS HE'S ALWAYS LOOKING OUT FOR ME AND ALL...
CHAPTER 6
MY HOME COOKING GIRLFRIEND
I JUST WANTED TO SHOW MY GRATITUDE!! SO, DON'T GET NO FUNNY IDEAS!!
Churio-chan's Premium Selection of Garbage
THE ONLY FUNNY IDEA HERE IS YOUR IDEA OF A PRESENT...
IF YOU WANT TO SHOW HIM YOUR GRATITUDE, WHY NOT TREAT HIM TO SOME HOME COOKING?
Trash is ick...
HOME COOK-ING?!
NEW
Jurassic Kitchen
NOW THEN! TODAY, WE'LL BE MAKING OYAKO-DON.

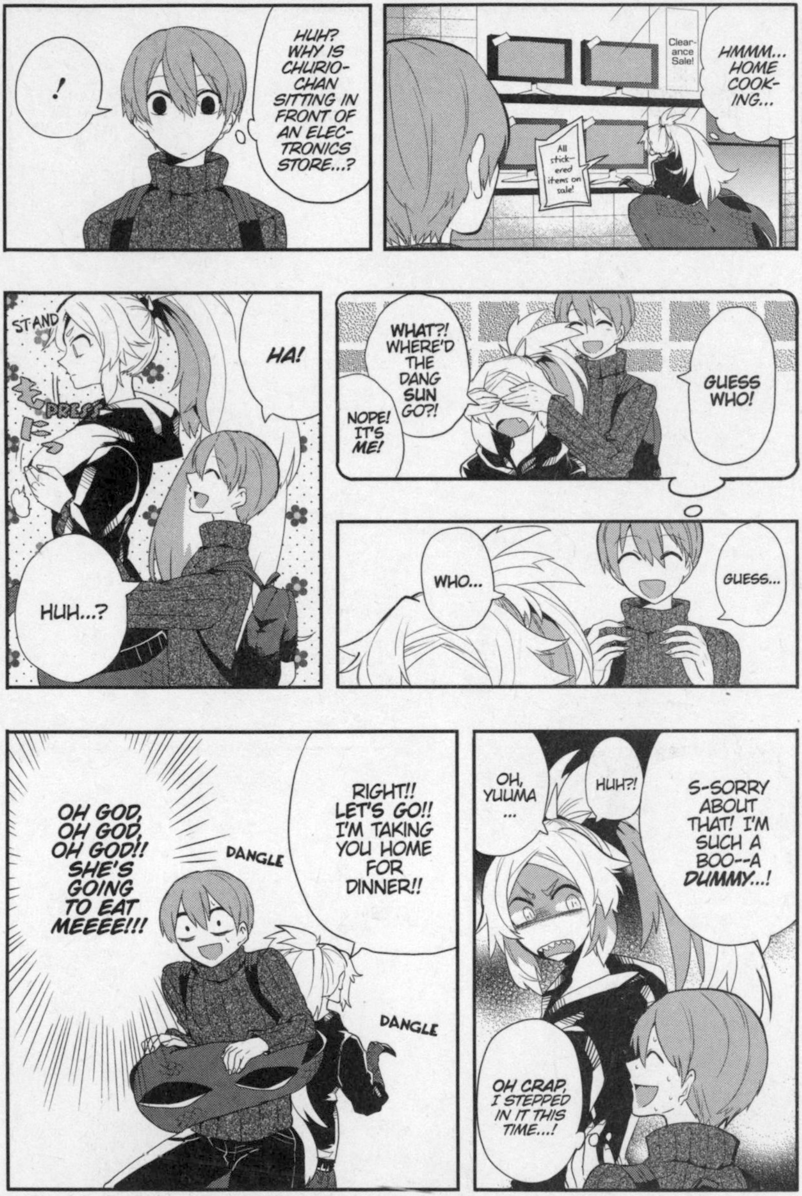
HMMM... HOME COOKING...
Clearance Sale!
All stickered items on sale!
!
HUH? WHY IS CHURIO-CHAN SITTING IN FRONT OF AN ELECTRONICS STORE...?
GUESS WHO!
WHAT?! WHERE'D THE DANG SUN GO?!
NOPE! IT'S ME!
GUESS...
WHO...
HA!
STAND
PRESS
HUH...?
S-SORRY ABOUT THAT! I'M SUCH A BOO--A DUMMY...!
HUH?!
OH, YUUMA ...
OH CRAP, I STEPPED IN IT THIS TIME...!
RIGHT!! LET'S GO!! I'M TAKING YOU HOME FOR DINNER!!
DANGLE
OH GOD, OH GOD, OH GOD!! SHE'S GOING TO EAT MEEEE!!!
DANGLE

EGGS

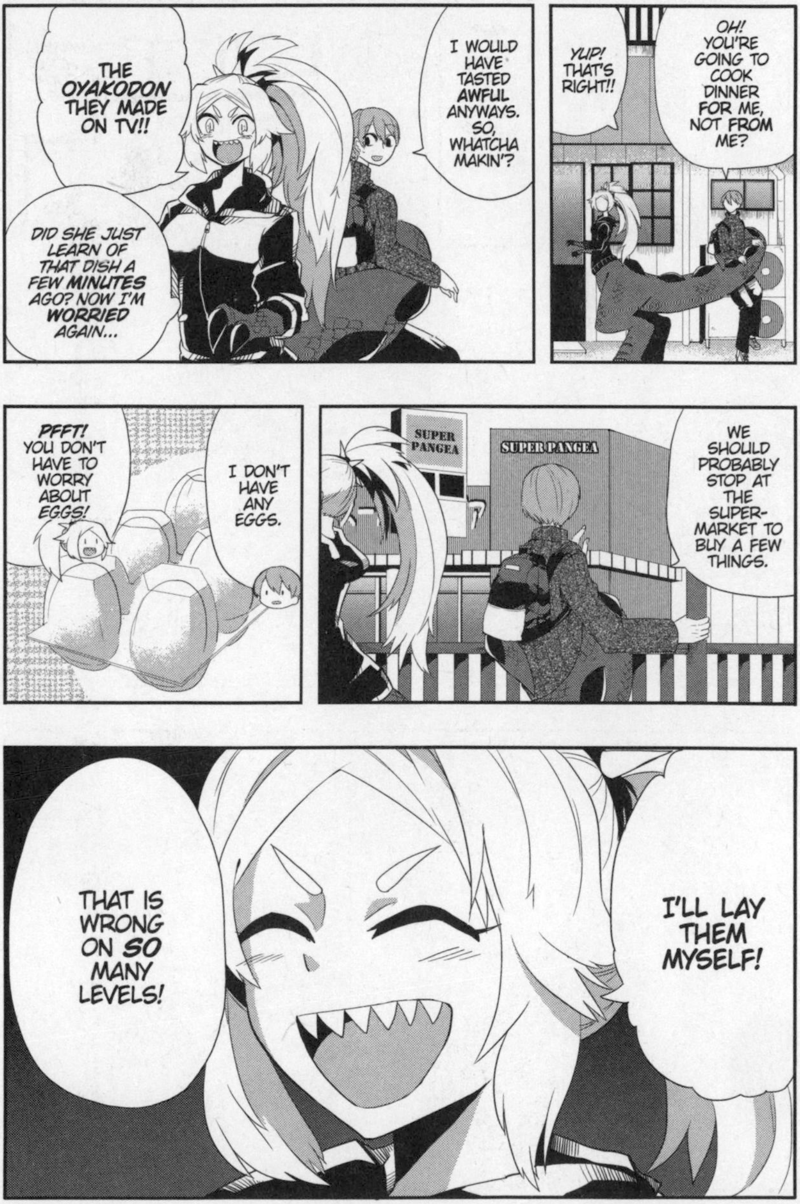
OH! YOU'RE GOING TO COOK DINNER FOR ME, NOT FROM ME?
YUP! THAT'S RIGHT!!
I WOULD HAVE TASTED AWFUL ANYWAYS. SO, WHATCHA MAKIN'?
THE OYAKODON THEY MADE ON TV!!
DID SHE JUST LEARN OF THAT DISH A FEW MINUTES AGO? NOW I'M WORRIED AGAIN...
WE SHOULD PROBABLY STOP AT THE SUPER-MARKET TO BUY A FEW THINGS.
SUPER PANGEA
SUPER PANGEA
I DON'T HAVE ANY EGGS.
PFFT! YOU DON'T HAVE TO WORRY ABOUT EGGS!
I'LL LAY THEM MYSELF!
THAT IS WRONG ON SO MANY LEVELS!

BATTLEFIELD

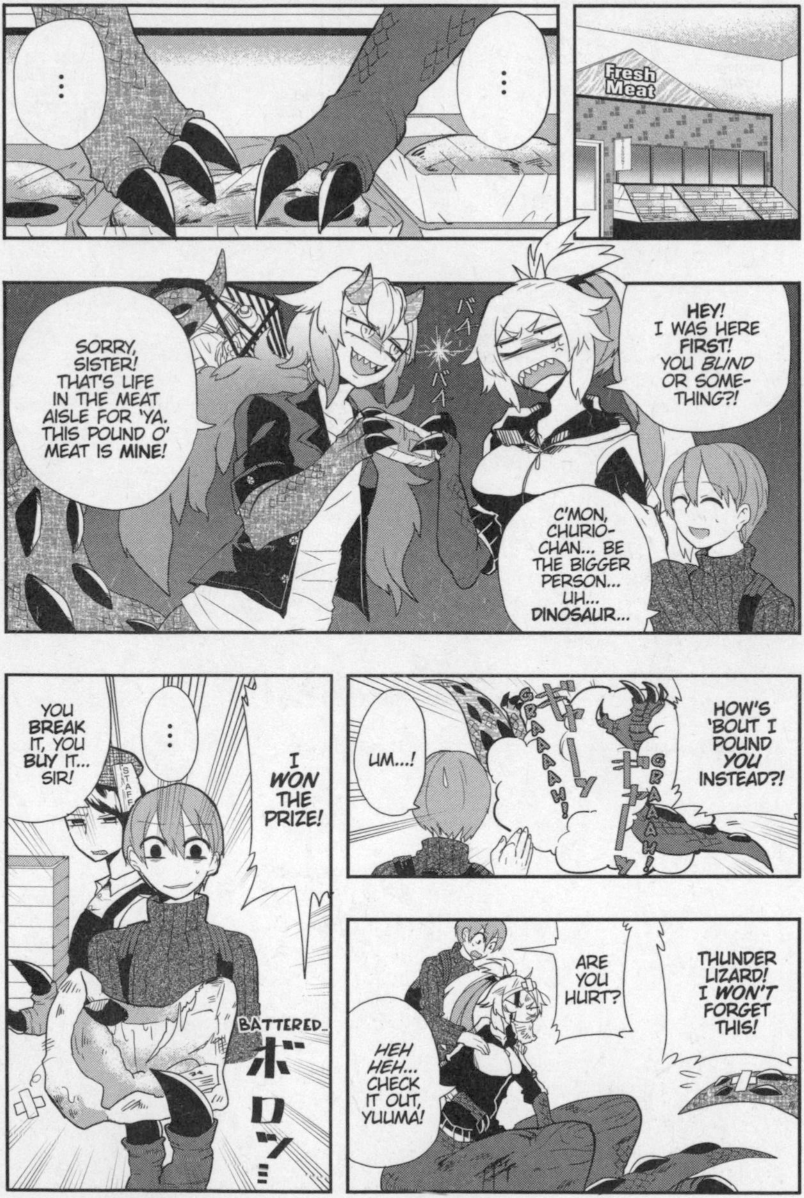
Fresh Meat
...
...
HEY! I WAS HERE FIRST! YOU *BLIND* OR SOME-THING?!
バイバイ
C'MON, CHURIO-CHAN... BE THE BIGGER PERSON... UH... DINOSAUR...
SORRY, SISTER! THAT'S LIFE IN THE MEAT AISLE FOR 'YA. THIS POUND O' MEAT IS MINE!
HOW'S 'BOUT I POUND *YOU* INSTEAD?!
GRAAAAH!
GRAAAAH!
UM...!
THUNDER LIZARD! I *WON'T* FORGET THIS!
ARE YOU HURT?
HEH HEH... CHECK IT OUT, YUUMA!
I *WON* THE PRIZE!
...
YOU BREAK IT, YOU BUY IT... SIR!
STAFF
BATTERED...
ボロッ

COOKING SKILL

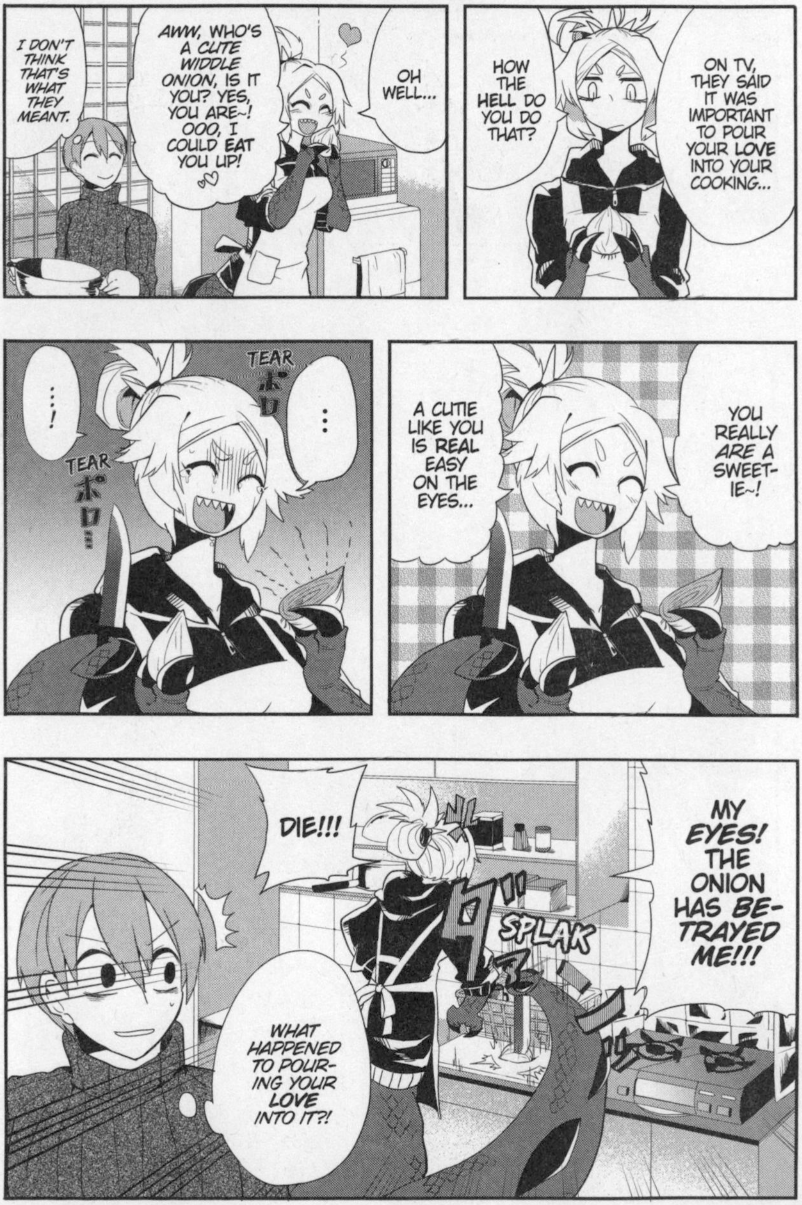

ON TV, THEY SAID IT WAS IMPORTANT TO POUR YOUR LOVE INTO YOUR COOKING...
HOW THE HELL DO YOU DO THAT?
OH WELL...
AWW, WHO'S A CUTE WIDDLE ONION, IS IT YOU? YES, YOU ARE~! OOO, I COULD EAT YOU UP!
I DON'T THINK THAT'S WHAT THEY MEANT.
YOU REALLY ARE A SWEET-IE~!
A CUTIE LIKE YOU IS REAL EASY ON THE EYES...
...
...!
TEAR
TEAR
MY EYES! THE ONION HAS BE-TRAYED ME!!!
SPLAK
DIE!!!
WHAT HAPPENED TO POUR-ING YOUR LOVE INTO IT?!

EXCITEMENT

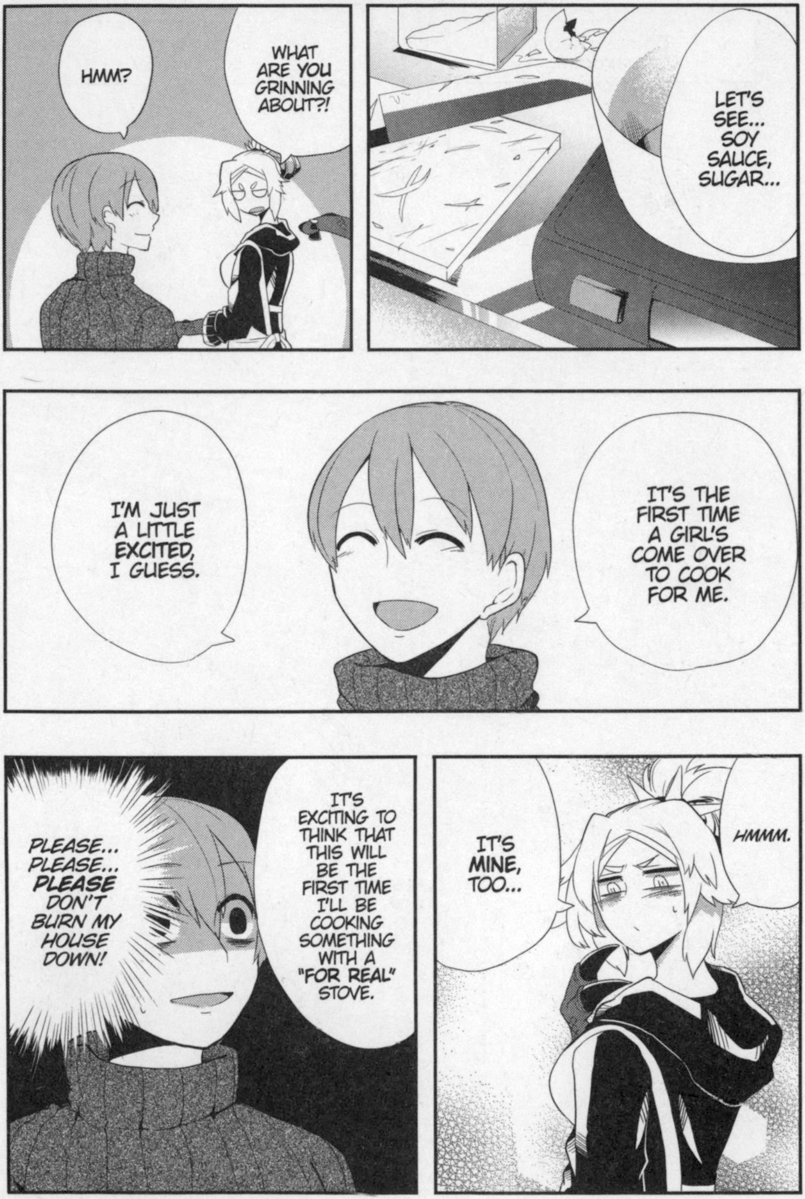
LET'S SEE... SOY SAUCE, SUGAR...
WHAT ARE YOU GRINNING ABOUT?!
HMM?
IT'S THE FIRST TIME A GIRL'S COME OVER TO COOK FOR ME.
I'M JUST A LITTLE EXCITED, I GUESS.
HMMM.
IT'S MINE, TOO...
IT'S EXCITING TO THINK THAT THIS WILL BE THE FIRST TIME I'LL BE COOKING SOMETHING WITH A "FOR REAL" STOVE.
PLEASE... PLEASE... **PLEASE** DON'T BURN MY HOUSE DOWN!

TIME TO EAT!

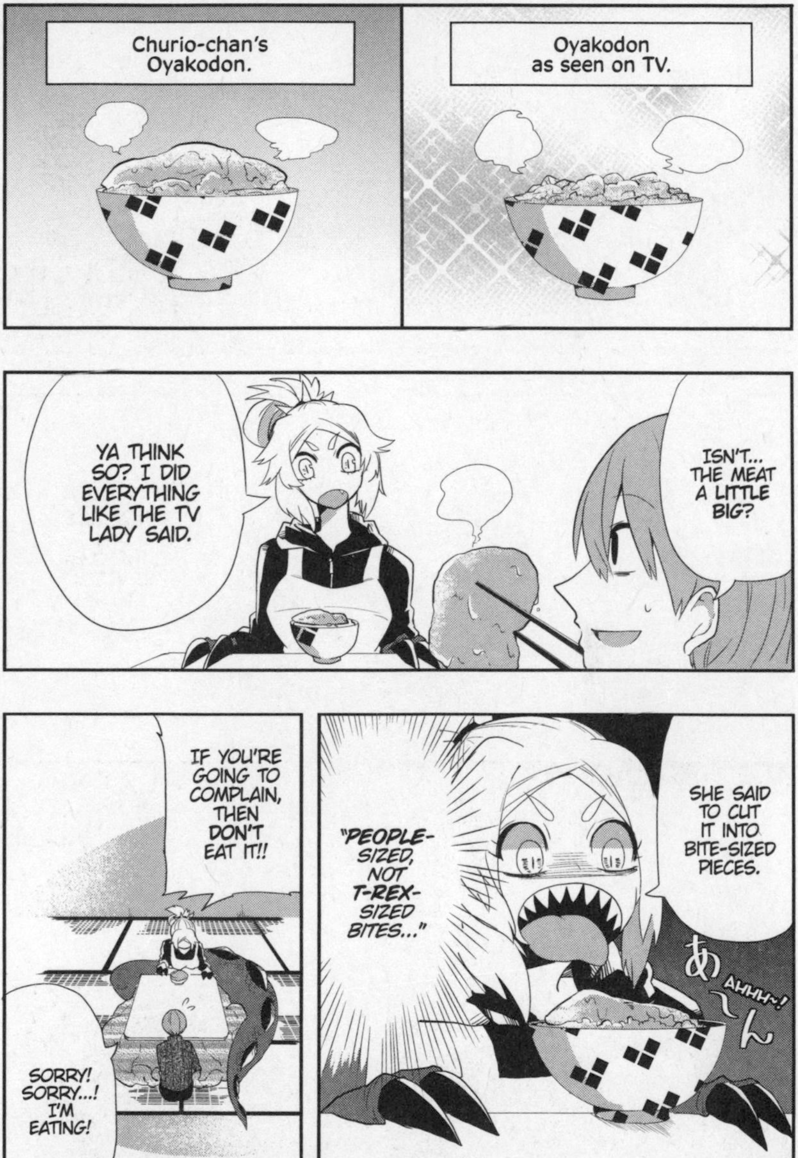
Oyakodon as seen on TV.
Churio-chan's Oyakodon.
ISN'T... THE MEAT A LITTLE BIG?
YA THINK SO? I DID EVERYTHING LIKE THE TV LADY SAID.
SHE SAID TO CUT IT INTO BITE-SIZED PIECES.
"PEOPLE-SIZED, NOT T-REX-SIZED BITES..."
あ～ん
AHHH~!
IF YOU'RE GOING TO COMPLAIN, THEN DON'T EAT IT!!
SORRY! SORRY...! I'M EATING!

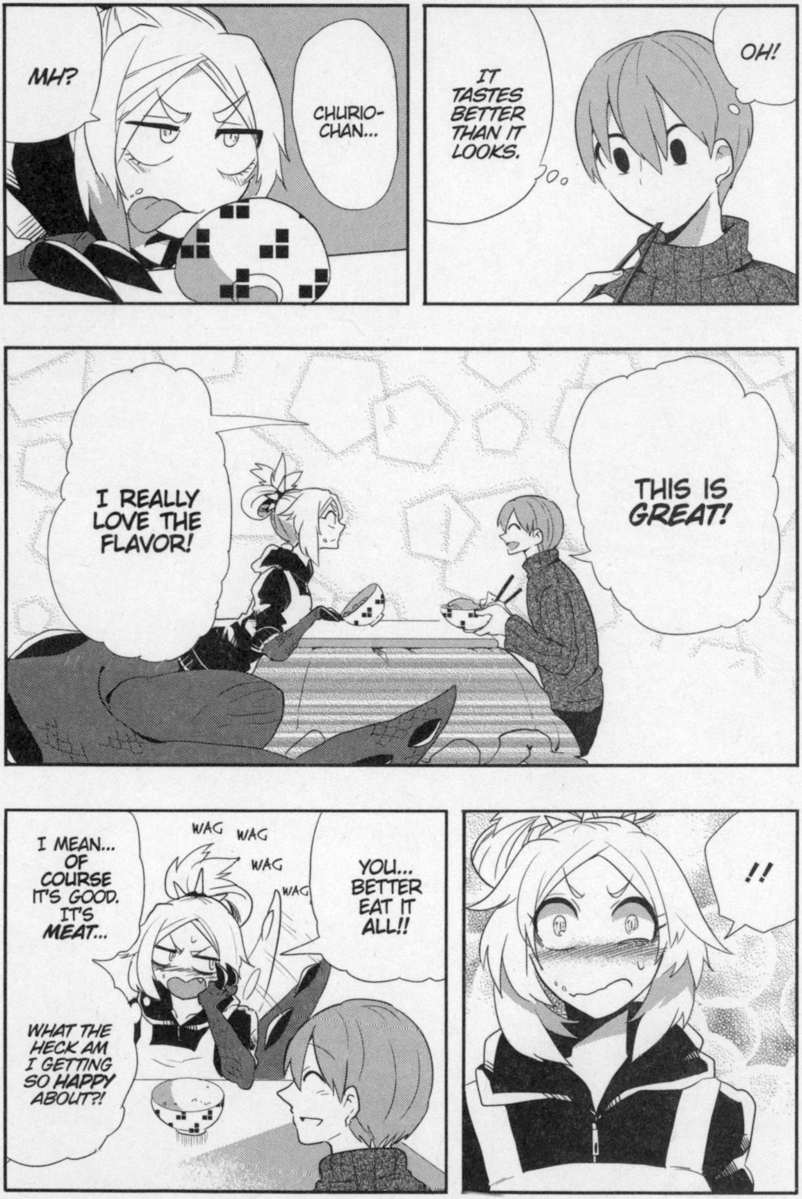
OH!
IT TASTES BETTER THAN IT LOOKS.
CHURIO-CHAN...
MH?
THIS IS GREAT!
I REALLY LOVE THE FLAVOR!
!!
YOU... BETTER EAT IT ALL!!
WAG WAG WAG WAG
I MEAN... OF COURSE IT'S GOOD. IT'S MEAT...
WHAT THE HECK AM I GETTING SO HAPPY ABOUT?!

My Girlfriend is a

T-REX

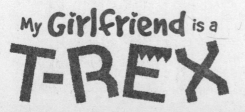

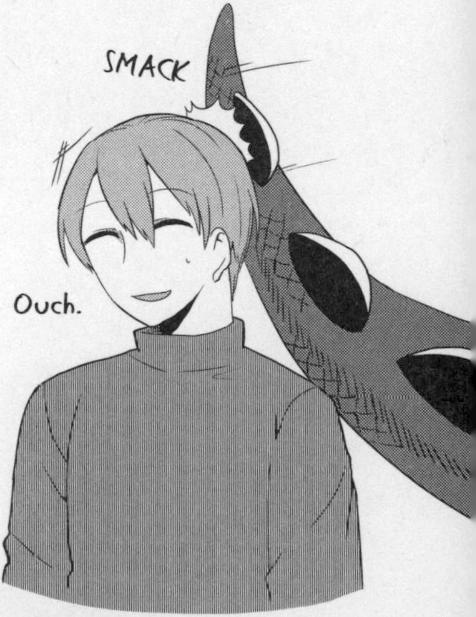
SMACK
Ouch.

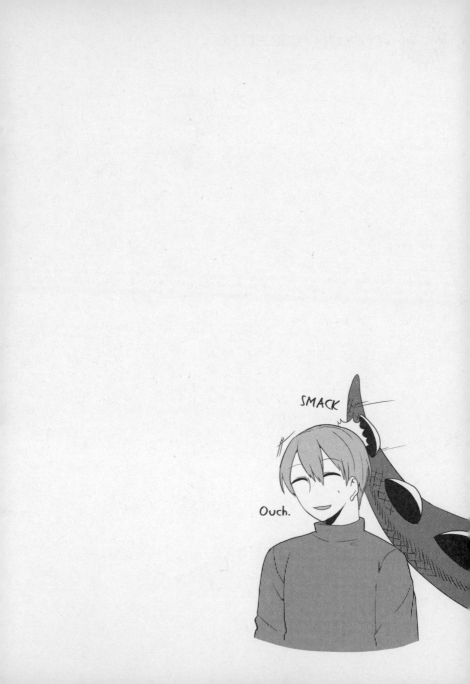

CHAPTER 7

MY CRANKY GIRLFRIEND

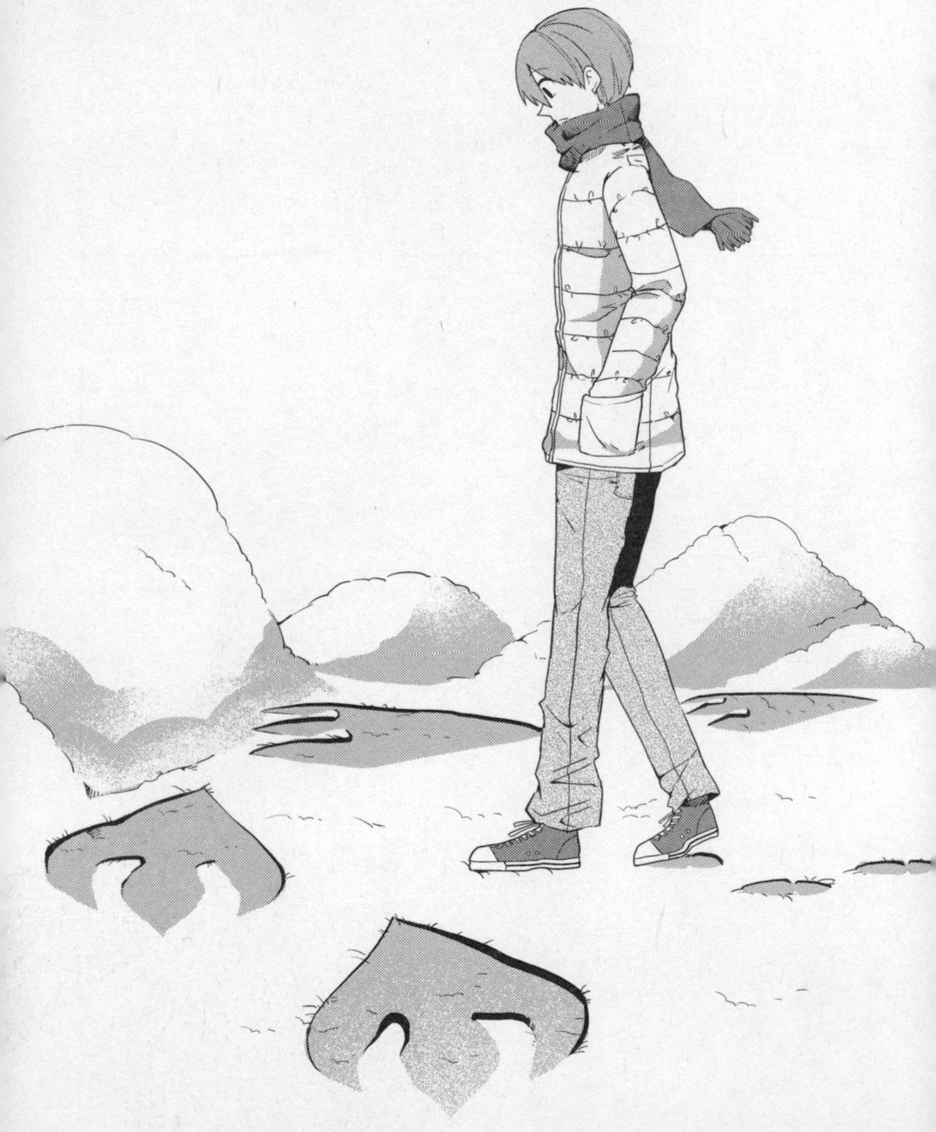

MUTUAL UNDERSTANDING

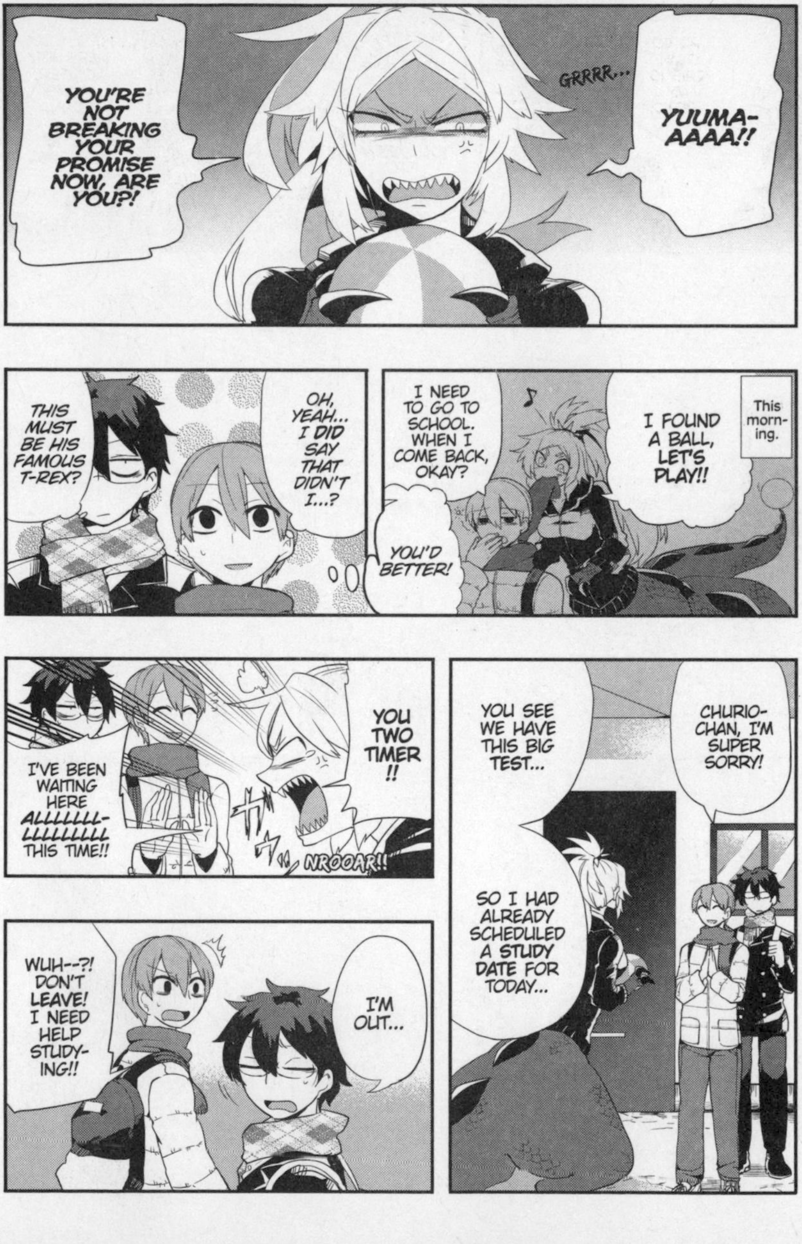
GRRRR...
YUUMA-AAAA!!
YOU'RE NOT BREAKING YOUR PROMISE NOW, ARE YOU?!
This morning.
I FOUND A BALL, LET'S PLAY!!
I NEED TO GO TO SCHOOL. WHEN I COME BACK, OKAY?
YOU'D BETTER!
OH, YEAH... I DID SAY THAT DIDN'T I...?
THIS MUST BE HIS FAMOUS T-REX?
CHURIO-CHAN, I'M SUPER SORRY!
YOU SEE WE HAVE THIS BIG TEST...
SO I HAD ALREADY SCHEDULED A STUDY DATE FOR TODAY...
YOU TWO TIMER!!
I'VE BEEN WAITING HERE ALLLLLLLL-LLLLLLLLL THIS TIME!!
NROOAR!!
I'M OUT...
WUH--?! DON'T LEAVE! I NEED HELP STUDY-ING!!

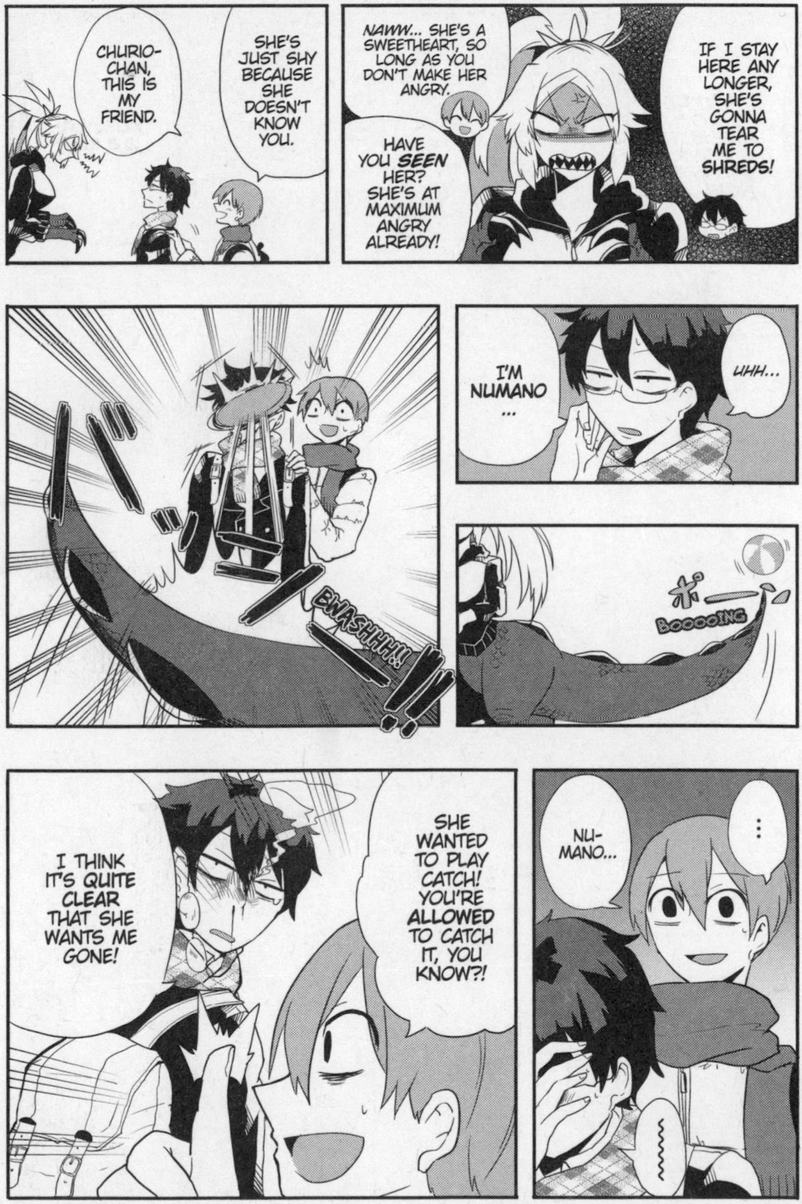
CHURIO-CHAN, THIS IS MY FRIEND.
SHE'S JUST SHY BECAUSE SHE DOESN'T KNOW YOU.
IF I STAY HERE ANY LONGER, SHE'S GONNA TEAR ME TO SHREDS!
NAWW... SHE'S A SWEETHEART, SO LONG AS YOU DON'T MAKE HER ANGRY.
HAVE YOU SEEN HER? SHE'S AT MAXIMUM ANGRY ALREADY!
UHH...
I'M NUMANO ...
BOOOOING
BWASHHH!!
...
NU-MANO...
SHE WANTED TO PLAY CATCH! YOU'RE ALLOWED TO CATCH IT, YOU KNOW?!
I THINK IT'S QUITE CLEAR THAT SHE WANTS ME GONE!

KOTATSU

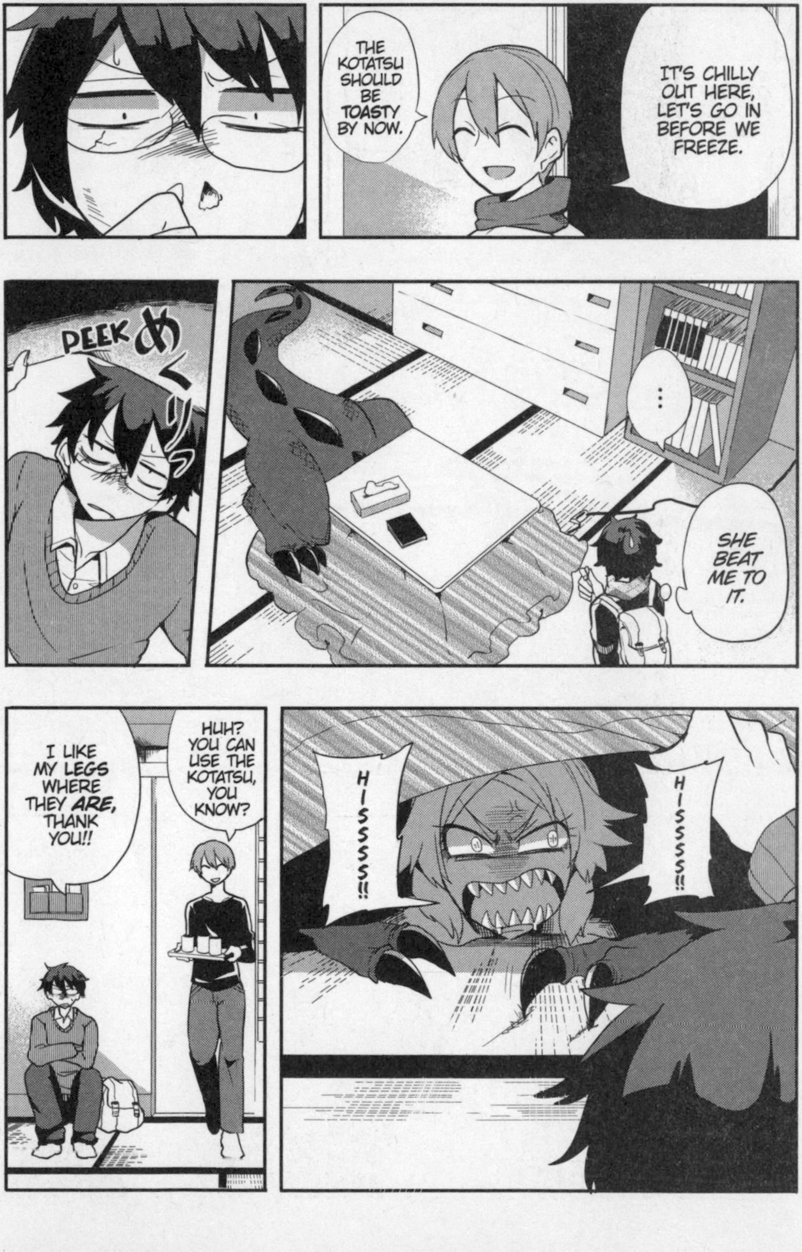
IT'S CHILLY OUT HERE, LET'S GO IN BEFORE WE FREEZE.
THE KOTATSU SHOULD BE TOASTY BY NOW.
...
SHE BEAT ME TO IT.
PEEK
HISSSS!!
HISSSS!!
HUH? YOU CAN USE THE KOTATSU, YOU KNOW?
I LIKE MY LEGS WHERE THEY ARE, THANK YOU!!

INSURANCE

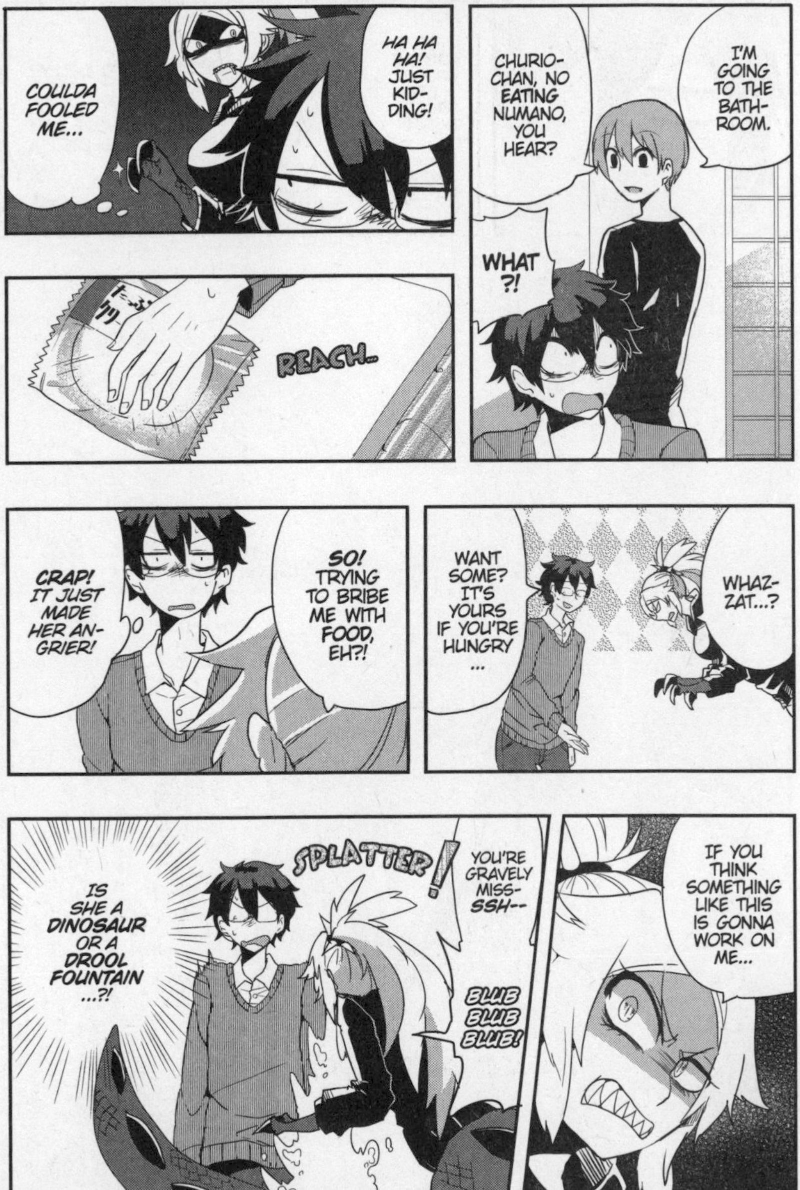

I'M GOING TO THE BATH-ROOM.
CHURIO-CHAN, NO EATING NUMANO, YOU HEAR?
WHAT?!
HA HA HA! JUST KID-DING!
COULDA FOOLED ME...
REACH..
WHAZ-ZAT...?
WANT SOME? IT'S YOURS IF YOU'RE HUNGRY ...
SO! TRYING TO BRIBE ME WITH FOOD, EH?!
CRAP! IT JUST MADE HER AN-GRIER!
IF YOU THINK SOMETHING LIKE THIS IS GONNA WORK ON ME...
YOU'RE GRAVELY MISS-SSH--
SPLATTER!
BLUB BLUB BLUB!
IS SHE A DINOSAUR OR A DROOL FOUNTAIN ...?!

OUT OF THE LOOP

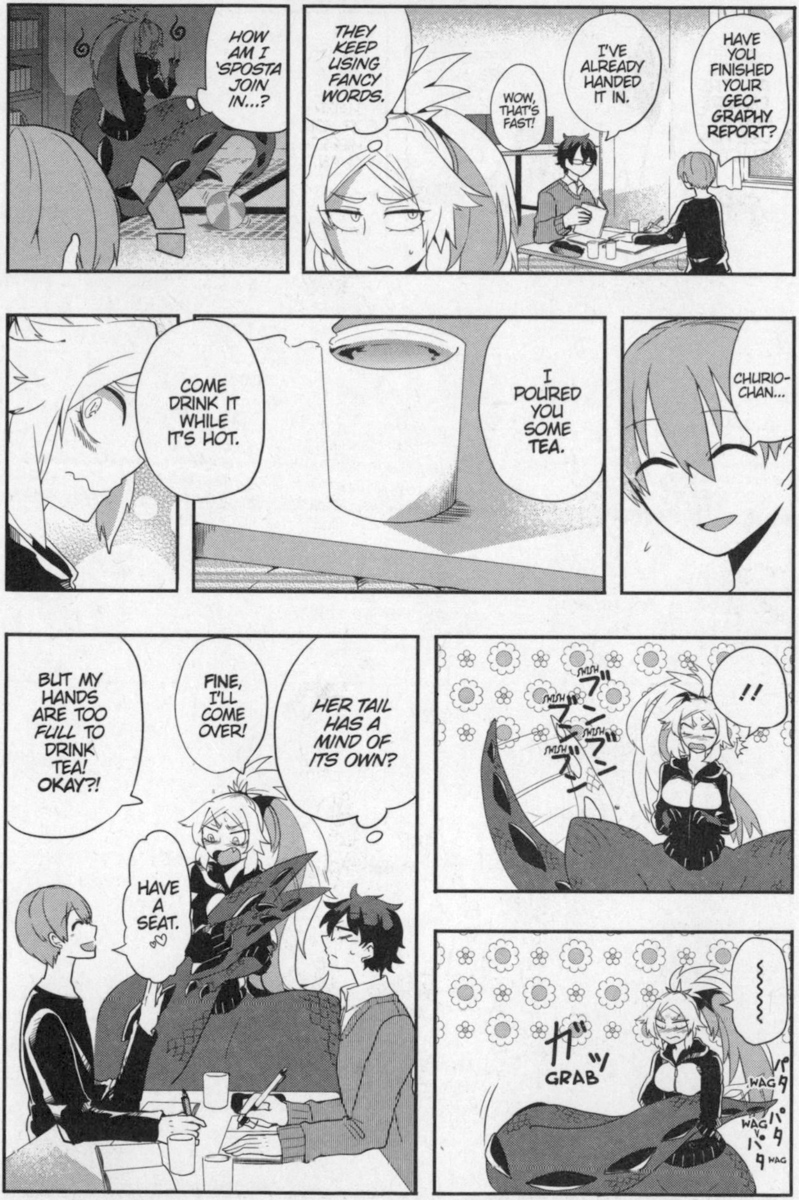
HAVE YOU FINISHED YOUR GEO-GRAPHY REPORT?
I'VE ALREADY HANDED IT IN.
WOW, THAT'S FAST!
THEY KEEP USING FANCY WORDS.
HOW AM I 'SPOSTA JOIN IN...?
CHURIO-CHAN...
I POURED YOU SOME TEA.
COME DRINK IT WHILE IT'S HOT.
SWISH
SWISH
SWISH
SWISH
!!
......
GRAB
WAG
WAG
WAG
HER TAIL HAS A MIND OF ITS OWN?
FINE, I'LL COME OVER!
BUT MY HANDS ARE TOO FULL TO DRINK TEA! OKAY?!
HAVE A SEAT.

THE JOY OF BOOKS

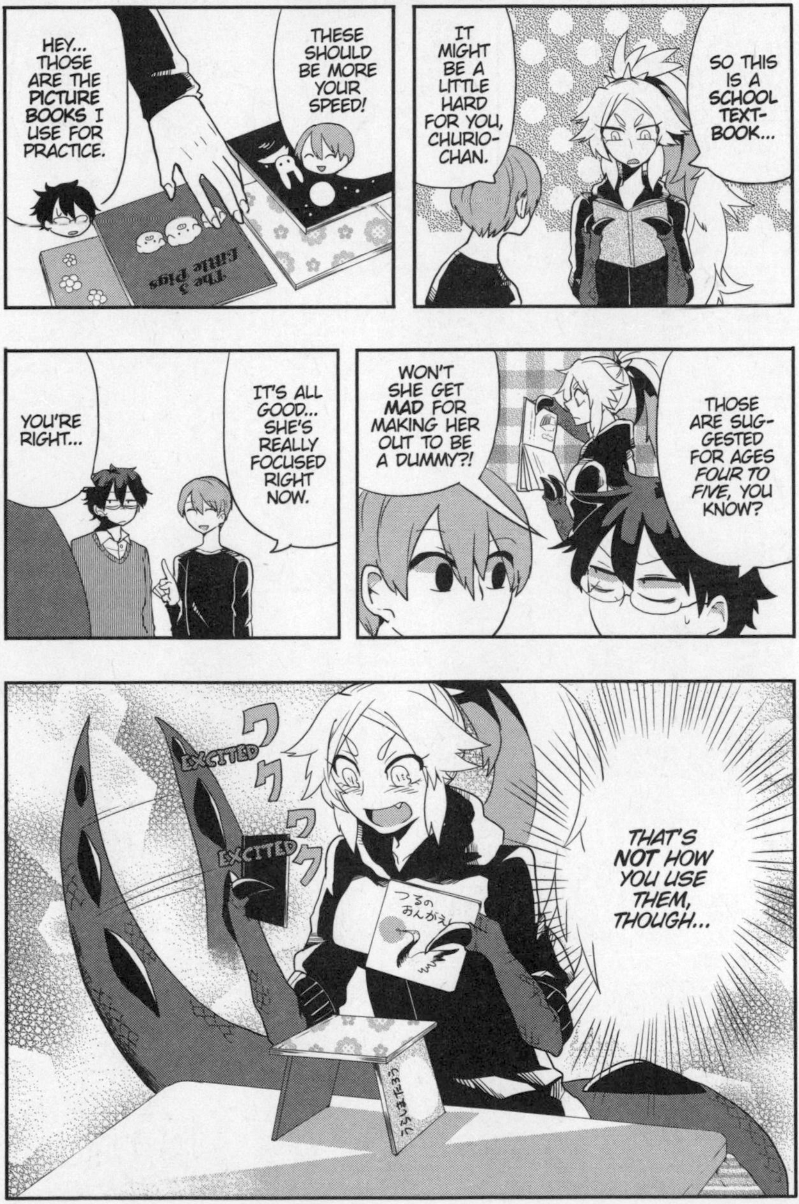
SO THIS IS A SCHOOL TEXT-BOOK...
IT MIGHT BE A LITTLE HARD FOR YOU, CHURIO-CHAN.
THESE SHOULD BE MORE YOUR SPEED!
HEY... THOSE ARE THE PICTURE BOOKS I USE FOR PRACTICE.
The 3 Little Pigs
THOSE ARE SUG-GESTED FOR AGES FOUR TO FIVE, YOU KNOW?
WON'T SHE GET MAD FOR MAKING HER OUT TO BE A DUMMY?!
IT'S ALL GOOD... SHE'S REALLY FOCUSED RIGHT NOW.
YOU'RE RIGHT...
EXCITED
ワクワク
EXCITED
つるのおんがえし
うらしまたろう
THAT'S NOT HOW YOU USE THEM, THOUGH...

MAKING UP

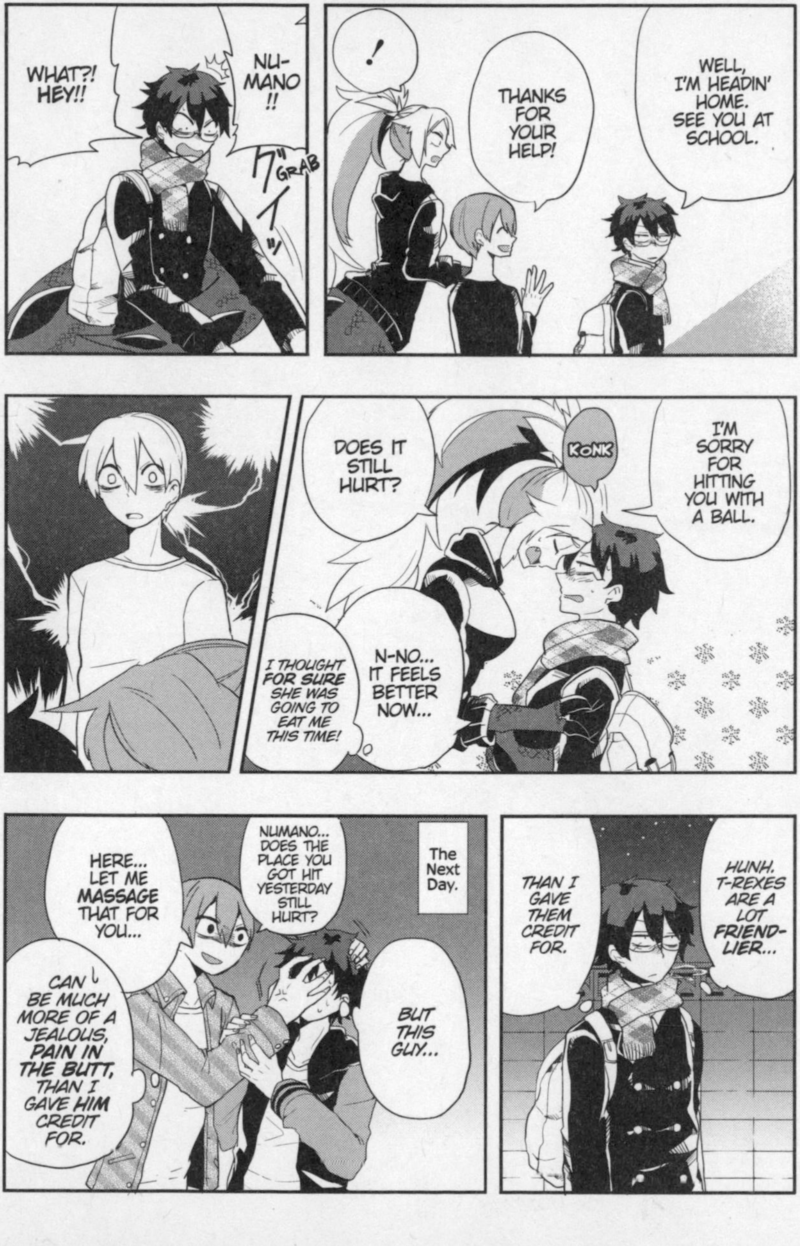
WELL, I'M HEADIN' HOME. SEE YOU AT SCHOOL.
THANKS FOR YOUR HELP!
!
NU-MANO !!
GRAB
WHAT?! HEY!!
I'M SORRY FOR HITTING YOU WITH A BALL.
KONK
DOES IT STILL HURT?
N-NO... IT FEELS BETTER NOW...
I THOUGHT FOR SURE SHE WAS GOING TO EAT ME THIS TIME!
HUNH. T-REXES ARE A LOT FRIENDLIER...
THAN I GAVE THEM CREDIT FOR.
The Next Day.
NUMANO... DOES THE PLACE YOU GOT HIT YESTERDAY STILL HURT?
HERE... LET ME MASSAGE THAT FOR YOU...
BUT THIS GUY...
CAN BE MUCH MORE OF A JEALOUS, PAIN IN THE BUTT, THAN I GAVE HIM CREDIT FOR.

My Girlfriend is a T-REX

I need new glasses...

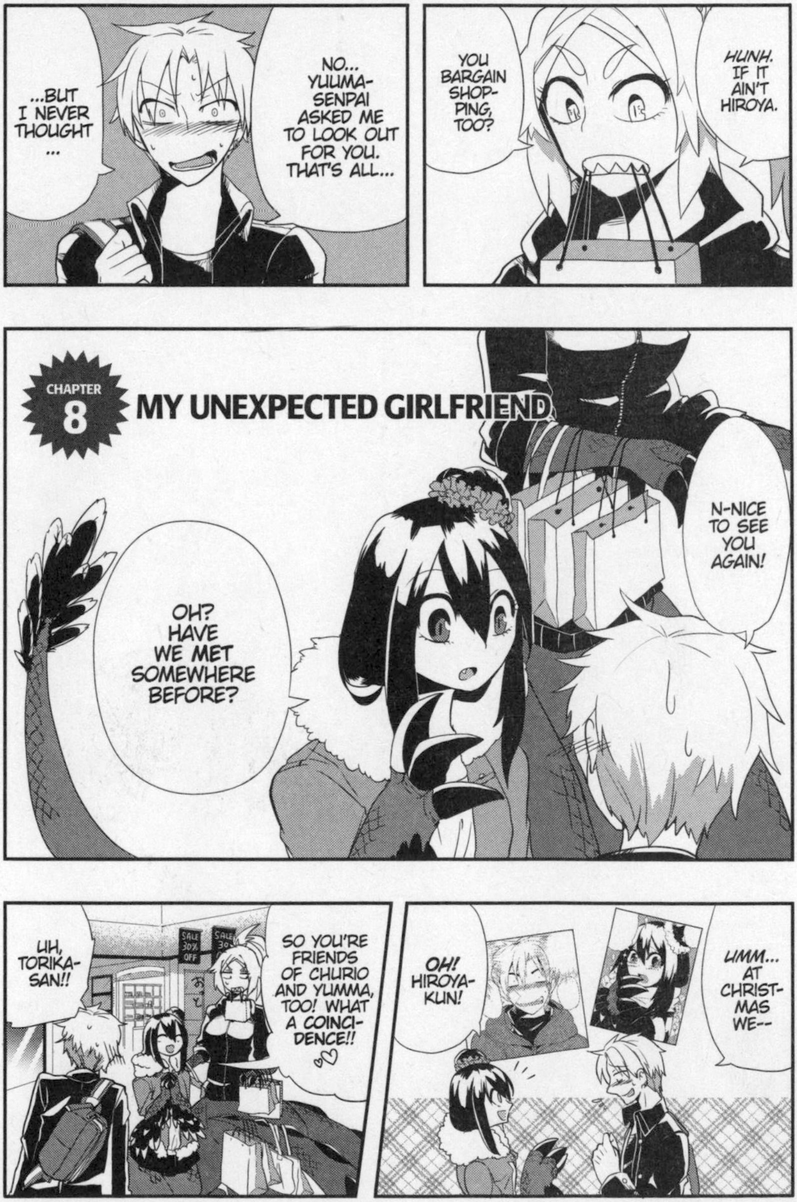
HUNH. IF IT AIN'T HIROYA.
YOU BARGAIN SHOP-PING, TOO?
NO... YUUMA-SENPAI ASKED ME TO LOOK OUT FOR YOU. THAT'S ALL...
...BUT I NEVER THOUGHT ...
CHAPTER 8
MY UNEXPECTED GIRLFRIEND
N-NICE TO SEE YOU AGAIN!
OH? HAVE WE MET SOMEWHERE BEFORE?
UMM... AT CHRIST-MAS WE--
OH! HIROYA-KUN!
SO YOU'RE FRIENDS OF CHURIO AND YUMMA, TOO! WHAT A COINCI-DENCE!!
SALE 30% OFF
UH, TORIKA-SAN!!

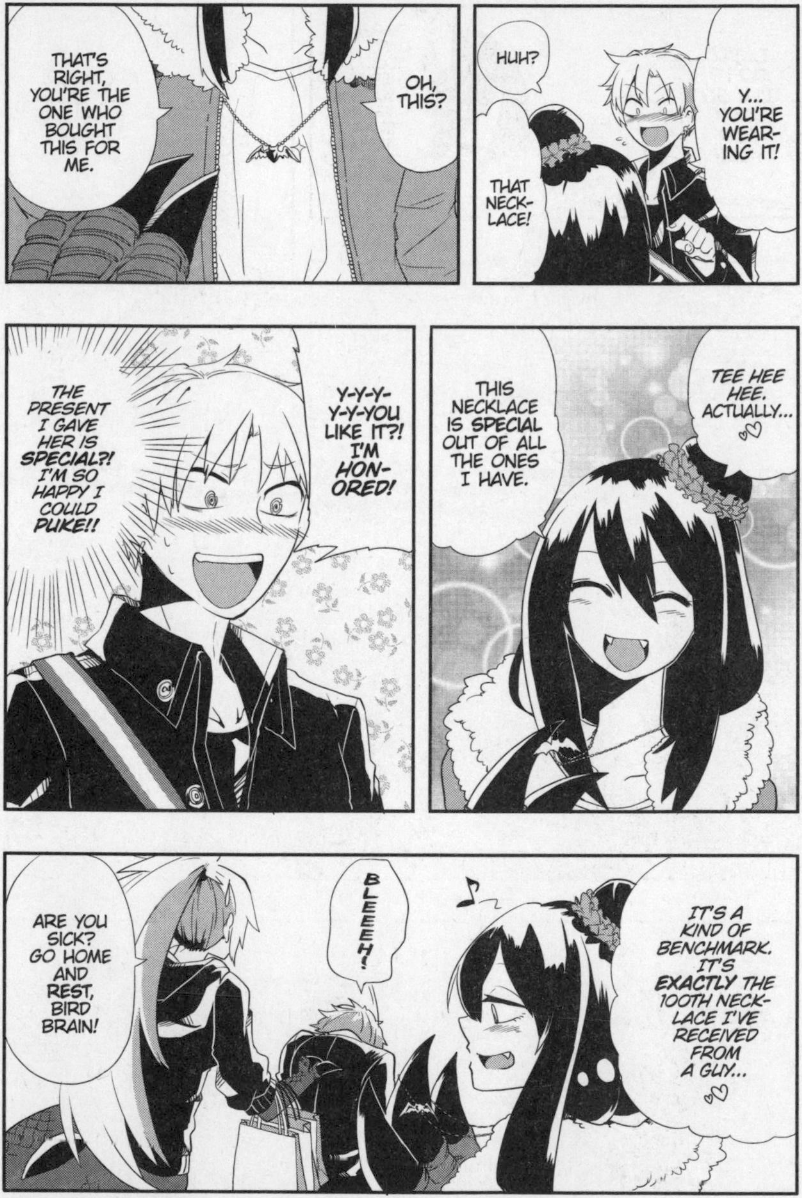
Y... YOU'RE WEARING IT!
HUH?
THAT NECKLACE!
OH, THIS?
THAT'S RIGHT, YOU'RE THE ONE WHO BOUGHT THIS FOR ME.
TEE HEE HEE. ACTUALLY... ♡
THIS NECKLACE IS SPECIAL OUT OF ALL THE ONES I HAVE.
Y-Y-Y-Y-Y-YOU LIKE IT?! I'M HONORED!
THE PRESENT I GAVE HER IS SPECIAL?! I'M SO HAPPY I COULD PUKE!!
IT'S A KIND OF BENCHMARK. IT'S EXACTLY THE 100TH NECKLACE I'VE RECEIVED FROM A GUY... ♡
BLEEEH!
ARE YOU SICK? GO HOME AND REST, BIRD BRAIN!

LOST AND FOUND

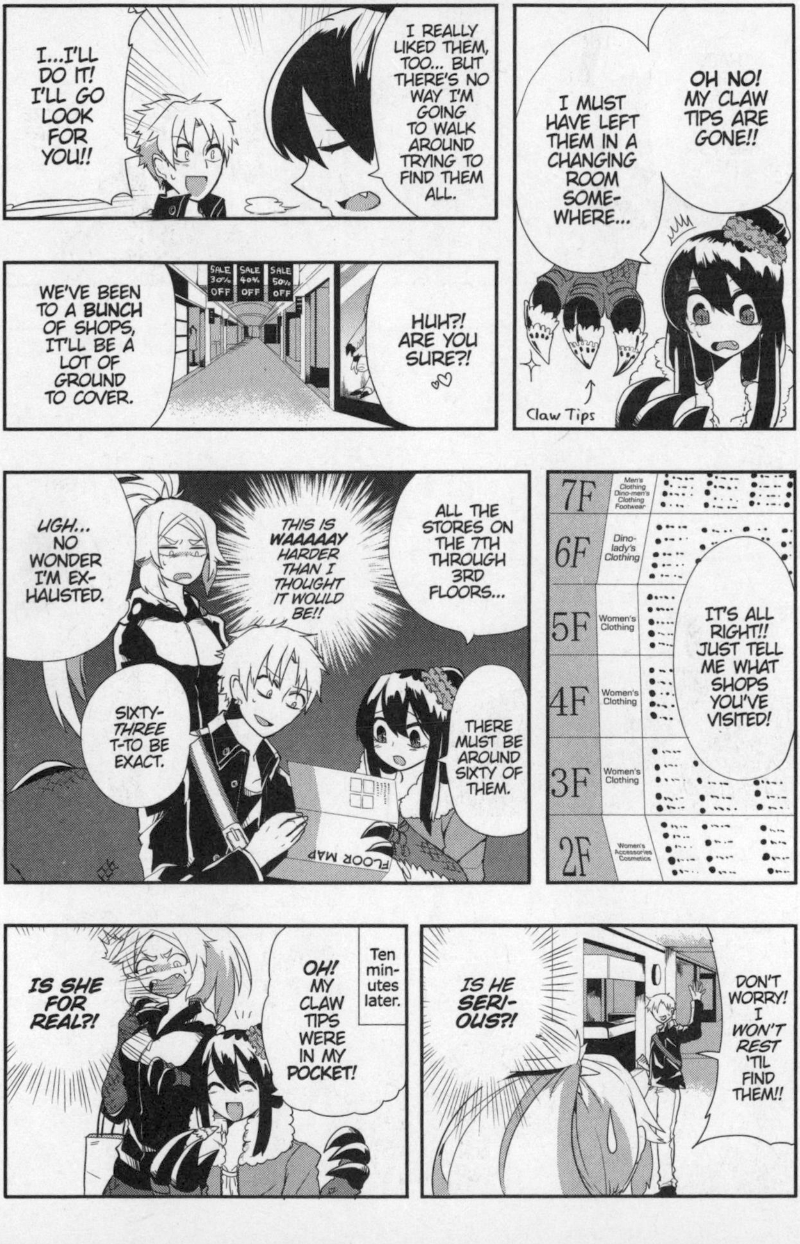
OH NO! MY CLAW TIPS ARE GONE!!
I MUST HAVE LEFT THEM IN A CHANGING ROOM SOME-WHERE...
Claw Tips
I REALLY LIKED THEM, TOO... BUT THERE'S NO WAY I'M GOING TO WALK AROUND TRYING TO FIND THEM ALL.
I...I'LL DO IT! I'LL GO LOOK FOR YOU!!
HUH?! ARE YOU SURE?! ♡
SALE 30% OFF
SALE 40% OFF
SALE 50% OFF
WE'VE BEEN TO A BUNCH OF SHOPS, IT'LL BE A LOT OF GROUND TO COVER.
IT'S ALL RIGHT!! JUST TELL ME WHAT SHOPS YOU'VE VISITED!
7F Men's Clothing Dino-men's Clothing Footwear
6F Dino-lady's Clothing
5F Women's Clothing
4F Women's Clothing
3F Women's Clothing
2F Women's Accessories Cosmetics
ALL THE STORES ON THE 7TH THROUGH 3RD FLOORS...
THERE MUST BE AROUND SIXTY OF THEM.
THIS IS WAAAAAY HARDER THAN I THOUGHT IT WOULD BE!!
SIXTY-THREE T-TO BE EXACT.
UGH... NO WONDER I'M EX-HAUSTED.
FLOOR MAP
DON'T WORRY! I WON'T REST 'TIL FIND THEM!!
IS HE SERI-OUS?!
Ten min-utes later.
OH! MY CLAW TIPS WERE IN MY POCKET!
IS SHE FOR REAL?!

REWARD

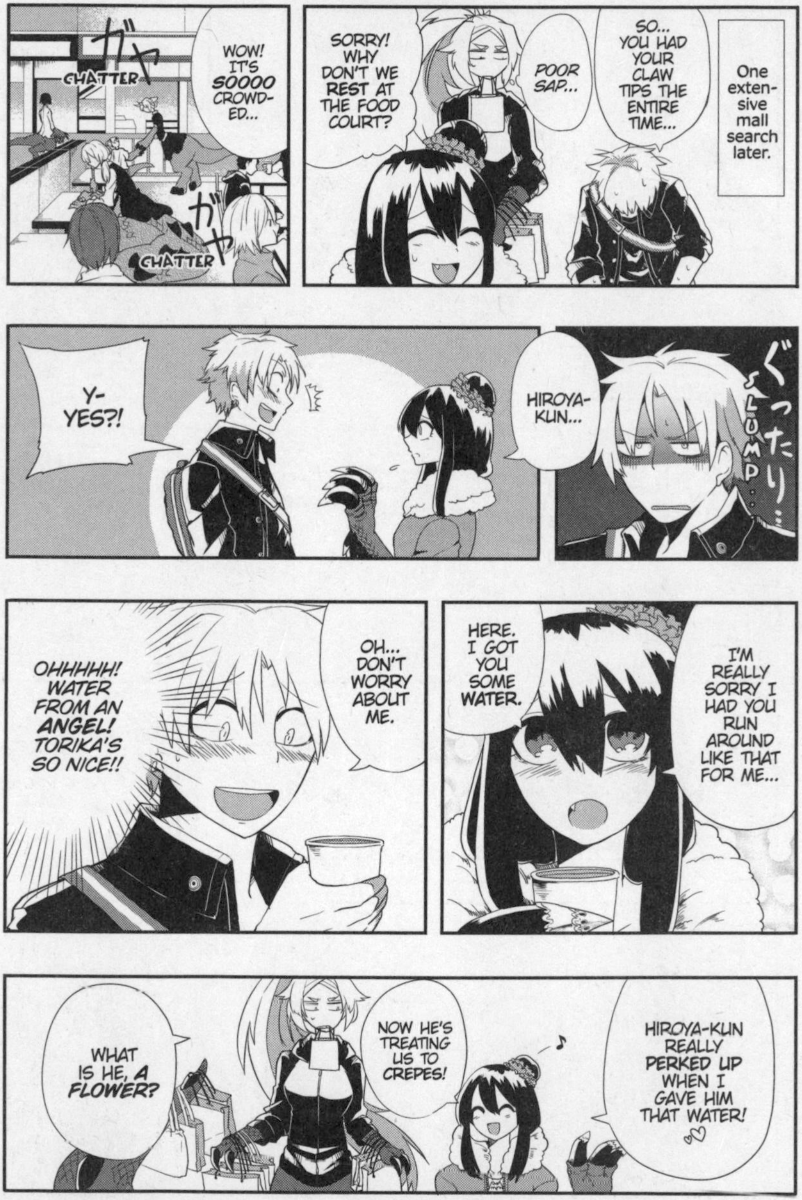
One extensive mall search later.
SO... YOU HAD YOUR CLAW TIPS THE ENTIRE TIME...
POOR SAP...
SORRY! WHY DON'T WE REST AT THE FOOD COURT?
WOW! IT'S SOOOO CROWDED...
ガヤ
CHATTER
ガヤ
CHATTER
ぐったり
SLUMP...
HIROYA-KUN...
Y-YES?!
I'M REALLY SORRY I HAD YOU RUN AROUND LIKE THAT FOR ME...
HERE. I GOT YOU SOME WATER.
OH... DON'T WORRY ABOUT ME.
OHHHHH! WATER FROM AN ANGEL! TORIKA'S SO NICE!!
HIROYA-KUN REALLY PERKED UP WHEN I GAVE HIM THAT WATER! ♡
NOW HE'S TREATING US TO CREPES!
WHAT IS HE, A FLOWER?

PLAYING FAVORITES

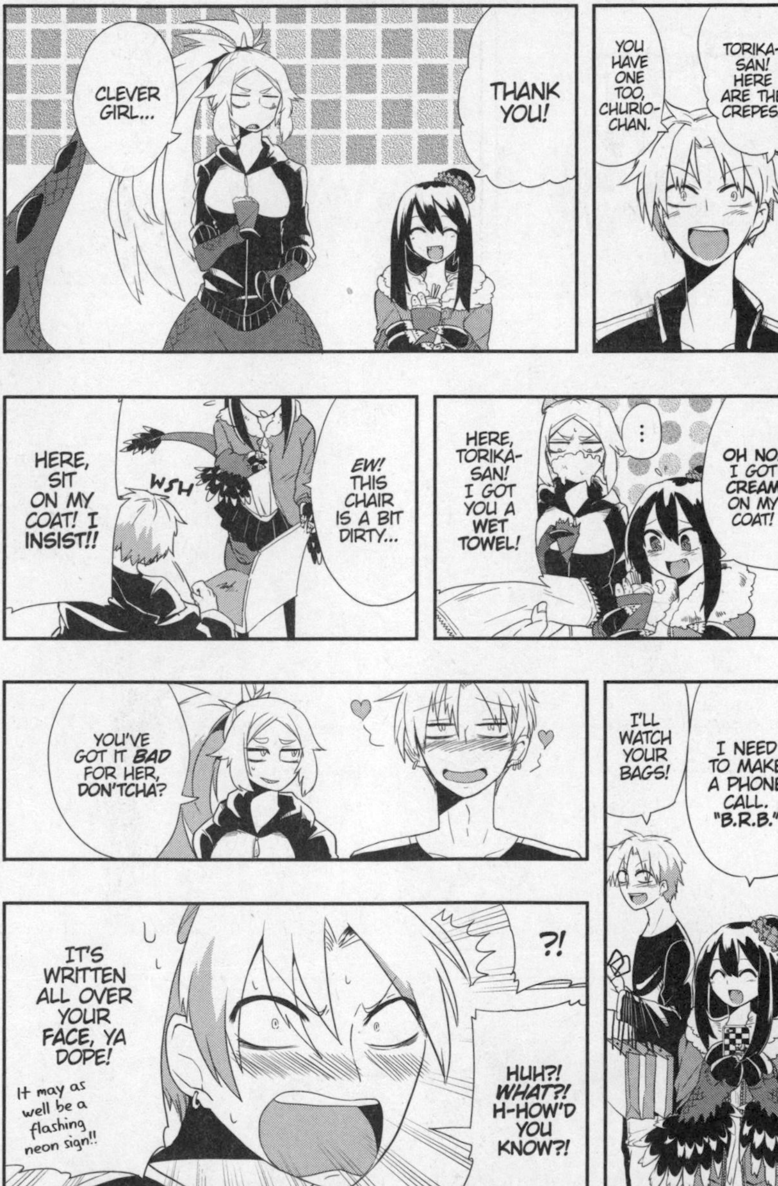
TORIKA-SAN! HERE ARE THE CREPES!
YOU HAVE ONE TOO, CHURIO-CHAN.
THANK YOU!
CLEVER GIRL...
OH NO! I GOT CREAM ON MY COAT!
...
HERE, TORIKA-SAN! I GOT YOU A WET TOWEL!
EW! THIS CHAIR IS A BIT DIRTY...
WSH
HERE, SIT ON MY COAT! I INSIST!!
I NEED TO MAKE A PHONE CALL. "B.R.B."
I'LL WATCH YOUR BAGS!
YOU'VE GOT IT *BAD* FOR HER, DON'TCHA?
?!
HUH?! *WHAT?!* H-HOW'D YOU KNOW?!
IT'S WRITTEN ALL OVER YOUR FACE, YA DOPE!
It may as well be a flashing neon sign!!

SCARED OF MICE

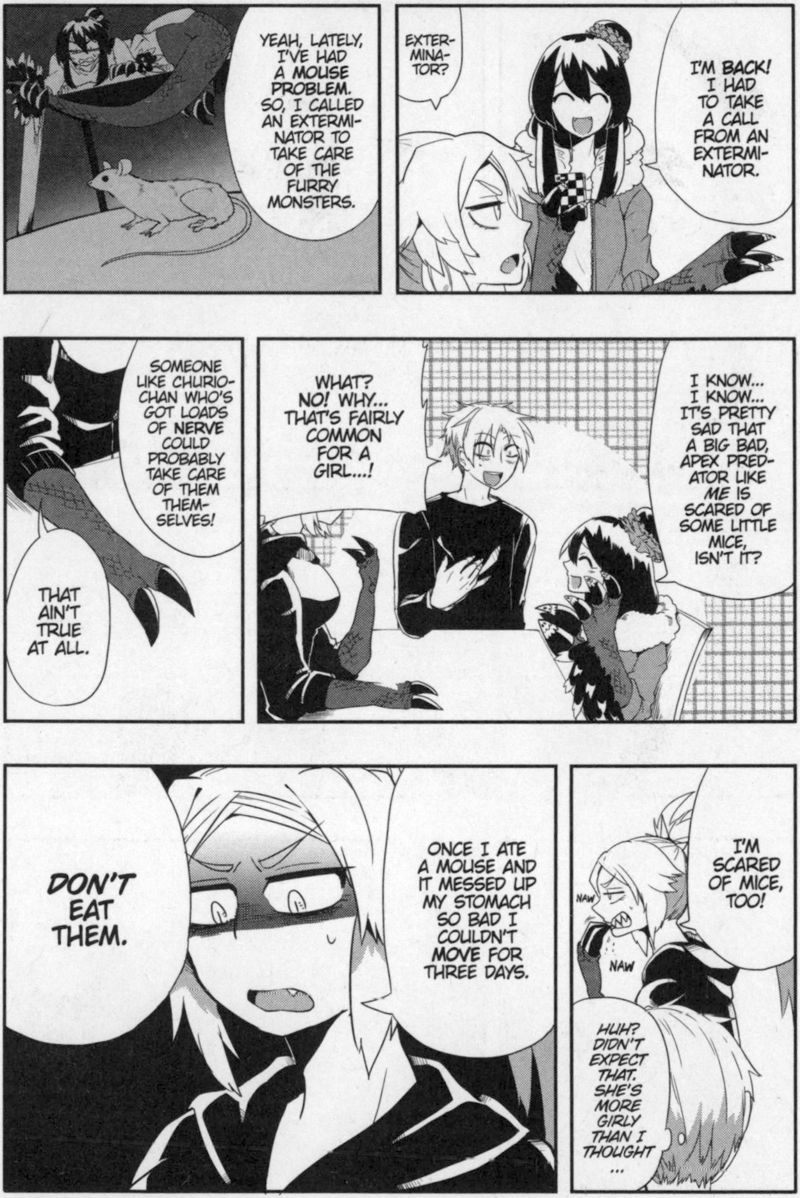
I'M BACK! I HAD TO TAKE A CALL FROM AN EXTERMINATOR.
EXTERMINATOR?
YEAH, LATELY, I'VE HAD A MOUSE PROBLEM. SO, I CALLED AN EXTERMINATOR TO TAKE CARE OF THE FURRY MONSTERS.
I KNOW... I KNOW... IT'S PRETTY SAD THAT A BIG BAD, APEX PREDATOR LIKE *ME* IS SCARED OF SOME LITTLE MICE, ISN'T IT?
WHAT? NO! WHY... THAT'S FAIRLY COMMON FOR A GIRL...!
SOMEONE LIKE CHURIO-CHAN WHO'S GOT LOADS OF NERVE COULD PROBABLY TAKE CARE OF THEM THEMSELVES!
THAT AIN'T TRUE AT ALL.
I'M SCARED OF MICE, TOO!
NAW
NAW
HUH? DIDN'T EXPECT THAT. SHE'S MORE GIRLY THAN I THOUGHT...
ONCE I ATE A MOUSE AND IT MESSED UP MY STOMACH SO BAD I COULDN'T MOVE FOR THREE DAYS.
***DON'T* EAT THEM.**

PRECIOUS OBJECTS

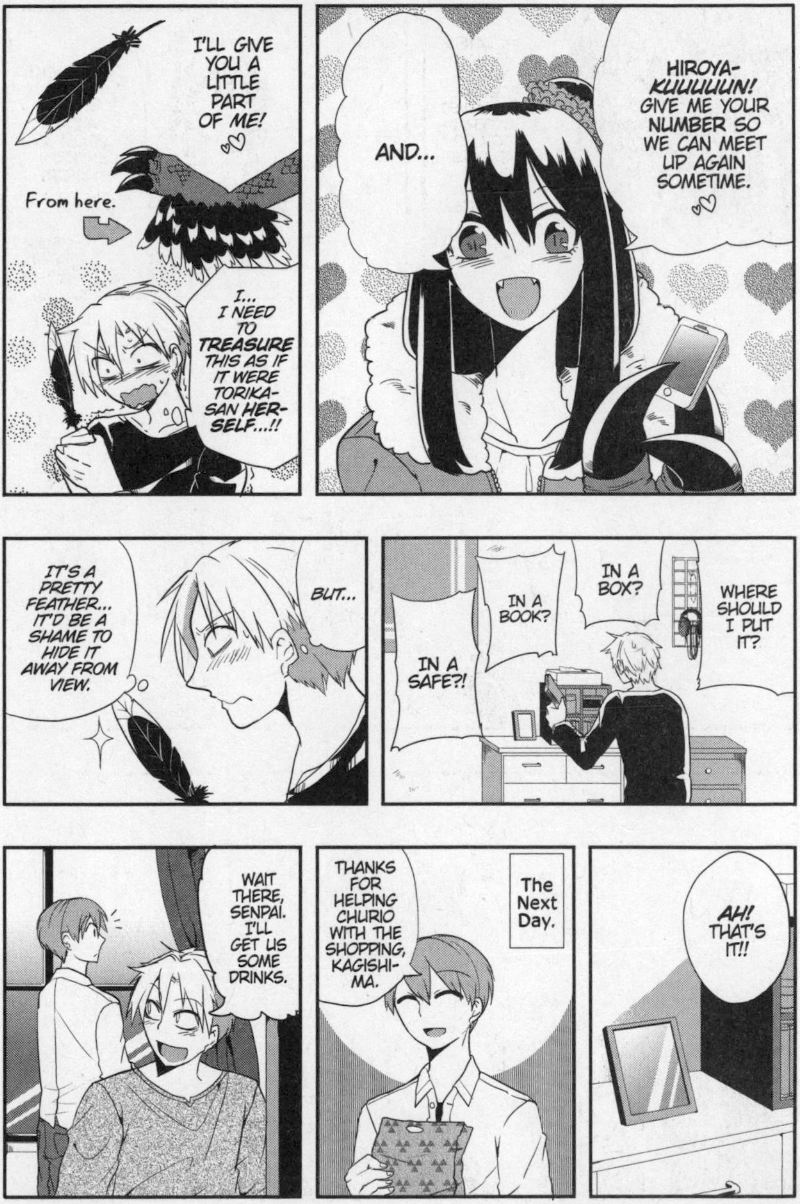
HIROYA-KUUUUUUN! GIVE ME YOUR NUMBER SO WE CAN MEET UP AGAIN SOMETIME.
AND...
I'LL GIVE YOU A LITTLE PART OF ME!
From here.
I... I NEED TO TREASURE THIS AS IF IT WERE TORIKA-SAN HERSELF...!!
WHERE SHOULD I PUT IT?
IN A BOX?
IN A BOOK?
IN A SAFE?!
BUT...
IT'S A PRETTY FEATHER... IT'D BE A SHAME TO HIDE IT AWAY FROM VIEW.
AH! THAT'S IT!!
The Next Day.
THANKS FOR HELPING CHURIO WITH THE SHOPPING, KAGISHIMA.
WAIT THERE, SENPAI. I'LL GET US SOME DRINKS.

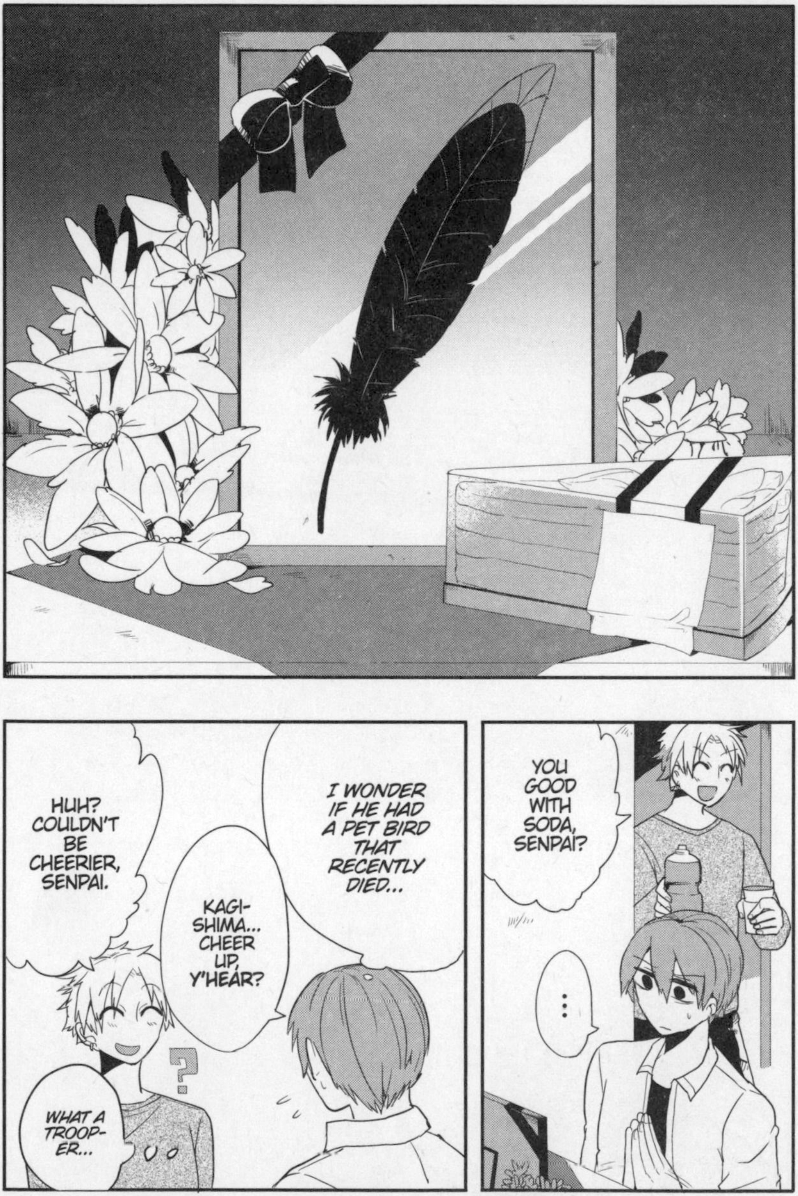
YOU GOOD WITH SODA, SENPAI?
...
I WONDER IF HE HAD A PET BIRD THAT RECENTLY DIED...
KAGI-SHIMA... CHEER UP, Y'HEAR?
HUH? COULDN'T BE CHEERIER, SENPAI.
?
WHAT A TROOP-ER...

My Girlfriend is a
T-REX

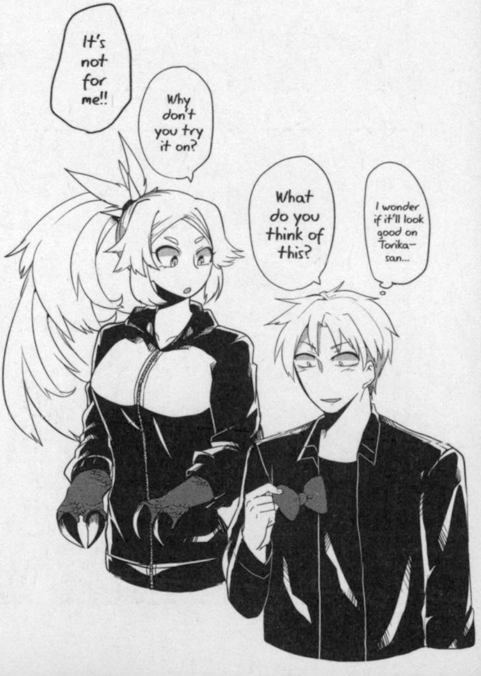
I wonder if it'll look good on Torika-san...
What do you think of this?
Why don't you try it on?
It's not for me!!

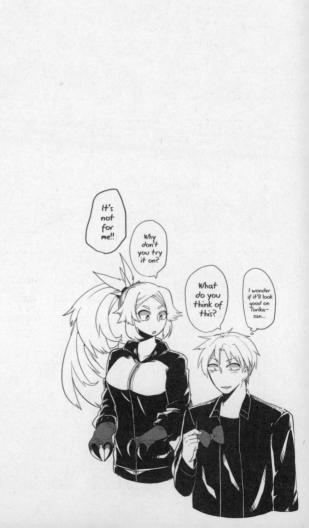

CHAPTER 9

MY LOVEY-DOVEY GIRLFRIEND

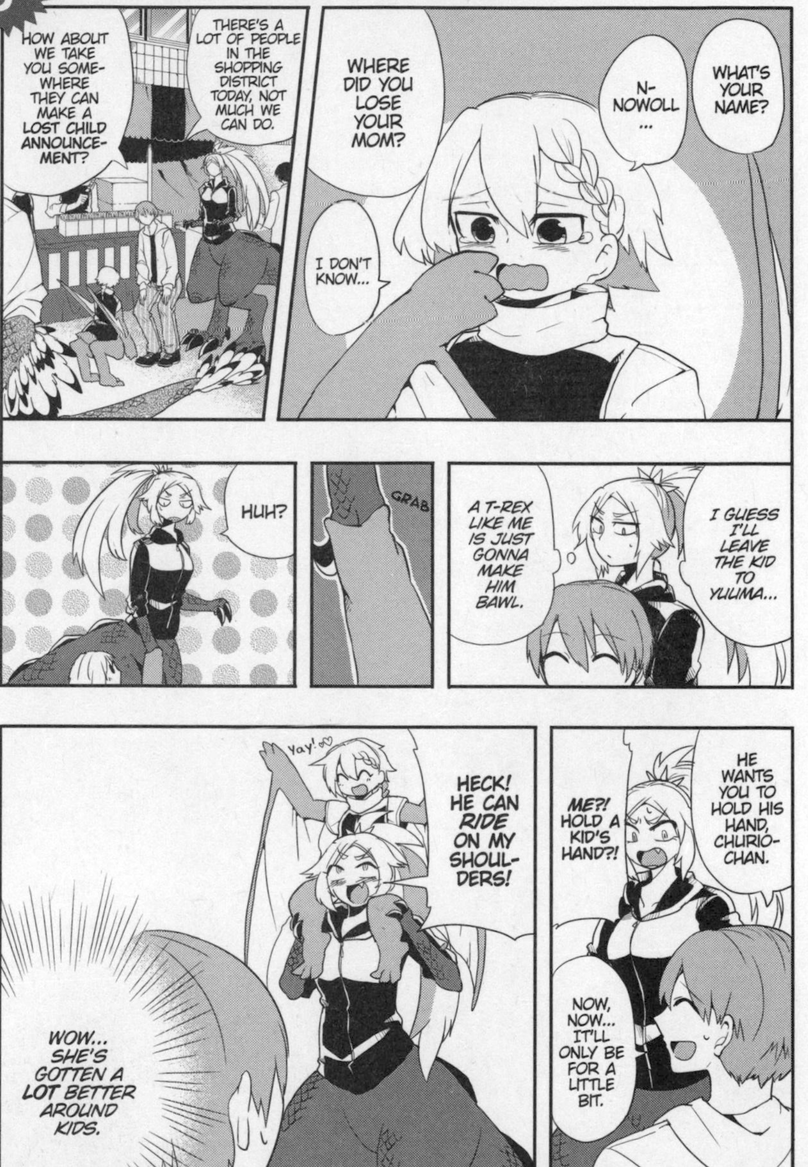
WHAT'S YOUR NAME?
N-NOWOLL ...
WHERE DID YOU LOSE YOUR MOM?
I DON'T KNOW...
THERE'S A LOT OF PEOPLE IN THE SHOPPING DISTRICT TODAY, NOT MUCH WE CAN DO.
HOW ABOUT WE TAKE YOU SOME-WHERE THEY CAN MAKE A LOST CHILD ANNOUNCE-MENT?
I GUESS I'LL LEAVE THE KID TO YUUMA...
A T-REX LIKE ME IS JUST GONNA MAKE HIM BAWL.
GRAB
HUH?
HE WANTS YOU TO HOLD HIS HAND, CHURIO-CHAN.
ME?! HOLD A KID'S HAND?!
NOW, NOW... IT'LL ONLY BE FOR A LITTLE BIT.
HECK! HE CAN RIDE ON MY SHOUL-DERS!
Yay!
WOW... SHE'S GOTTEN A LOT BETTER AROUND KIDS.

PRIMAL INSTINCTS

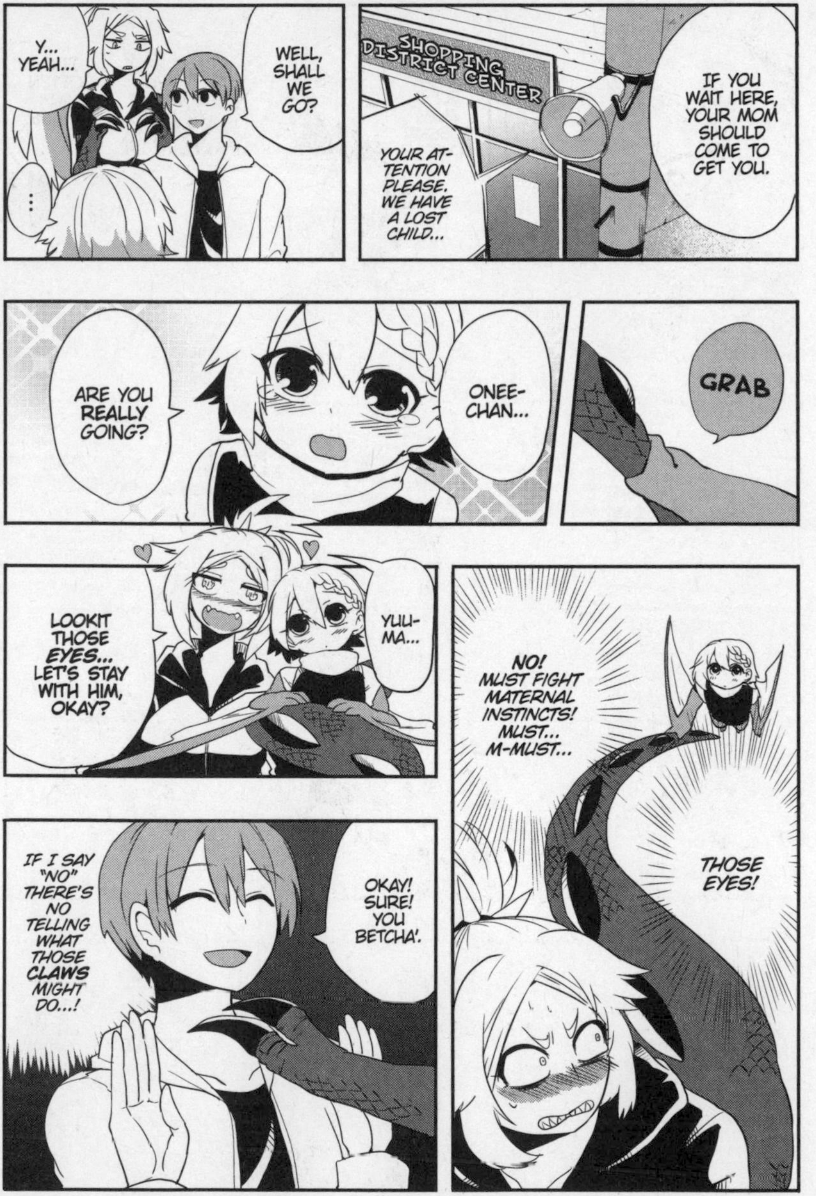
SHOPPING DISTRICT CENTER
YOUR ATTENTION PLEASE. WE HAVE A LOST CHILD...
IF YOU WAIT HERE, YOUR MOM SHOULD COME TO GET YOU.
WELL, SHALL WE GO?
Y... YEAH...
...
GRAB
ONEE-CHAN...
ARE YOU REALLY GOING?
NO! MUST FIGHT MATERNAL INSTINCTS! MUST... M-MUST...
THOSE EYES!
YUU-MA...
LOOKIT THOSE EYES... LET'S STAY WITH HIM, OKAY?
OKAY! SURE! YOU BETCHA'.
IF I SAY "NO" THERE'S NO TELLING WHAT THOSE CLAWS MIGHT DO...!

YUUMA AND NOWOLL-KUN

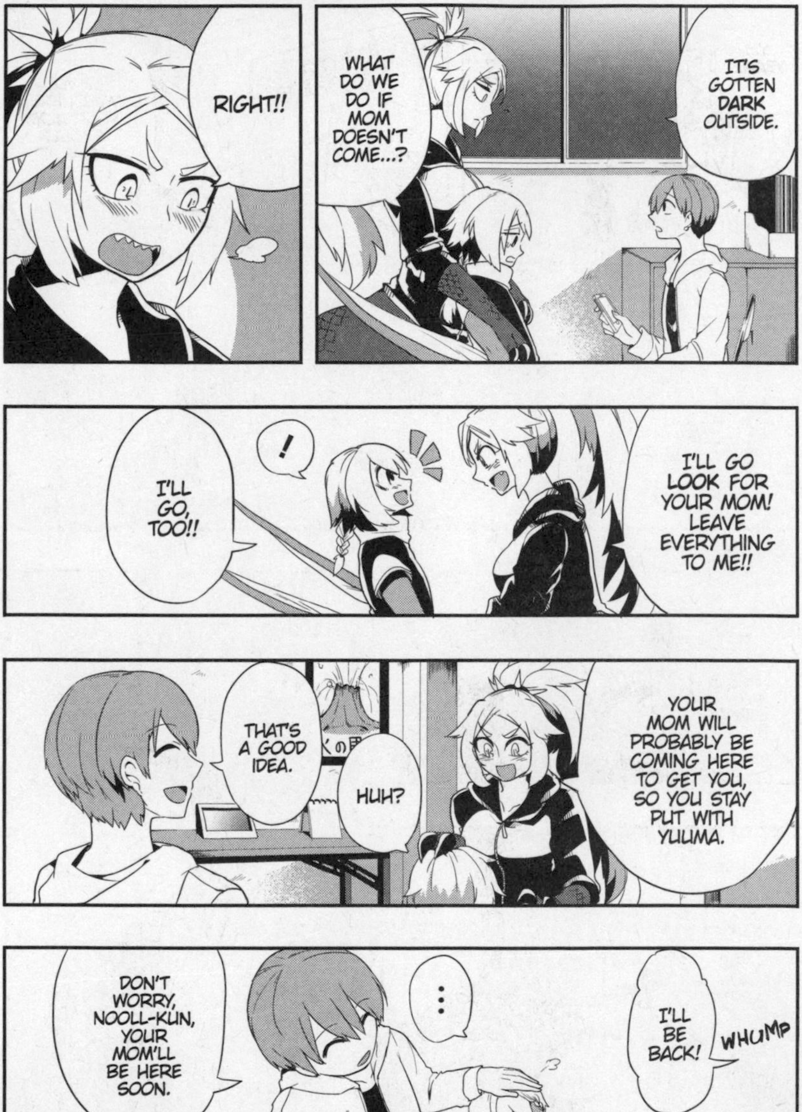
IT'S GOTTEN DARK OUTSIDE.
WHAT DO WE DO IF MOM DOESN'T COME...?
RIGHT!!
I'LL GO LOOK FOR YOUR MOM! LEAVE EVERYTHING TO ME!!
!
I'LL GO, TOO!!
YOUR MOM WILL PROBABLY BE COMING HERE TO GET YOU, SO YOU STAY PUT WITH YUUMA.
HUH?
THAT'S A GOOD IDEA.
I'LL BE BACK!
WHUMP
WHUMP
...
DON'T WORRY, NOOLL-KUN, YOUR MOM'LL BE HERE SOON.

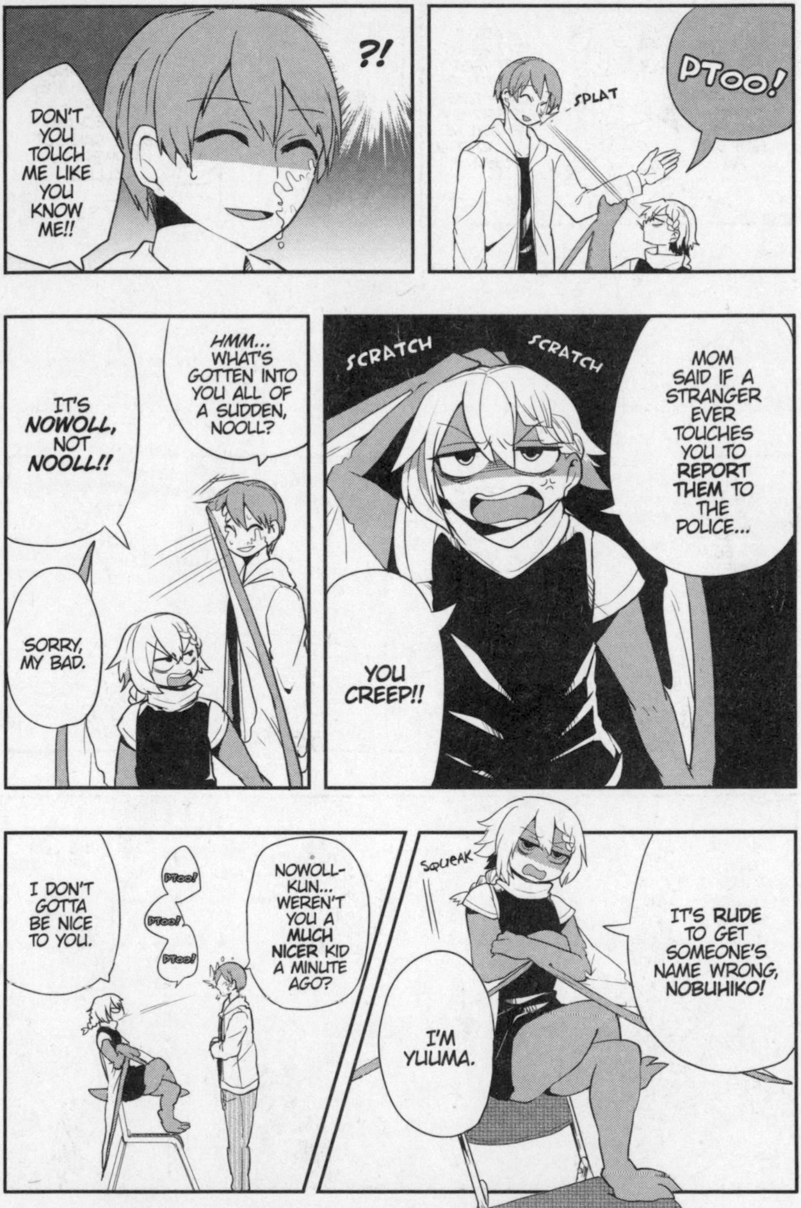
PTOO!
SPLAT
?!
DON'T YOU TOUCH ME LIKE YOU KNOW ME!!
SCRATCH
SCRATCH
MOM SAID IF A STRANGER EVER TOUCHES YOU TO REPORT THEM TO THE POLICE...
YOU CREEP!!
HMM... WHAT'S GOTTEN INTO YOU ALL OF A SUDDEN, NOOLL?
IT'S NOWOLL, NOT NOOLL!!
SORRY, MY BAD.
SQUEAK
IT'S RUDE TO GET SOMEONE'S NAME WRONG, NOBUHIKO!
I'M YUUMA.
NOWOLL-KUN... WEREN'T YOU A MUCH NICER KID A MINUTE AGO?
PTOO!
PTOO!
PTOO!
I DON'T GOTTA BE NICE TO YOU.

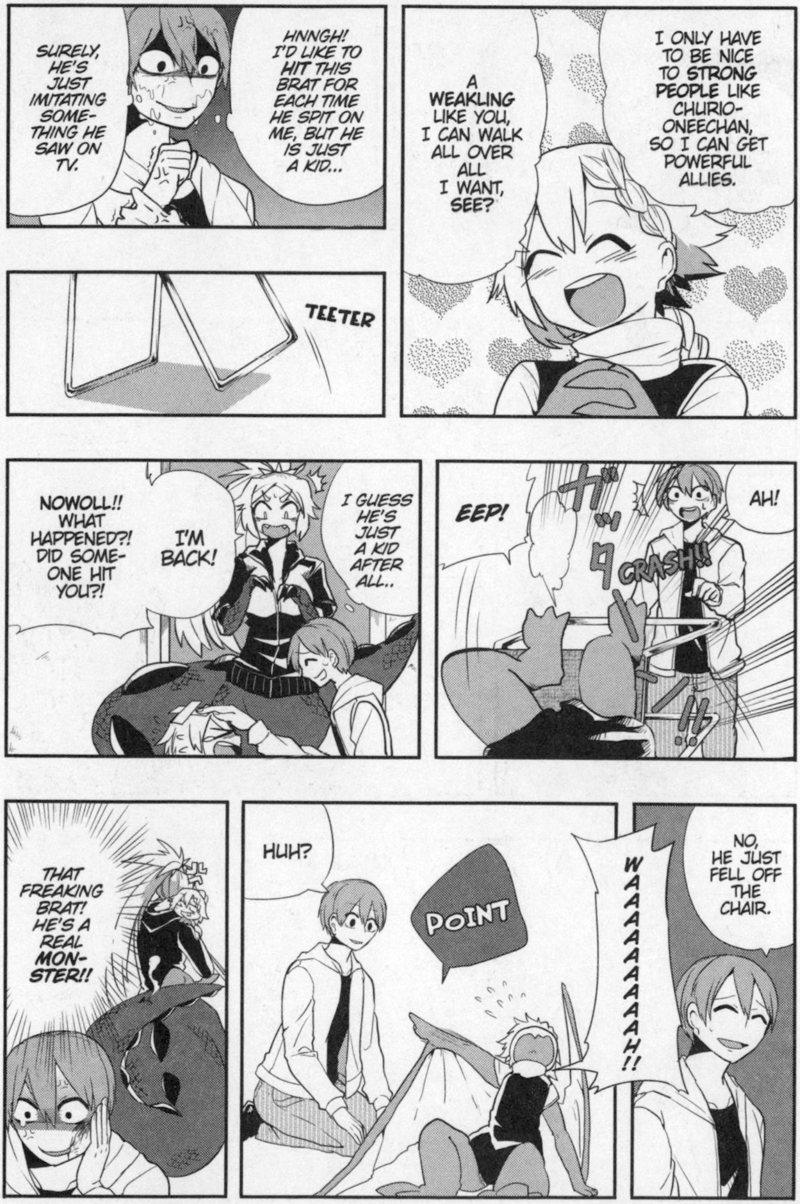

I ONLY HAVE TO BE NICE TO STRONG PEOPLE LIKE CHURIO-ONEECHAN, SO I CAN GET POWERFUL ALLIES.
A WEAKLING LIKE YOU, I CAN WALK ALL OVER ALL I WANT, SEE?
HNNGH! I'D LIKE TO HIT THIS BRAT FOR EACH TIME HE SPIT ON ME, BUT HE IS JUST A KID...
SURELY, HE'S JUST IMITATING SOME-THING HE SAW ON TV.
TEETER
AH!
EEP!
CRASH!!
I GUESS HE'S JUST A KID AFTER ALL..
I'M BACK!
NOWOLL!! WHAT HAPPENED?! DID SOME-ONE HIT YOU?!
NO, HE JUST FELL OFF THE CHAIR.
WAAAAAAAAAAH!!
POINT
HUH?
THAT FREAKING BRAT! HE'S A REAL MON-STER!!

LET'S TALK IT OVER

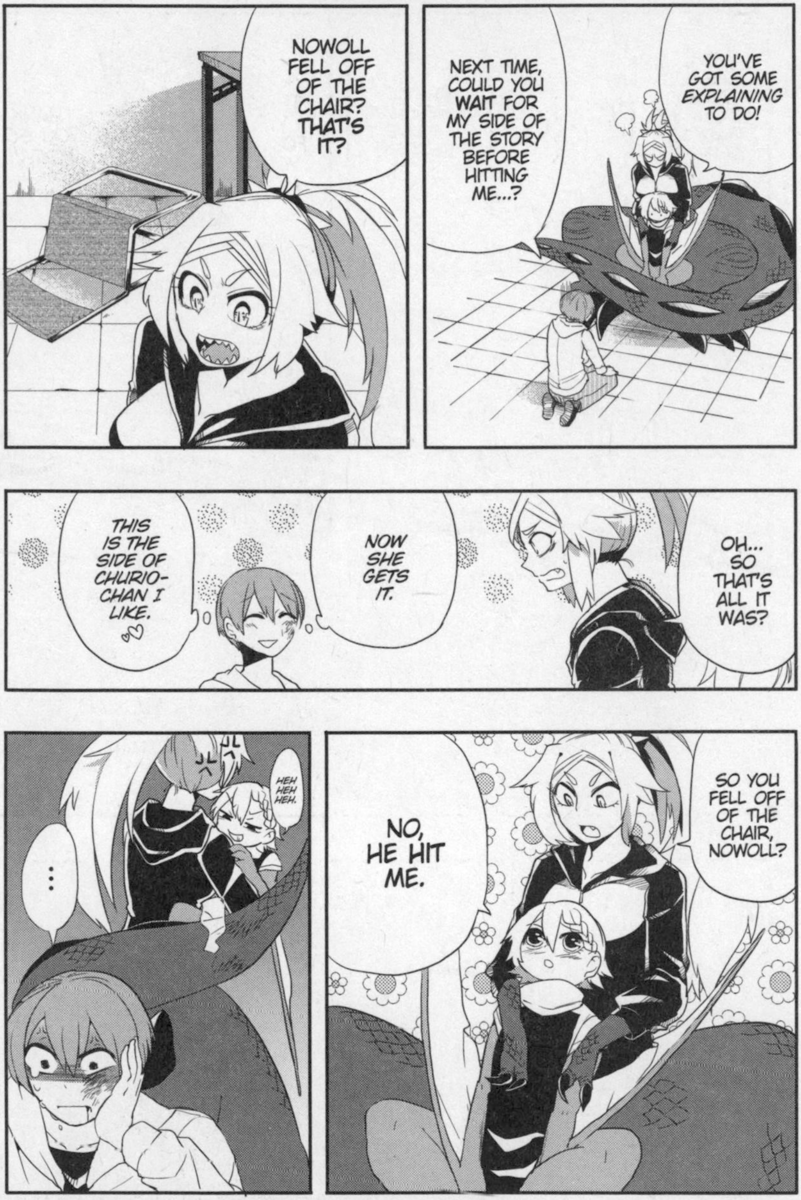
YOU'VE GOT SOME EXPLAINING TO DO!
NEXT TIME, COULD YOU WAIT FOR MY SIDE OF THE STORY BEFORE HITTING ME...?
NOWOLL FELL OFF OF THE CHAIR? THAT'S IT?
OH... SO THAT'S ALL IT WAS?
NOW SHE GETS IT.
THIS IS THE SIDE OF CHURIO-CHAN I LIKE. ♡
SO YOU FELL OFF OF THE CHAIR, NOWOLL?
NO, HE HIT ME.
HEH HEH HEH.
...

RESTRAINT

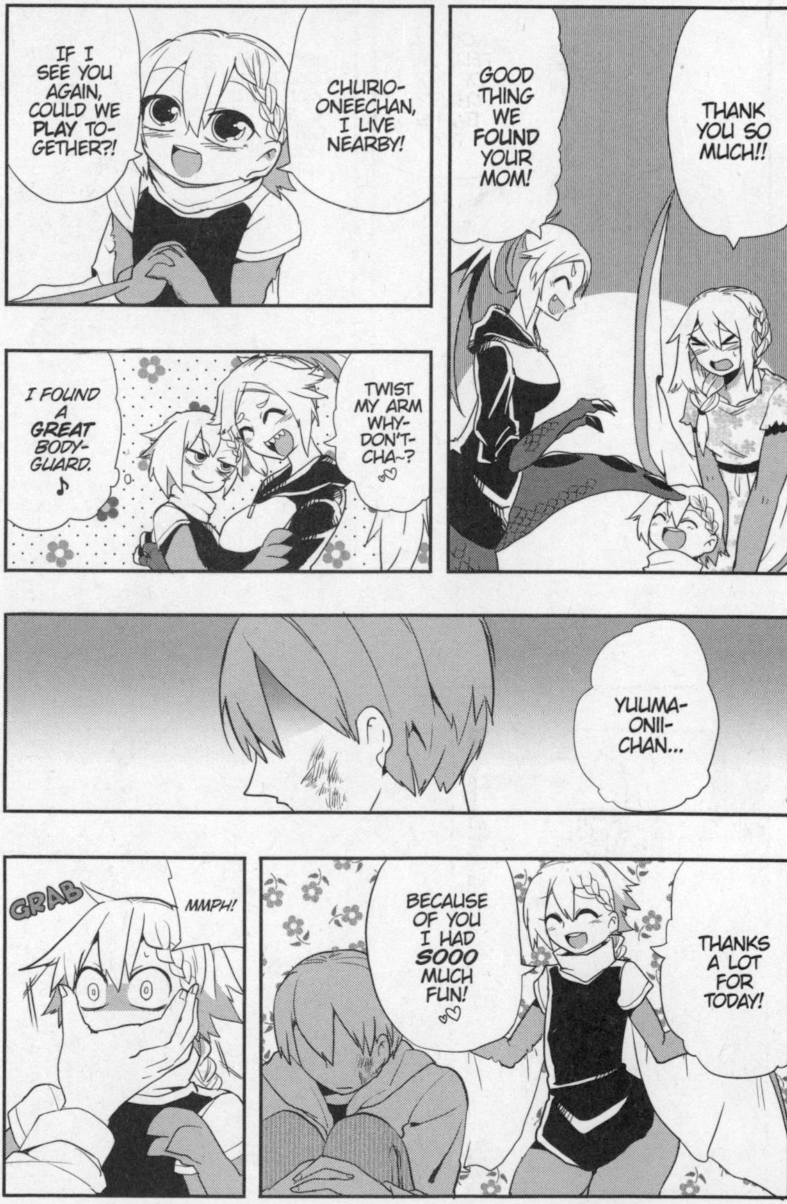
THANK YOU SO MUCH!!
GOOD THING WE FOUND YOUR MOM!
CHURIO-ONEECHAN, I LIVE NEARBY!
IF I SEE YOU AGAIN, COULD WE PLAY TO-GETHER?!
TWIST MY ARM WHY-DON'T-CHA~? ♡
I FOUND A GREAT BODY-GUARD. ♪
YUUMA-ONII-CHAN...
THANKS A LOT FOR TODAY!
BECAUSE OF YOU I HAD SOOO MUCH FUN! ♡
MMPH!
GRAB

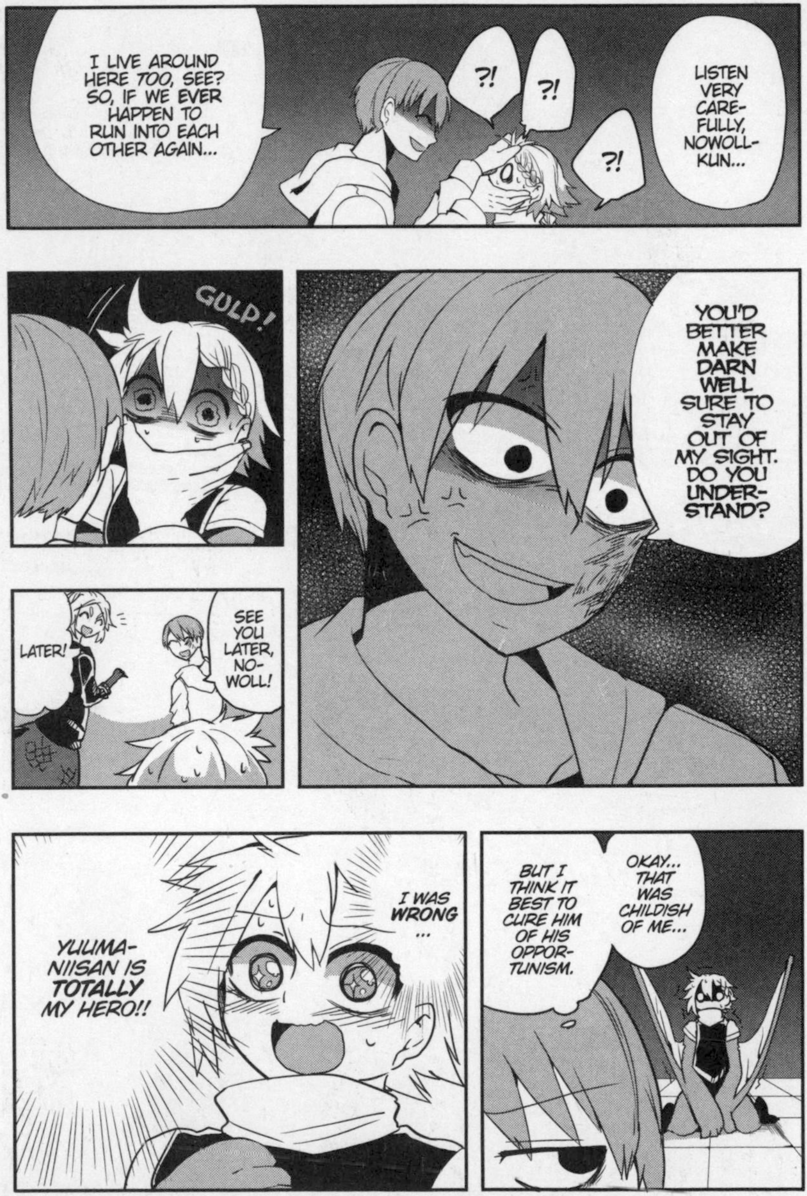
LISTEN VERY CARE-FULLY, NOWOLL-KUN...
?!
?!
?!
I LIVE AROUND HERE TOO, SEE? SO, IF WE EVER HAPPEN TO RUN INTO EACH OTHER AGAIN...
YOU'D BETTER MAKE DARN WELL SURE TO STAY OUT OF MY SIGHT. DO YOU UNDER-STAND?
GULP!
SEE YOU LATER, NO-WOLL!
LATER!
OKAY... THAT WAS CHILDISH OF ME...
BUT I THINK IT BEST TO CURE HIM OF HIS OPPOR-TUNISM.
I WAS WRONG ...
YUUMA-NIISAN IS TOTALLY MY HERO!!

My Girlfriend is a

T-REX

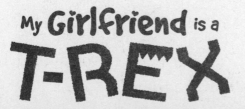

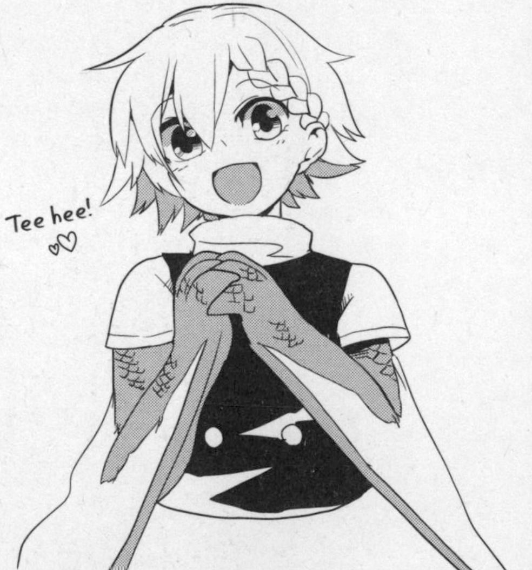
Tee hee! ♡♡

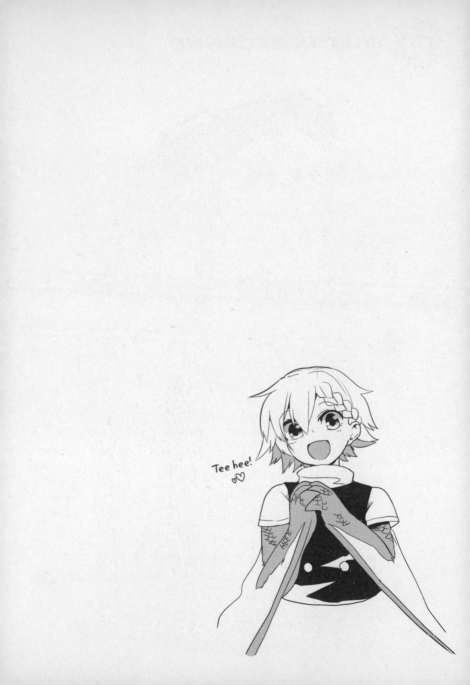

CHAPTER 10

MY MODERNIZING GIRLFRIEND

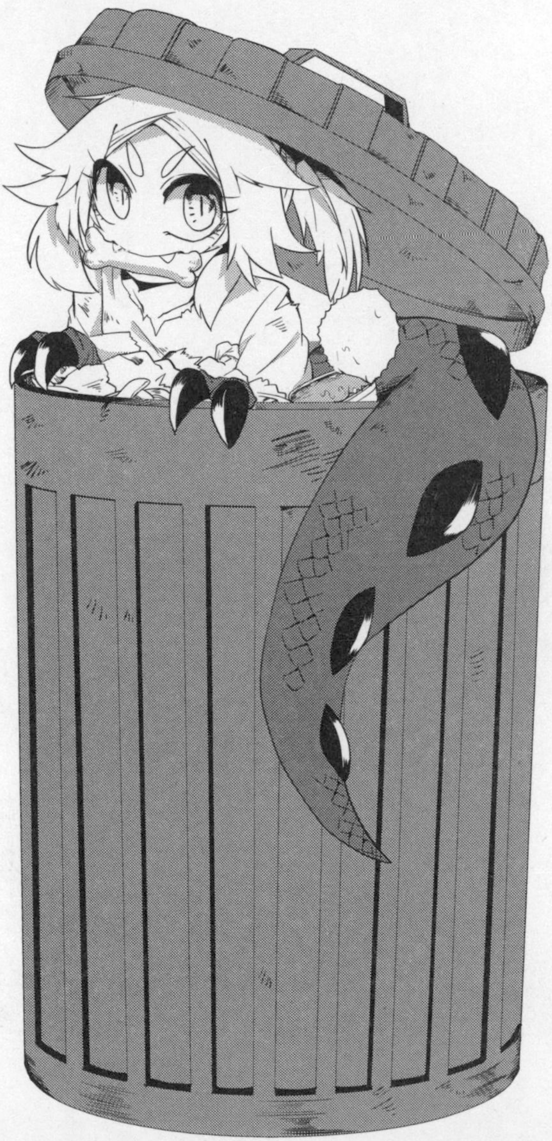

CRISIS

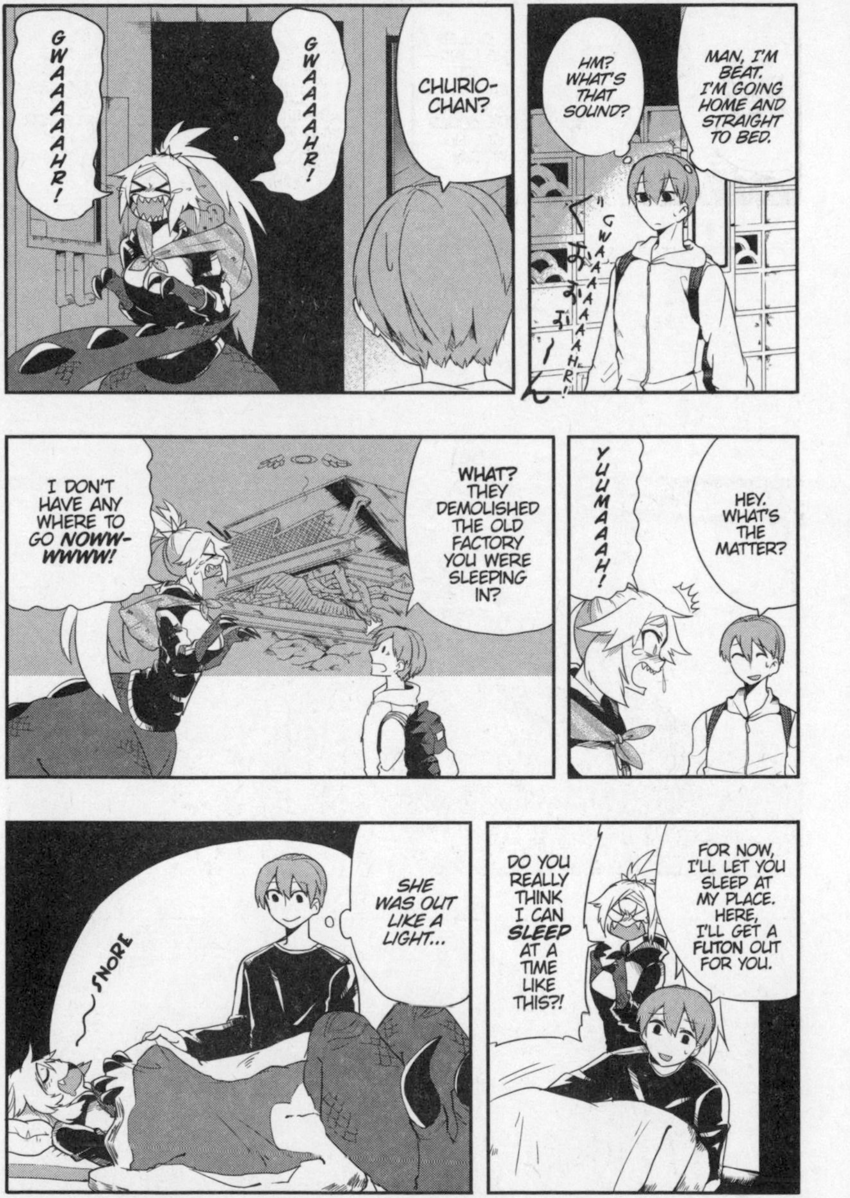
MAN, I'M BEAT. I'M GOING HOME AND STRAIGHT TO BED.
HM? WHAT'S THAT SOUND?
GWAAAAAAHR!
CHURIO-CHAN?
GWAAAAAAHR!
GWAAAAAAHR!
HEY. WHAT'S THE MATTER?
YUUMAAAAH!
WHAT? THEY DEMOLISHED THE OLD FACTORY YOU WERE SLEEPING IN?
I DON'T HAVE ANY WHERE TO GO **NOWW-WWWW!**
FOR NOW, I'LL LET YOU SLEEP AT MY PLACE. HERE, I'LL GET A FUTON OUT FOR YOU.
DO YOU REALLY THINK I CAN **SLEEP** AT A TIME LIKE THIS?!
SHE WAS OUT LIKE A LIGHT...
SNORE

FATE

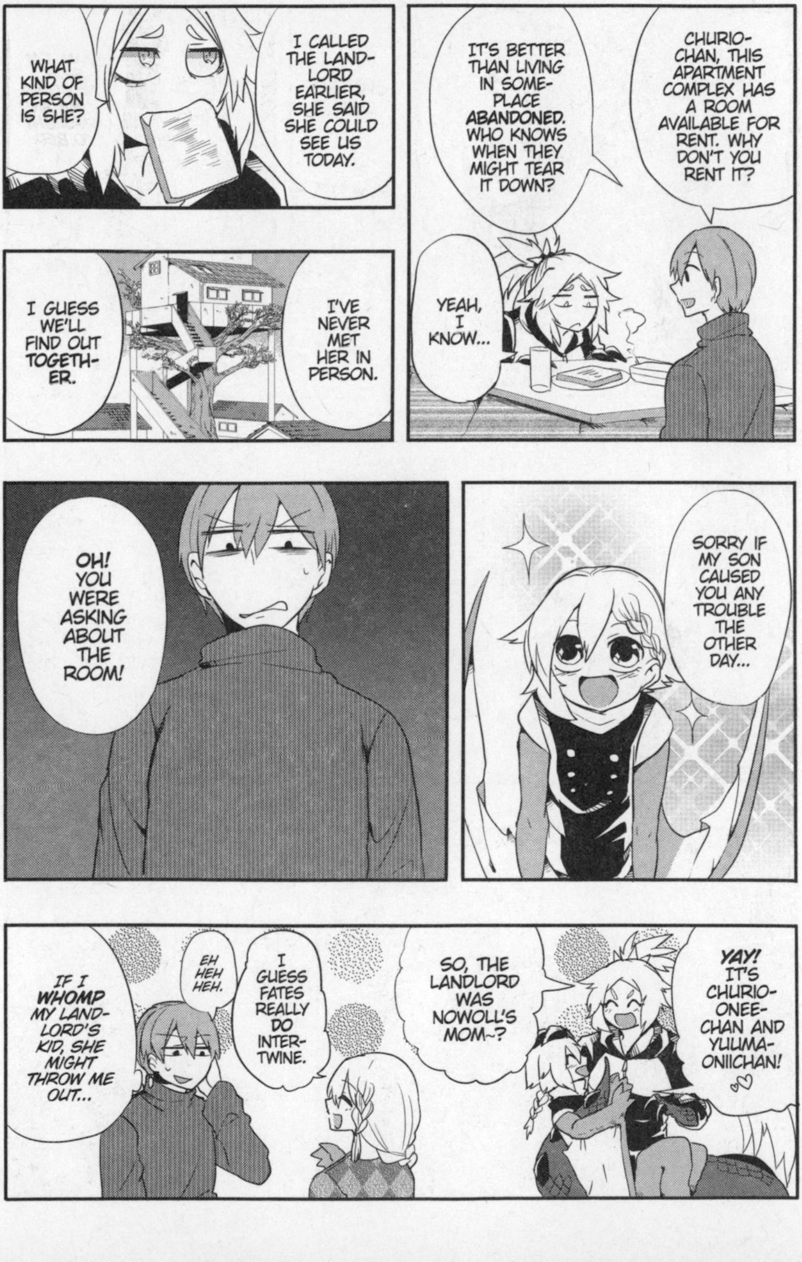
CHURIO-CHAN, THIS APARTMENT COMPLEX HAS A ROOM AVAILABLE FOR RENT. WHY DON'T YOU RENT IT?
IT'S BETTER THAN LIVING IN SOMEPLACE **ABANDONED**. WHO KNOWS WHEN THEY MIGHT TEAR IT DOWN?
YEAH, I KNOW...
I CALLED THE LANDLORD EARLIER, SHE SAID SHE COULD SEE US TODAY.
WHAT KIND OF PERSON IS SHE?
I'VE NEVER MET HER IN PERSON.
I GUESS WE'LL FIND OUT TOGETHER.
SORRY IF MY SON CAUSED YOU ANY TROUBLE THE OTHER DAY...
OH! YOU WERE ASKING ABOUT THE ROOM!
YAY! IT'S CHURIO-ONEE-CHAN AND YUUMA-ONIICHAN!
SO, THE LANDLORD WAS NOWOLL'S MOM~?
I GUESS FATES REALLY DO INTERTWINE.
EH HEH HEH.
*IF I **WHOMP** MY LANDLORD'S KID, SHE MIGHT THROW ME OUT...*

APPEAL

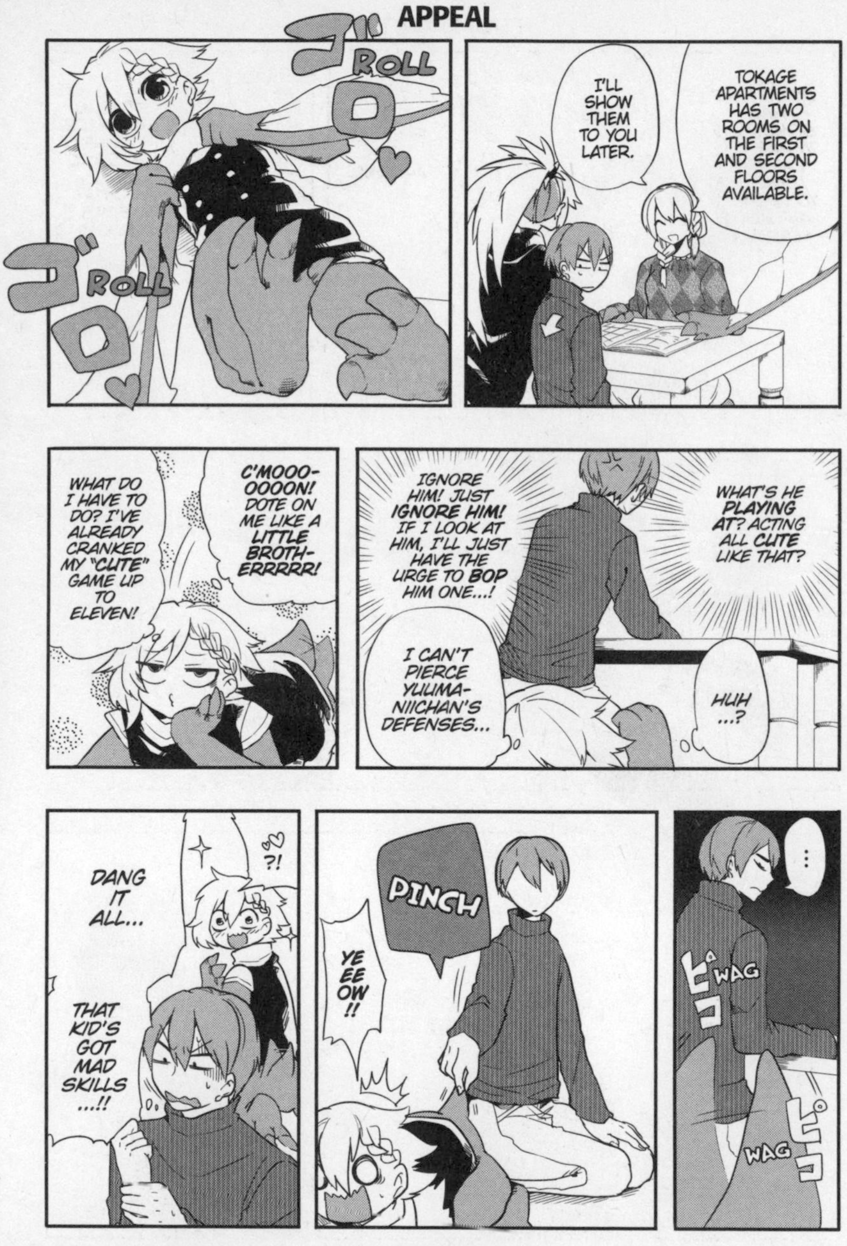
TOKAGE APARTMENTS HAS TWO ROOMS ON THE FIRST AND SECOND FLOORS AVAILABLE.
I'LL SHOW THEM TO YOU LATER.
ゴロ ROLL
ゴロ ROLL
WHAT'S HE PLAYING AT? ACTING ALL CUTE LIKE THAT?
IGNORE HIM! JUST IGNORE HIM! IF I LOOK AT HIM, I'LL JUST HAVE THE URGE TO BOP HIM ONE...!
HUH ...?
I CAN'T PIERCE YUUMA-NIICHAN'S DEFENSES...
C'MOOOO-OOOON! DOTE ON ME LIKE A LITTLE BROTH-ERRRRR!
WHAT DO I HAVE TO DO? I'VE ALREADY CRANKED MY "CUTE" GAME UP TO ELEVEN!
...
ピコ WAG
ピコ WAG
PINCH
YE EE OW !!
?!
DANG IT ALL...
THAT KID'S GOT MAD SKILLS ...!!

EVALUATION

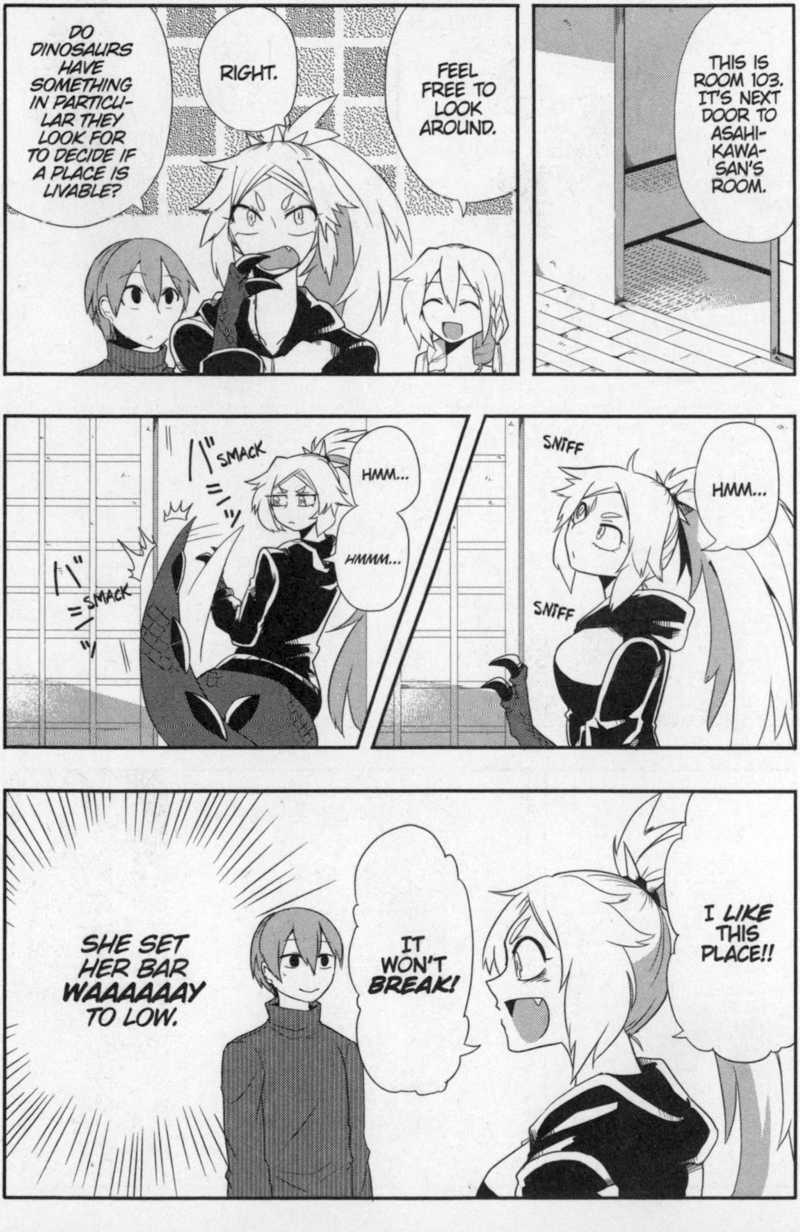
THIS IS ROOM 103. IT'S NEXT DOOR TO ASAHIKAWA-SAN'S ROOM.
FEEL FREE TO LOOK AROUND.
RIGHT.
DO DINOSAURS HAVE SOMETHING IN PARTICULAR THEY LOOK FOR TO DECIDE IF A PLACE IS LIVABLE?
SNIFF
HMM...
SNIFF
HMM...
HMMM...
バ SMACK
バ SMACK
I *LIKE* THIS PLACE!!
IT WON'T ***BREAK!***
SHE SET HER BAR ***WAAAAAAY*** TO LOW.

KEYS

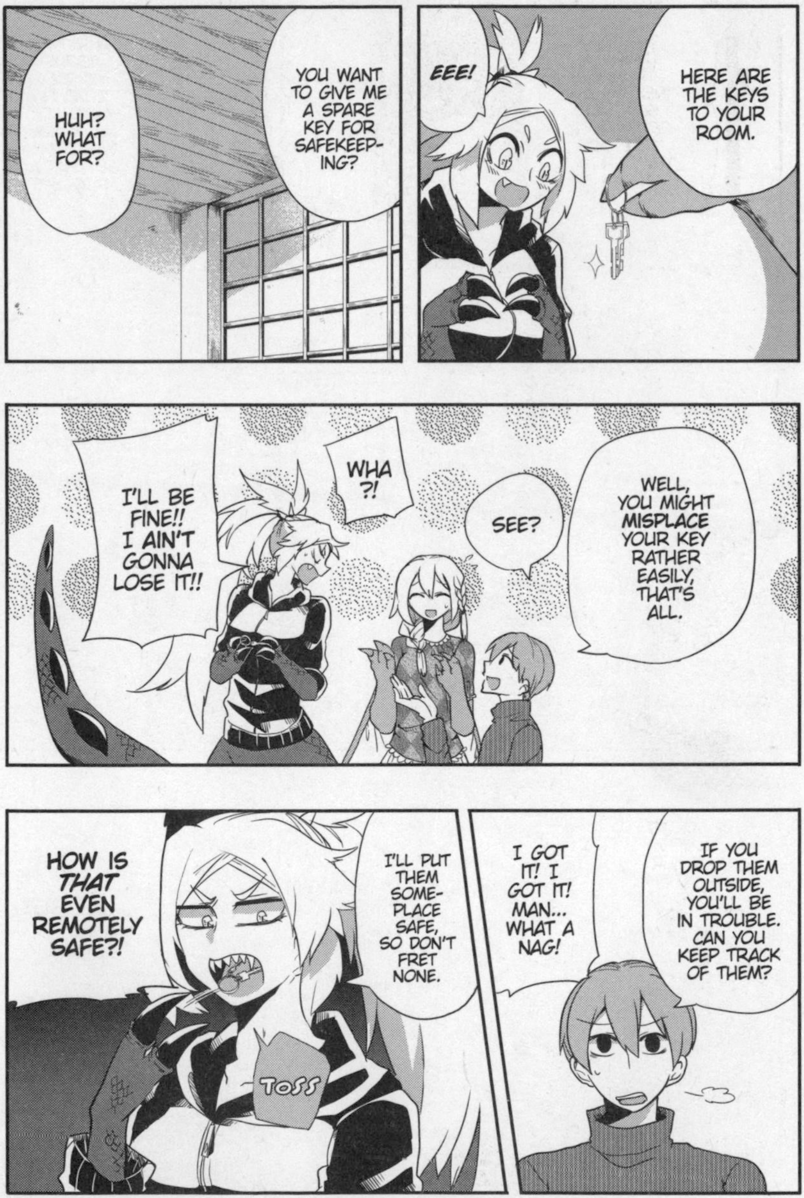
HERE ARE THE KEYS TO YOUR ROOM.
EEE!
YOU WANT TO GIVE ME A SPARE KEY FOR SAFEKEEP-ING?
HUH? WHAT FOR?
WELL, YOU MIGHT MISPLACE YOUR KEY RATHER EASILY, THAT'S ALL.
SEE?
WHA?!
I'LL BE FINE!! I AIN'T GONNA LOSE IT!!
IF YOU DROP THEM OUTSIDE, YOU'LL BE IN TROUBLE. CAN YOU KEEP TRACK OF THEM?
I GOT IT! I GOT IT! MAN... WHAT A NAG!
I'LL PUT THEM SOME-PLACE SAFE, SO DON'T FRET NONE.
TOSS
HOW IS *THAT* EVEN REMOTELY SAFE?!

THE REASON

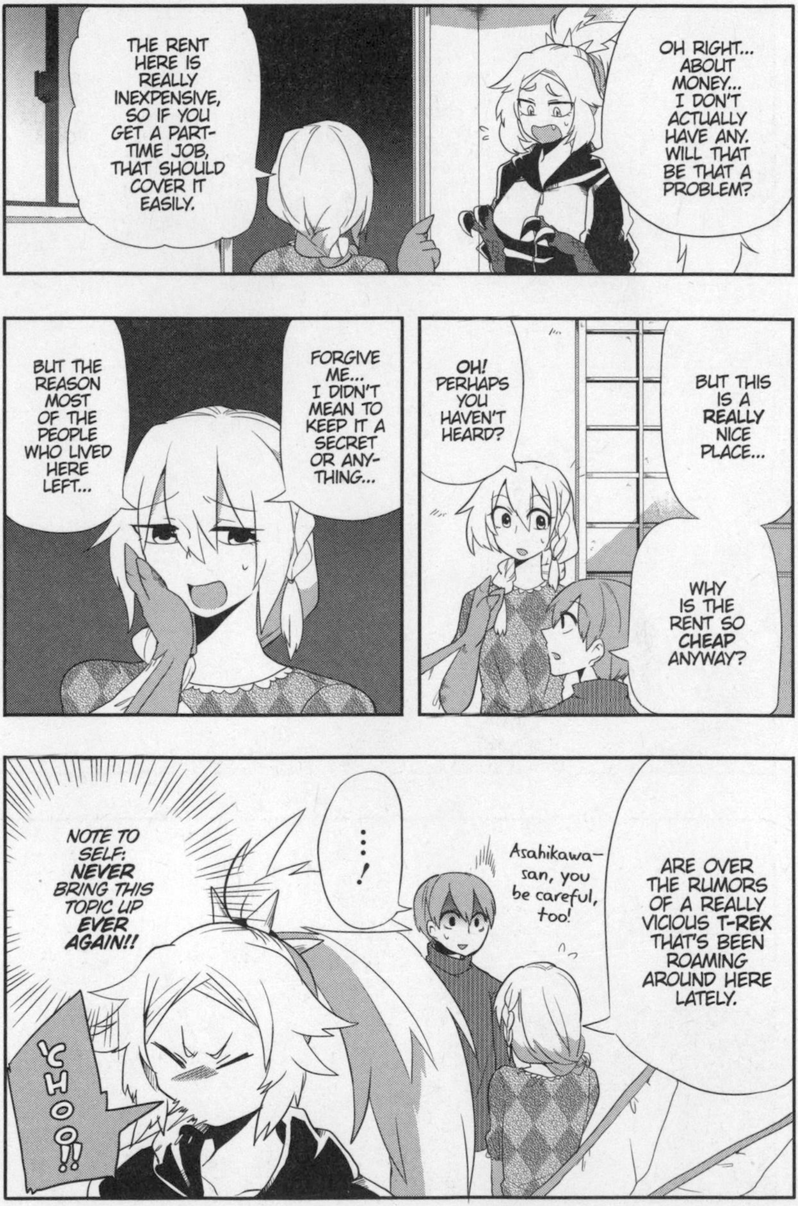
OH RIGHT... ABOUT MONEY... I DON'T ACTUALLY HAVE ANY. WILL THAT BE THAT A PROBLEM?
THE RENT HERE IS REALLY INEXPENSIVE, SO IF YOU GET A PART-TIME JOB, THAT SHOULD COVER IT EASILY.
BUT THIS IS A REALLY NICE PLACE...
WHY IS THE RENT SO CHEAP ANYWAY?
OH! PERHAPS YOU HAVEN'T HEARD?
FORGIVE ME... I DIDN'T MEAN TO KEEP IT A SECRET OR ANY-THING...
BUT THE REASON MOST OF THE PEOPLE WHO LIVED HERE LEFT...
ARE OVER THE RUMORS OF A REALLY VICIOUS T-REX THAT'S BEEN ROAMING AROUND HERE LATELY.
Asahikawa-san, you be careful, too!
...!
NOTE TO SELF: NEVER BRING THIS TOPIC UP EVER AGAIN!!
'CHOO!!

NEIGHBORS

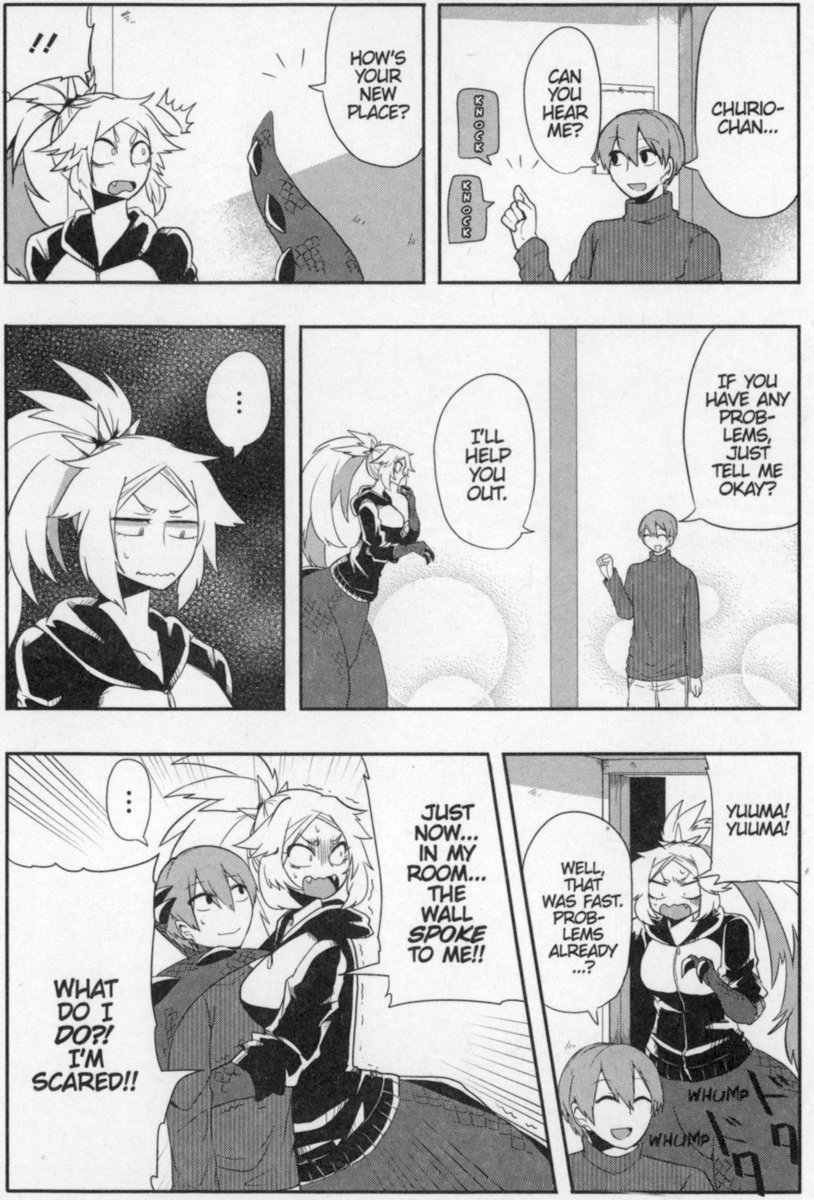
CHURIO-CHAN...
CAN YOU HEAR ME?
KNOCK
KNOCK
HOW'S YOUR NEW PLACE?
!!
IF YOU HAVE ANY PROB-LEMS, JUST TELL ME OKAY?
I'LL HELP YOU OUT.
...
YUUMA! YUUMA!
WELL, THAT WAS FAST. PROB-LEMS ALREADY ...?
WHUMP
WHUMP
JUST NOW... IN MY ROOM... THE WALL SPOKE TO ME!!
...
WHAT DO I DO?! I'M SCARED!!

My Girlfriend is a
T-REX

CHAPTER 11 MY GIRLFRIEND THE PART-TIMER

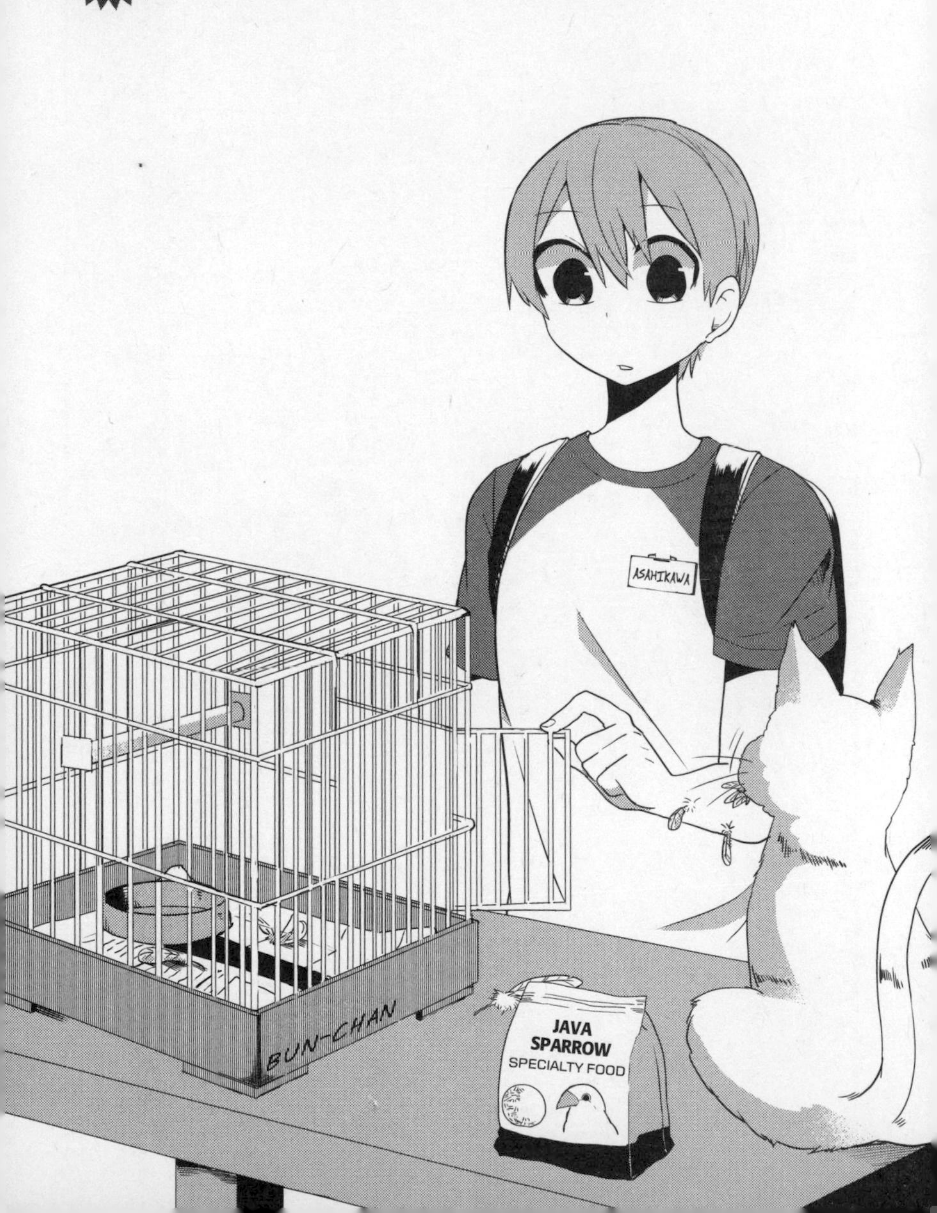
ASAHIKAWA
BUN-CHAN
JAVA
SPARROW
SPECIALTY FOOD

RESUME

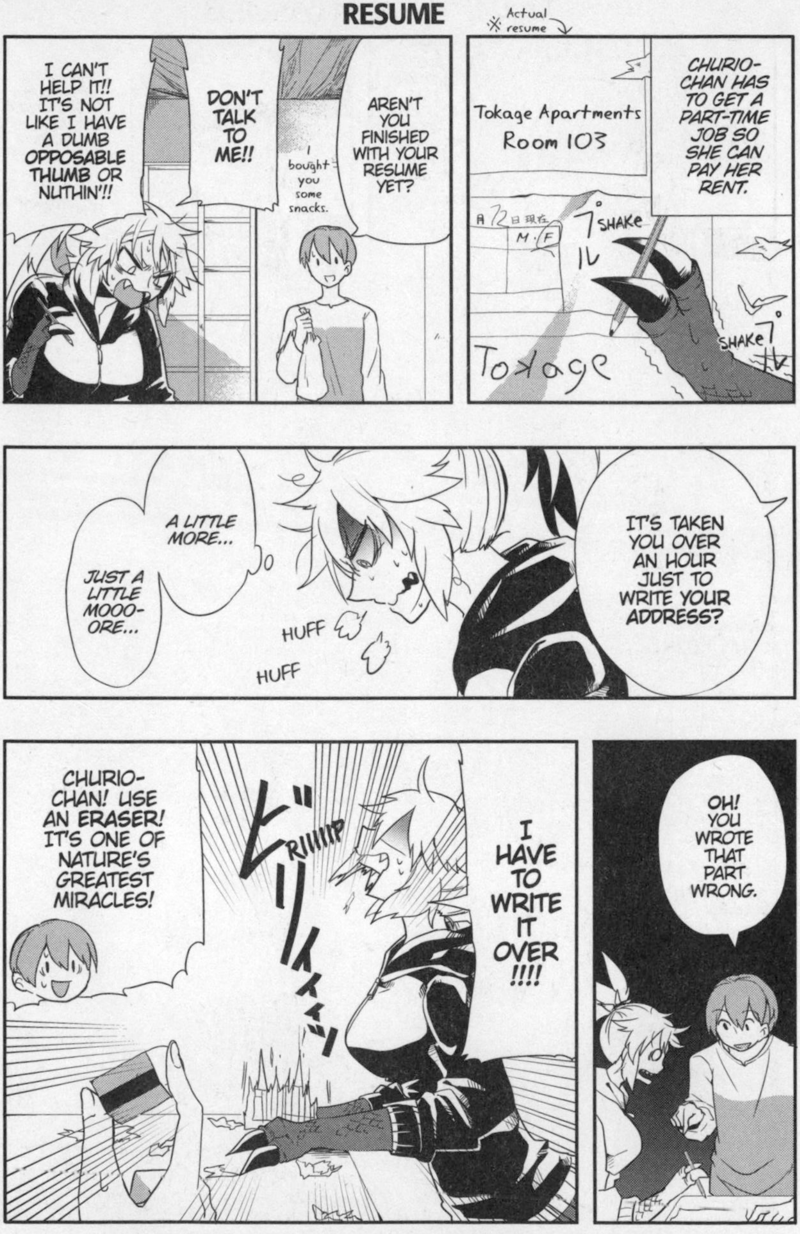
※ Actual resume
CHURIO-CHAN HAS TO GET A PART-TIME JOB SO SHE CAN PAY HER RENT.
Tokage Apartments
Room 103
月 12 日現在
M・F
プル SHAKE
SHAKE プル
Tokage
AREN'T YOU FINISHED WITH YOUR RESUME YET?
I bought you some snacks.
DON'T TALK TO ME!!
I CAN'T HELP IT!! IT'S NOT LIKE I HAVE A DUMB OPPOSABLE THUMB OR NUTHIN'!!
IT'S TAKEN YOU OVER AN HOUR JUST TO WRITE YOUR ADDRESS?
HUFF
HUFF
A LITTLE MORE...
JUST A LITTLE MOOOO-ORE...
OH! YOU WROTE THAT PART WRONG.
I HAVE TO WRITE IT OVER!!!!
RIIIIIP
CHURIO-CHAN! USE AN ERASER! IT'S ONE OF NATURE'S GREATEST MIRACLES!

KRAM, THE ANKYLOSAURUS

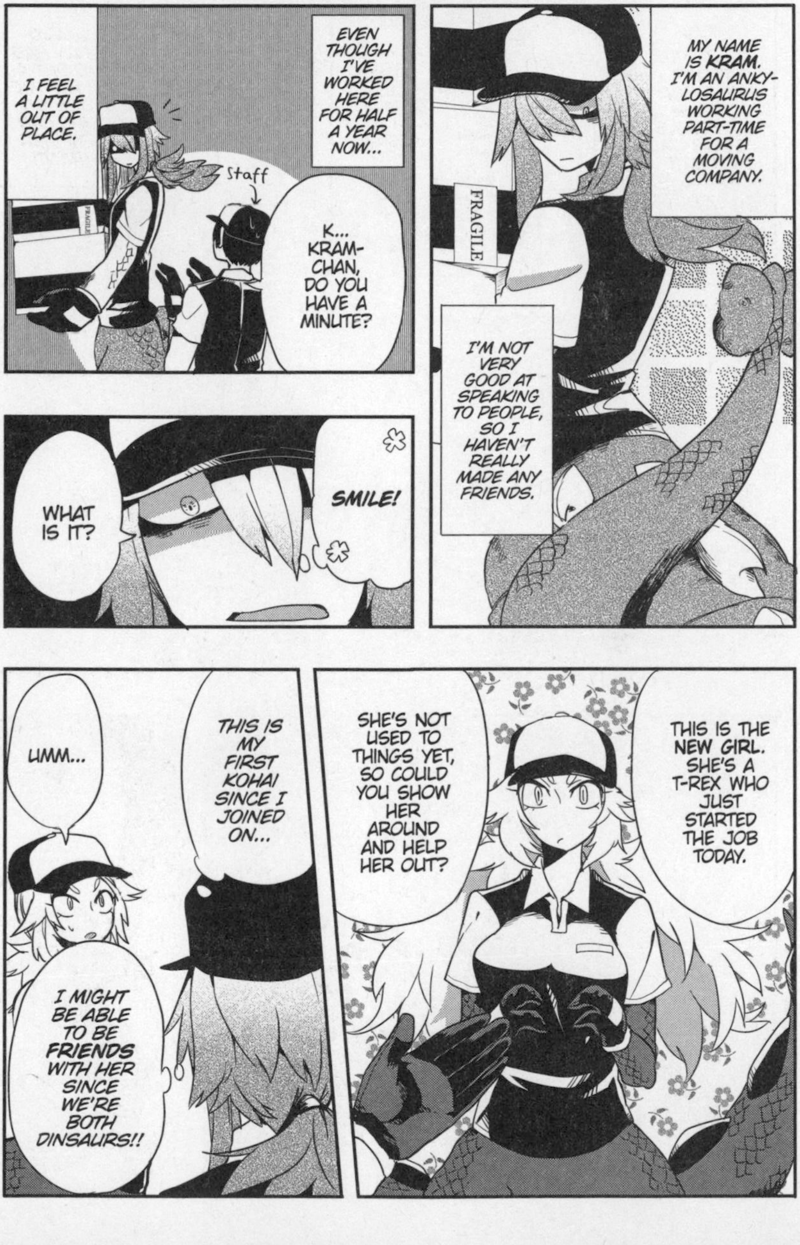
MY NAME IS KRAM. I'M AN ANKY-LOSAURUS WORKING PART-TIME FOR A MOVING COMPANY.
FRAGILE
I'M NOT VERY GOOD AT SPEAKING TO PEOPLE, SO I HAVEN'T REALLY MADE ANY FRIENDS.
EVEN THOUGH I'VE WORKED HERE FOR HALF A YEAR NOW...
I FEEL A LITTLE OUT OF PLACE.
Staff
K... KRAM-CHAN, DO YOU HAVE A MINUTE?
SMILE!
WHAT IS IT?
THIS IS THE NEW GIRL. SHE'S A T-REX WHO JUST STARTED THE JOB TODAY.
SHE'S NOT USED TO THINGS YET, SO COULD YOU SHOW HER AROUND AND HELP HER OUT?
THIS IS MY FIRST KOHAI SINCE I JOINED ON...
UMM...
I MIGHT BE ABLE TO BE FRIENDS WITH HER SINCE WE'RE BOTH DINSAURS!!

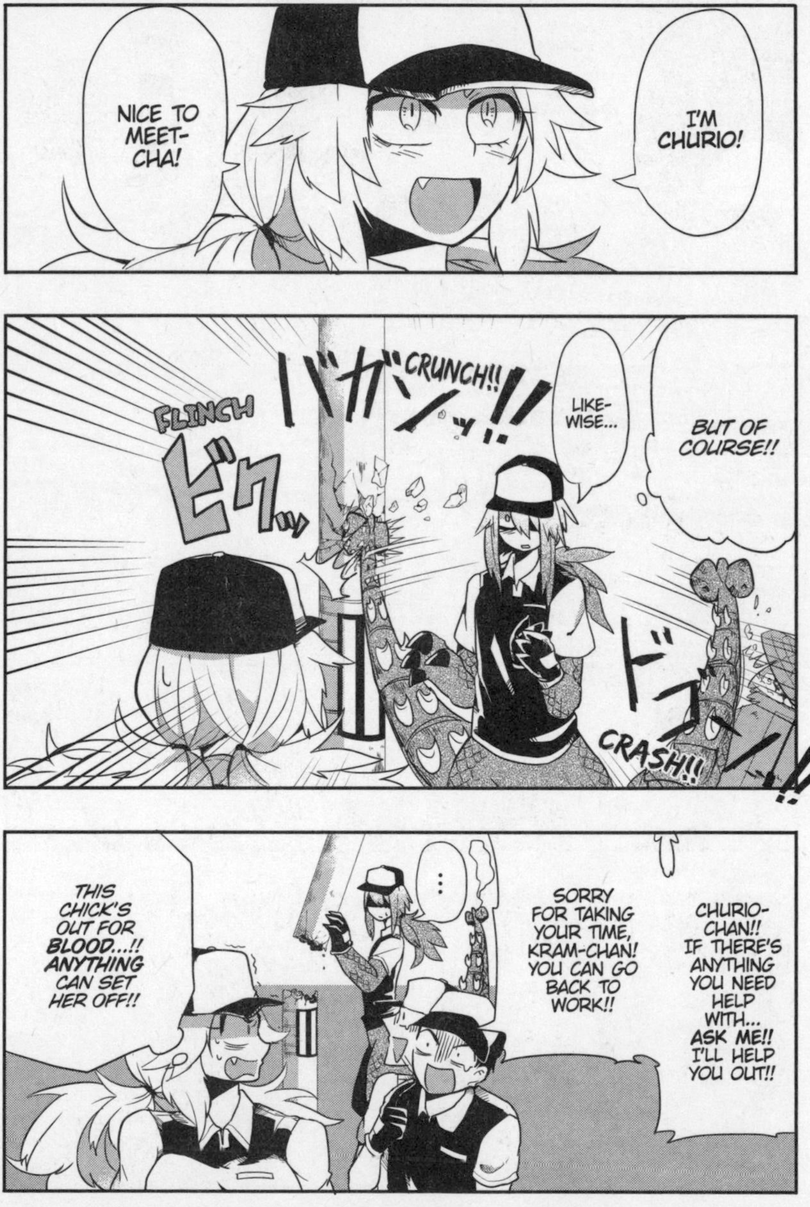
I'M CHURIO!
NICE TO MEET-CHA!
BUT OF COURSE!!
LIKE-WISE...
CRASH!!
CRUNCH!!
FLINCH
CHURIO-CHAN!! IF THERE'S ANYTHING YOU NEED HELP WITH... ASK ME!! I'LL HELP YOU OUT!!
SORRY FOR TAKING YOUR TIME, KRAM-CHAN! YOU CAN GO BACK TO WORK!!
...
THIS CHICK'S OUT FOR BLOOD...!! ANYTHING CAN SET HER OFF!!

KRAM'S SMILE

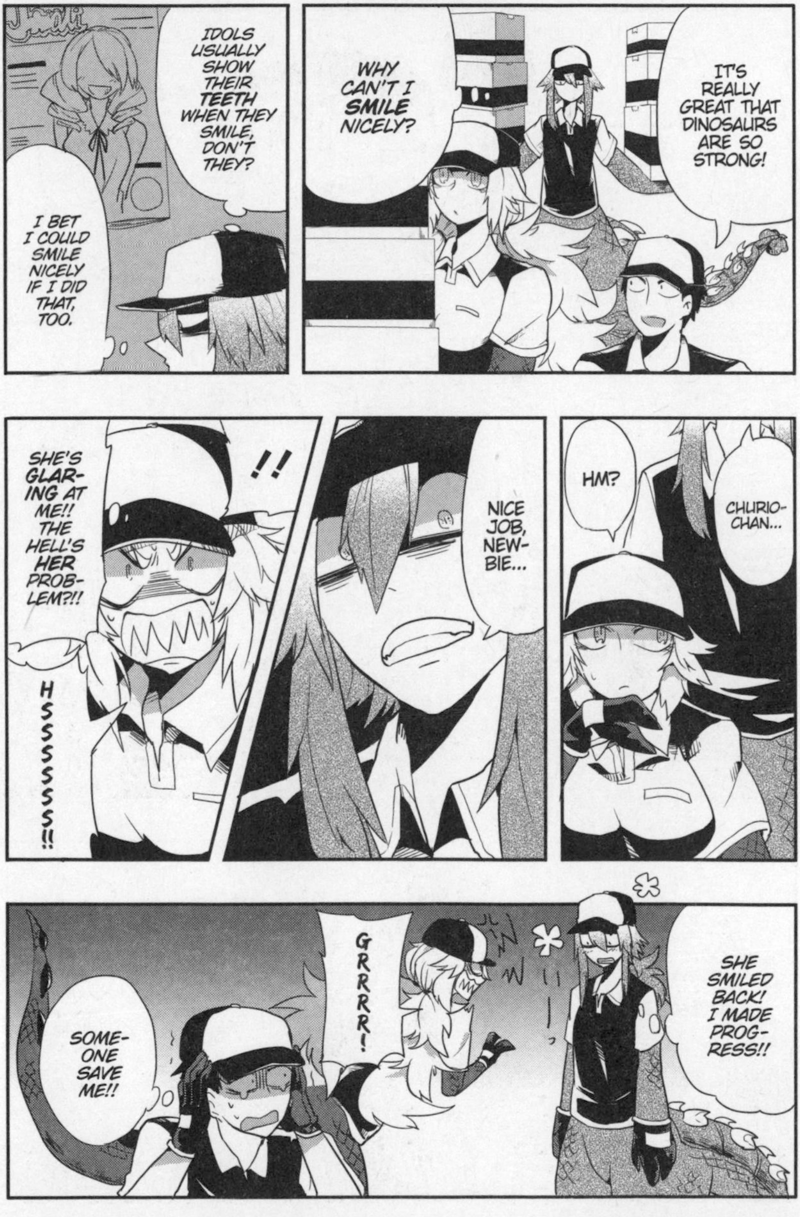
IT'S REALLY GREAT THAT DINOSAURS ARE SO STRONG!
WHY CAN'T I SMILE NICELY?
IDOLS USUALLY SHOW THEIR TEETH WHEN THEY SMILE, DON'T THEY?
I BET I COULD SMILE NICELY IF I DID THAT, TOO.
CHURIO-CHAN...
HM?
NICE JOB, NEWBIE...
!!
SHE'S GLARING AT ME!! THE HELL'S HER PROBLEM?!!
HSSSSSS!!
SHE SMILED BACK! I MADE PROGRESS!!
GRRRR!
SOMEONE SAVE ME!!

SELF SACRIFICE

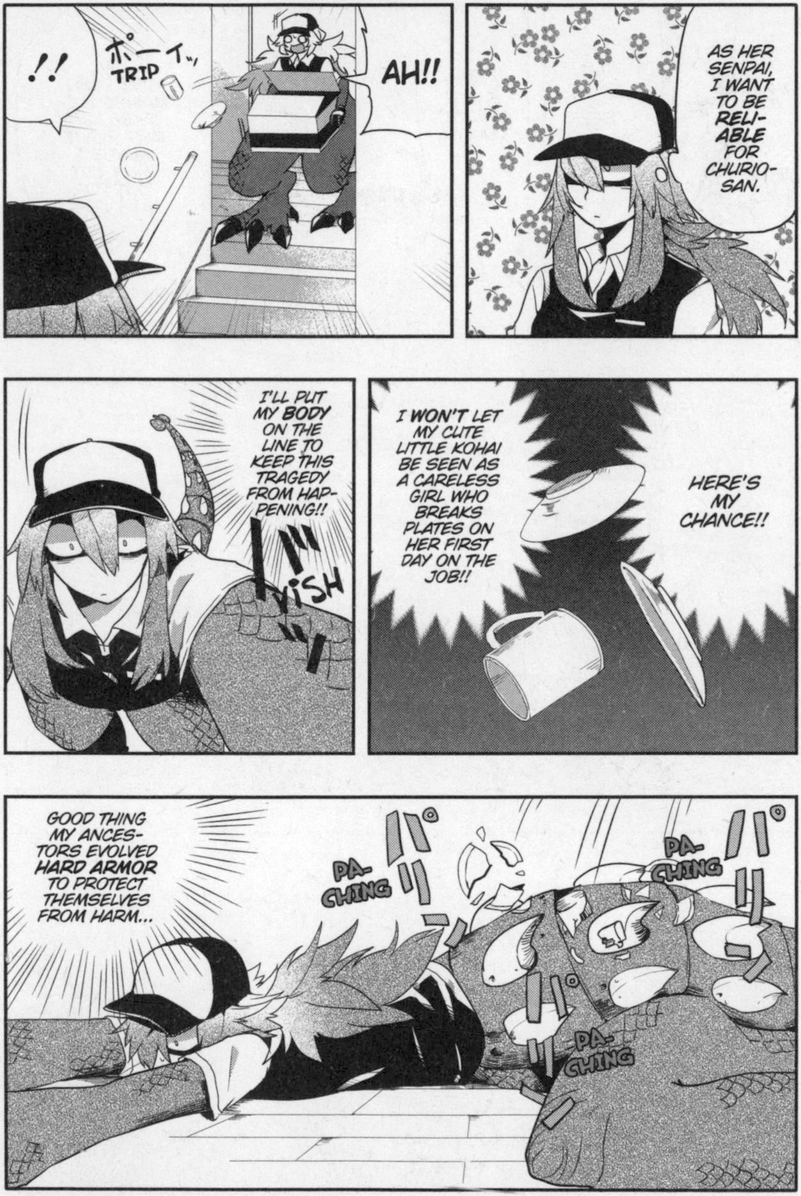
AS HER SENPAI, I WANT TO BE RELIABLE FOR CHURIO-SAN.
AH!!
ポーイッ
TRIP
!!
HERE'S MY CHANCE!!
I WON'T LET MY CUTE LITTLE KOHAI BE SEEN AS A CARELESS GIRL WHO BREAKS PLATES ON HER FIRST DAY ON THE JOB!!
I'LL PUT MY BODY ON THE LINE TO KEEP THIS TRAGEDY FROM HAPPENING!!
バッ
WISH
パリ
PA-CHING
パリ
PA-CHING
GOOD THING MY ANCESTORS EVOLVED HARD ARMOR TO PROTECT THEMSELVES FROM HARM...
パリ
PA-CHING

SLEIGHT OF HAND

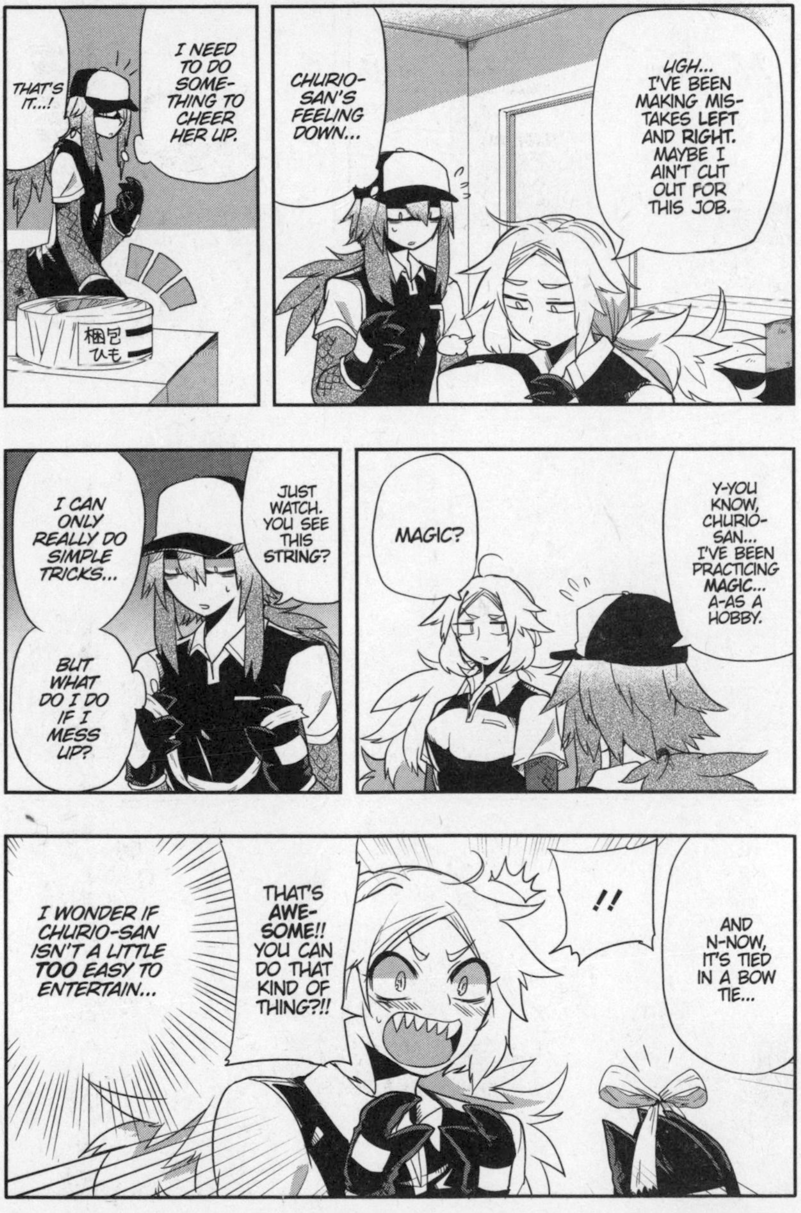

UGH... I'VE BEEN MAKING MIS-TAKES LEFT AND RIGHT. MAYBE I AIN'T CUT OUT FOR THIS JOB.
CHURIO-SAN'S FEELING DOWN...
I NEED TO DO SOME-THING TO CHEER HER UP.
THAT'S IT...!
梱包ひも
Y-YOU KNOW, CHURIO-SAN... I'VE BEEN PRACTICING MAGIC... A-AS A HOBBY.
MAGIC?
JUST WATCH. YOU SEE THIS STRING?
I CAN ONLY REALLY DO SIMPLE TRICKS...
BUT WHAT DO I DO IF I MESS UP?
AND N-NOW, IT'S TIED IN A BOW TIE...
!!
THAT'S AWE-SOME!! YOU CAN DO THAT KIND OF THING?!!
I WONDER IF CHURIO-SAN ISN'T A LITTLE TOO EASY TO ENTERTAIN...

ROTTEN FATE

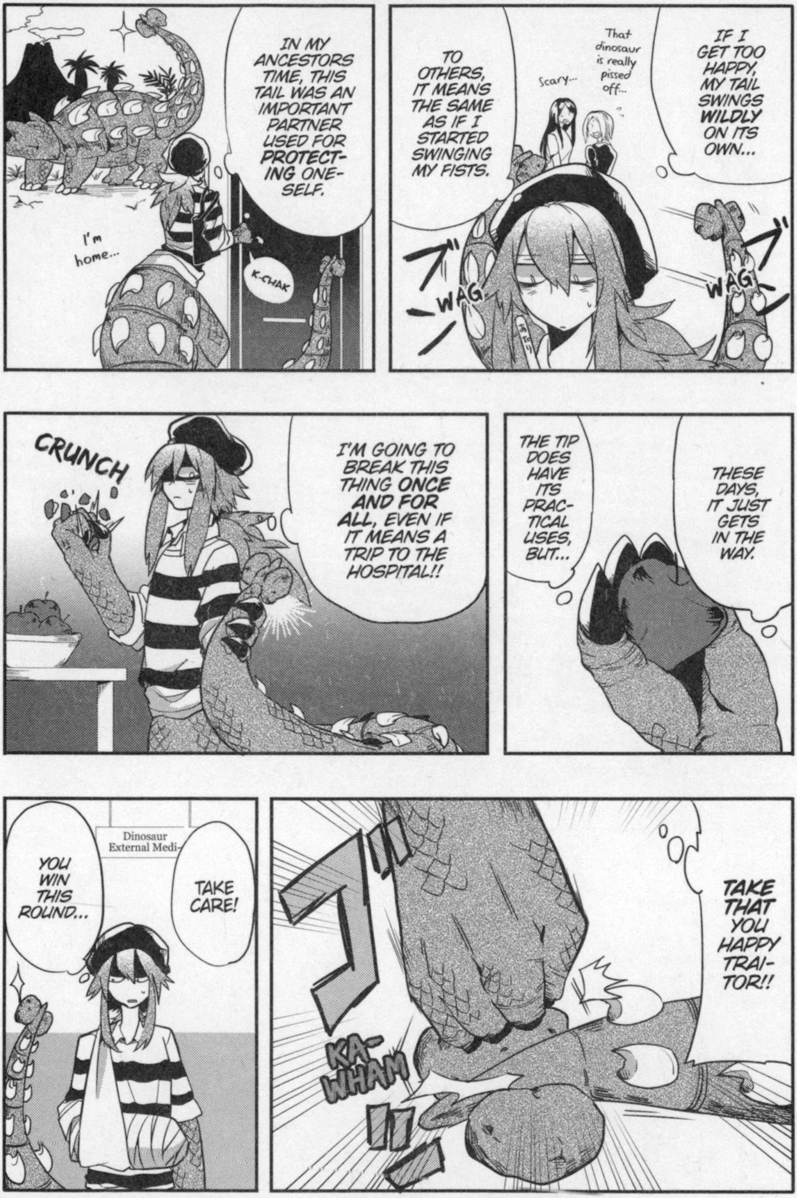
IF I GET TOO HAPPY, MY TAIL SWINGS WILDLY ON ITS OWN...
That dinosaur is really pissed off...
Scary...
TO OTHERS, IT MEANS THE SAME AS IF I STARTED SWINGING MY FISTS.
WAG
WAG
IN MY ANCESTORS TIME, THIS TAIL WAS AN IMPORTANT PARTNER USED FOR PROTECTING ONE-SELF.
K-CHAK
I'm home...
THESE DAYS, IT JUST GETS IN THE WAY.
THE TIP DOES HAVE ITS PRACTICAL USES, BUT...
I'M GOING TO BREAK THIS THING ONCE AND FOR ALL, EVEN IF IT MEANS A TRIP TO THE HOSPITAL!!
CRUNCH
TAKE THAT YOU HAPPY TRAITOR!!
KA-WHAM!!
TAKE CARE!
YOU WIN THIS ROUND...
Dinosaur External Medi-

My Girlfriend is a T-REX

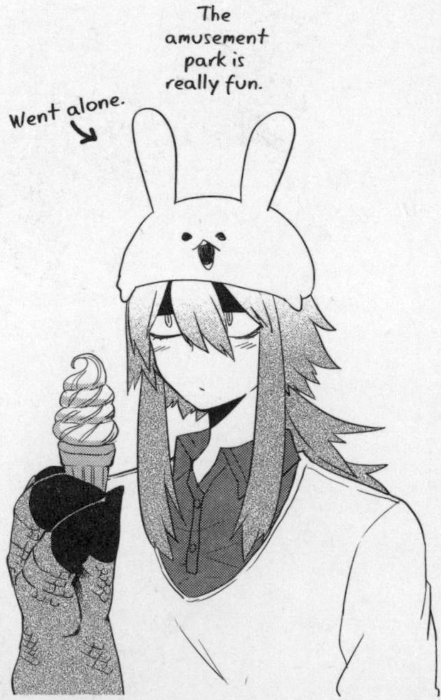
The amusement park is really fun.
Went alone.

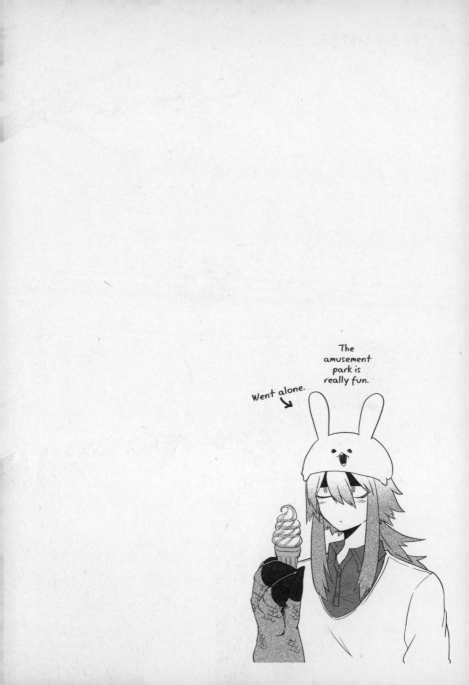

CHAPTER 12 MY GIRLFRIEND & MY DARK PAST

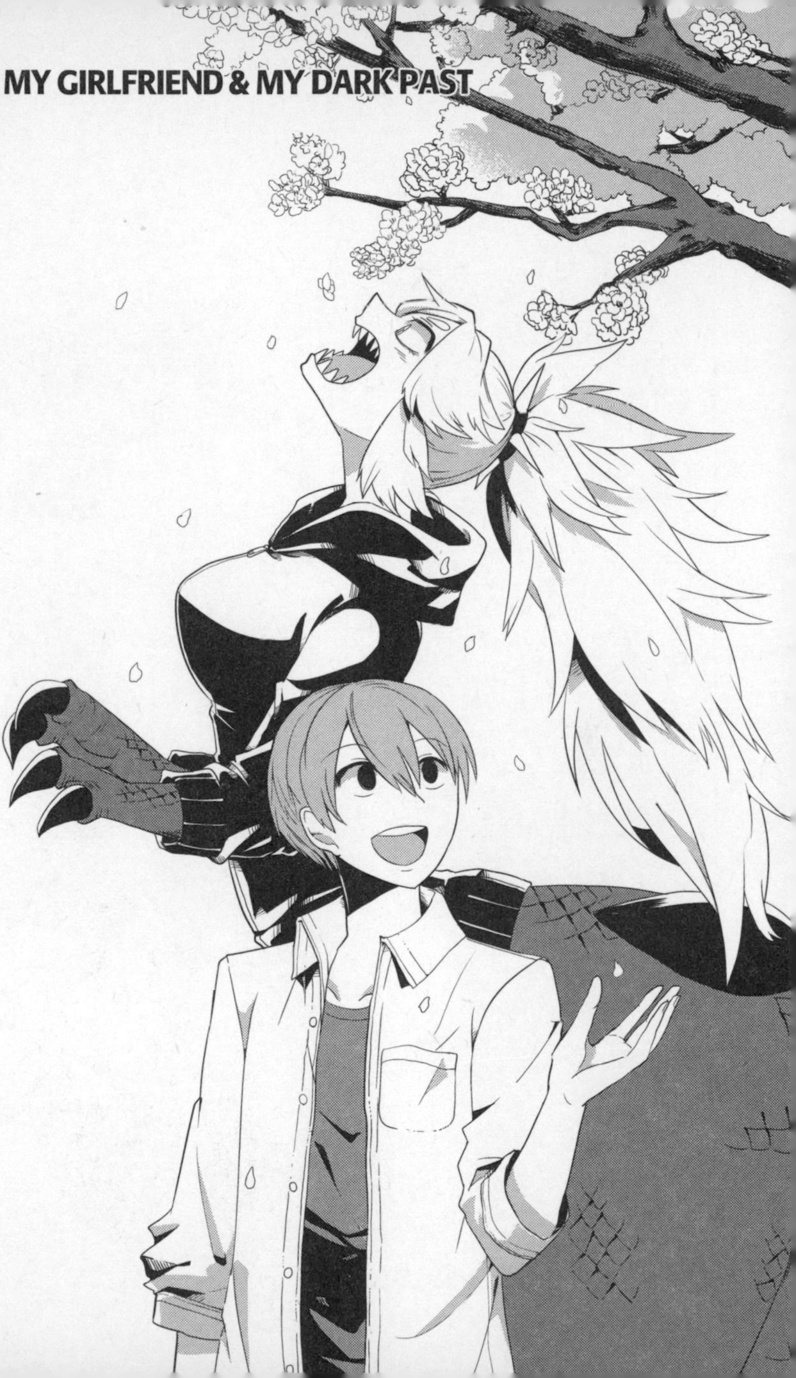

MASSAGE

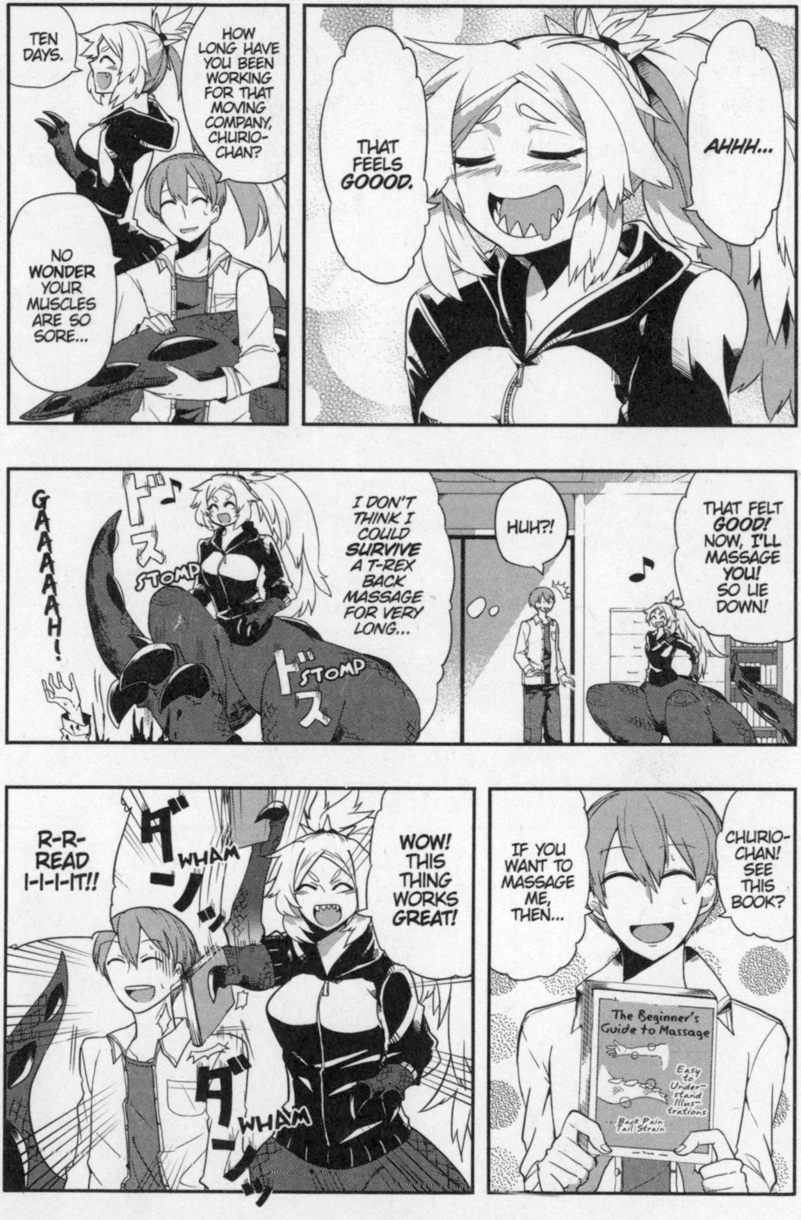
AHHH...
THAT FEELS GOOOD.
HOW LONG HAVE YOU BEEN WORKING FOR THAT MOVING COMPANY, CHURIO-CHAN?
TEN DAYS.
NO WONDER YOUR MUSCLES ARE SO SORE...
THAT FELT GOOD! NOW, I'LL MASSAGE YOU! SO LIE DOWN!
HUH?!
I DON'T THINK I COULD SURVIVE A T-REX BACK MASSAGE FOR VERY LONG...
STOMP
STOMP
GAAAAAAH!
CHURIO-CHAN! SEE THIS BOOK?
IF YOU WANT TO MASSAGE ME, THEN...
The Beginner's Guide to Massage
Easy to Understand Illustrations
Back Pain
Tail Strain
WOW! THIS THING WORKS GREAT!
WHAM
WHAM
R-R-READ I-I-I-IT!!

DESTINED

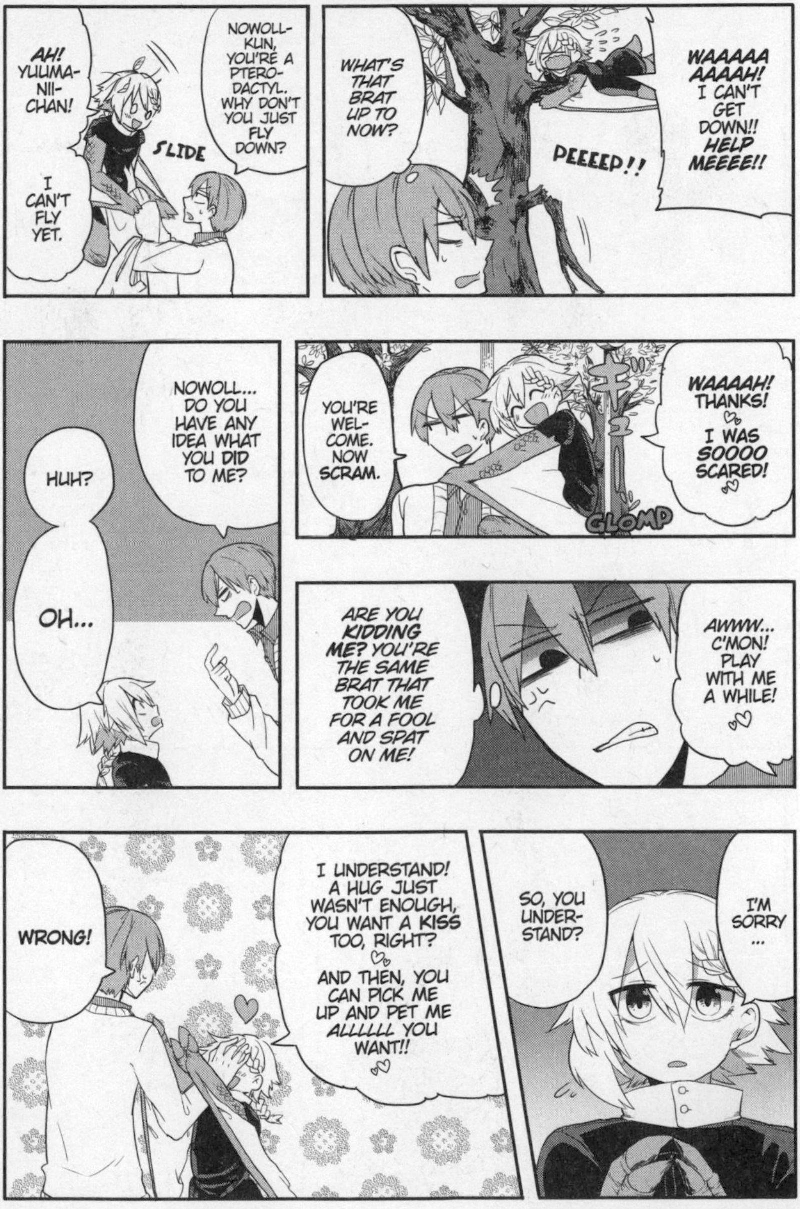

WAAAAA AAAAH! I CAN'T GET DOWN!! HELP MEEEE!!
PEEEEP!!
WHAT'S THAT BRAT UP TO NOW?
NOWOLL-KUN, YOU'RE A PTERO-DACTYL. WHY DON'T YOU JUST FLY DOWN?
SLIDE
AH! YUUMA-NII-CHAN!
I CAN'T FLY YET.
WAAAAH! THANKS! I WAS SOOOO SCARED!
GLOMP
YOU'RE WEL-COME. NOW SCRAM.
AWWW... C'MON! PLAY WITH ME A WHILE!
ARE YOU KIDDING ME? YOU'RE THE SAME BRAT THAT TOOK ME FOR A FOOL AND SPAT ON ME!
NOWOLL... DO YOU HAVE ANY IDEA WHAT YOU DID TO ME?
HUH?
OH...
I'M SORRY ...
SO, YOU UNDER-STAND?
I UNDERSTAND! A HUG JUST WASN'T ENOUGH, YOU WANT A KISS TOO, RIGHT? AND THEN, YOU CAN PICK ME UP AND PET ME ALLLLLL YOU WANT!!
WRONG!

FOUL MOUTHED BRATS

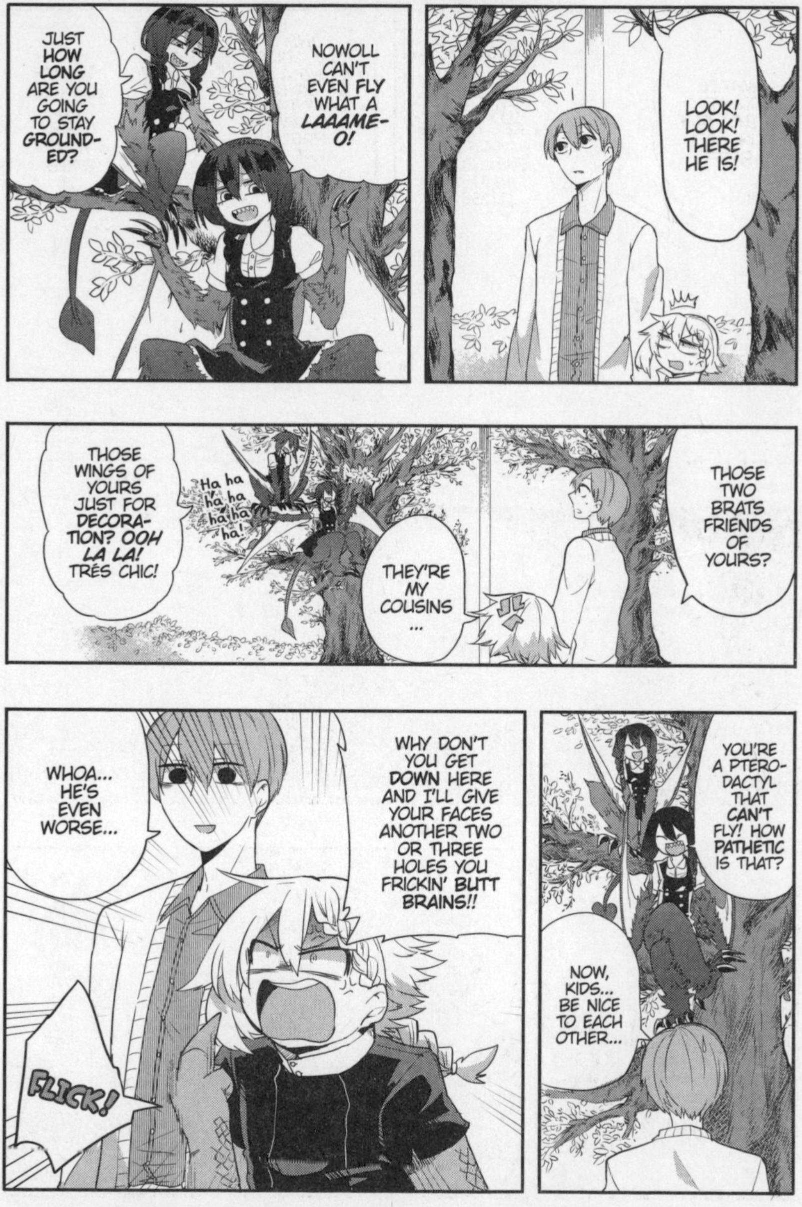
LOOK! LOOK! THERE HE IS!
NOWOLL CAN'T EVEN FLY WHAT A LAAAME-O!
JUST HOW LONG ARE YOU GOING TO STAY GROUNDED?
THOSE TWO BRATS FRIENDS OF YOURS?
THEY'RE MY COUSINS ...
Ha ha ha ha ha ha ha!
THOSE WINGS OF YOURS JUST FOR DECORATION? OOH LA LA! TRÉS CHIC!
YOU'RE A PTERODACTYL THAT CAN'T FLY! HOW PATHETIC IS THAT?
NOW, KIDS... BE NICE TO EACH OTHER...
WHY DON'T YOU GET DOWN HERE AND I'LL GIVE YOUR FACES ANOTHER TWO OR THREE HOLES YOU FRICKIN' BUTT BRAINS!!
WHOA... HE'S EVEN WORSE...
FLICK!

A CHANCE PRESENTS ITSELF

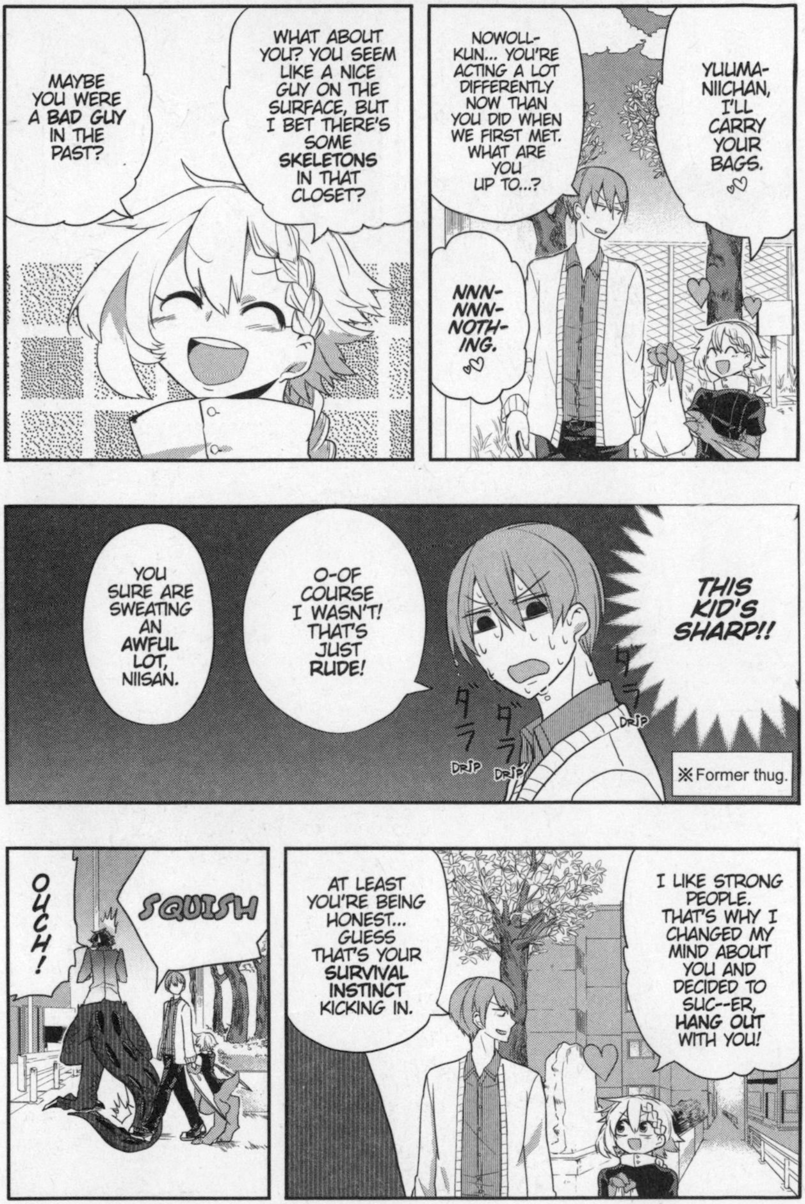
YUUMA-NIICHAN, I'LL CARRY YOUR BAGS. ♡
NOWOLL-KUN... YOU'RE ACTING A LOT DIFFERENTLY NOW THAN YOU DID WHEN WE FIRST MET. WHAT ARE YOU UP TO...?
NNN-NNN-NOTHING. ♡
WHAT ABOUT YOU? YOU SEEM LIKE A NICE GUY ON THE SURFACE, BUT I BET THERE'S SOME SKELETONS IN THAT CLOSET?
MAYBE YOU WERE A BAD GUY IN THE PAST?
THIS KID'S SHARP!!
ダラ
DRIP
O-OF COURSE I WASN'T! THAT'S JUST RUDE!
ダラ
DRIP
ダラ
DRIP
YOU SURE ARE SWEATING AN AWFUL LOT, NIISAN.
※Former thug.
I LIKE STRONG PEOPLE. THAT'S WHY I CHANGED MY MIND ABOUT YOU AND DECIDED TO SUC--ER, HANG OUT WITH YOU!
AT LEAST YOU'RE BEING HONEST... GUESS THAT'S YOUR SURVIVAL INSTINCT KICKING IN.
SQUISH
OUCH!

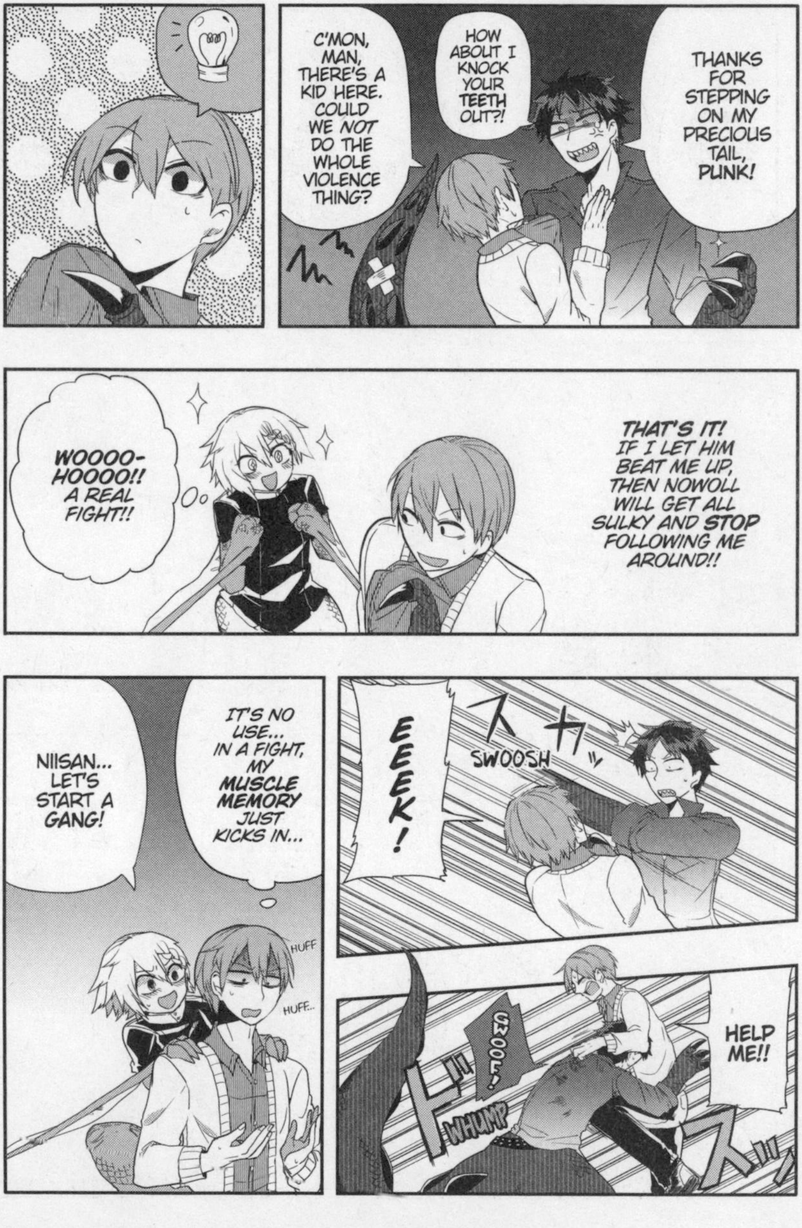
THANKS FOR STEPPING ON MY PRECIOUS TAIL, PUNK!
HOW ABOUT I KNOCK YOUR TEETH OUT?!
C'MON, MAN, THERE'S A KID HERE. COULD WE *NOT* DO THE WHOLE VIOLENCE THING?
THAT'S IT! *IF I LET HIM BEAT ME UP, THEN NOWOLL WILL GET ALL SULKY AND* **STOP** *FOLLOWING ME AROUND!!*
WOOOO-HOOOO!! A REAL FIGHT!!
スカッ
SWOOSH
EEEK!
HELP ME!!
GWOOF!
ドッ
WHUMP
ズッ
IT'S NO USE... IN A FIGHT, MY **MUSCLE MEMORY** JUST KICKS IN...
NIISAN... LET'S START A GANG!
HUFF
HUFF...

DARK PAST

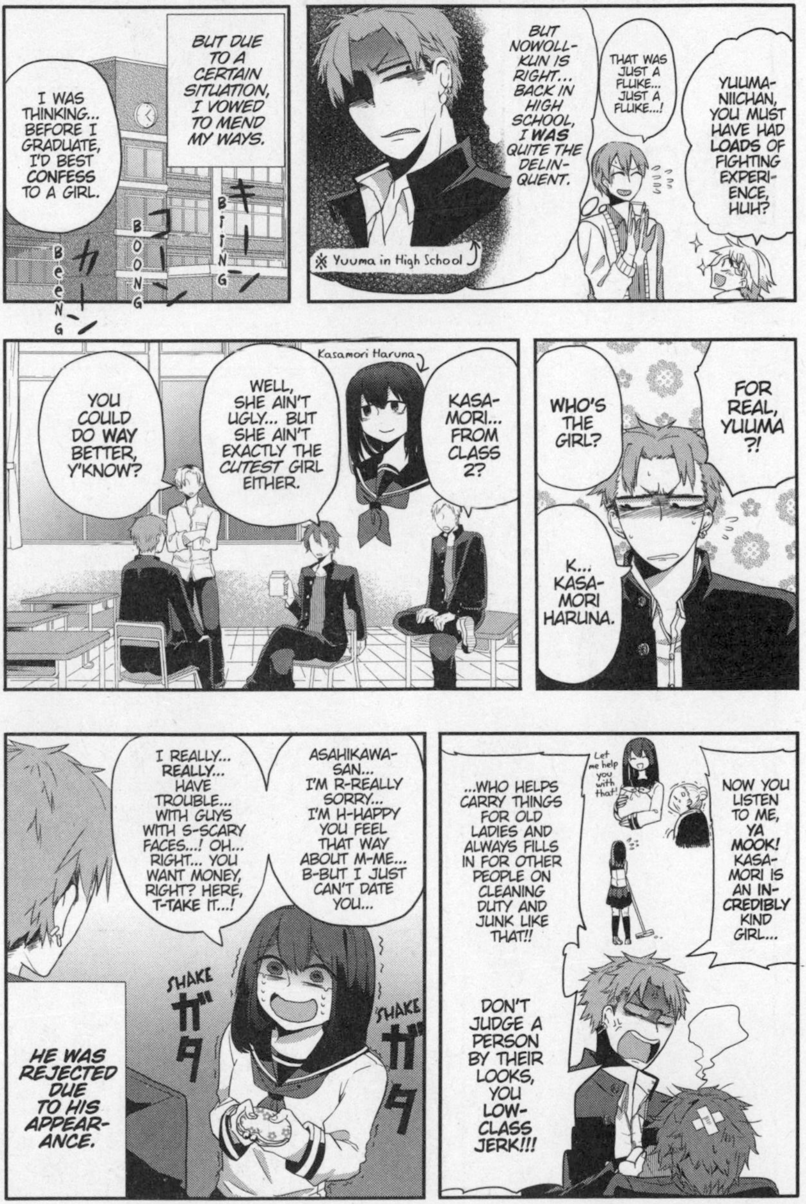
YUUMA-NIICHAN, YOU MUST HAVE HAD LOADS OF FIGHTING EXPERIENCE, HUH?
THAT WAS JUST A FLUKE... JUST A FLUKE...!
BUT NOWOLL-KUN IS RIGHT... BACK IN HIGH SCHOOL, I WAS QUITE THE DELINQUENT.
※ Yuuma in High School
BUT DUE TO A CERTAIN SITUATION, I VOWED TO MEND MY WAYS.
I WAS THINKING... BEFORE I GRADUATE, I'D BEST CONFESS TO A GIRL.
キーン BIING
コーン BOONG
カーン BEENG
FOR REAL, YUUMA?!
WHO'S THE GIRL?
K... KASAMORI HARUNA.
KASAMORI... FROM CLASS 2?
Kasamori Haruna
WELL, SHE AIN'T UGLY... BUT SHE AIN'T EXACTLY THE CUTEST GIRL EITHER.
YOU COULD DO WAY BETTER, Y'KNOW?
NOW YOU LISTEN TO ME, YA MOOK! KASAMORI IS AN INCREDIBLY KIND GIRL...
Let me help you with that!
...WHO HELPS CARRY THINGS FOR OLD LADIES AND ALWAYS FILLS IN FOR OTHER PEOPLE ON CLEANING DUTY AND JUNK LIKE THAT!!
DON'T JUDGE A PERSON BY THEIR LOOKS, YOU LOW-CLASS JERK!!!
ASAHIKAWA-SAN... I'M R-REALLY SORRY... I'M H-HAPPY YOU FEEL THAT WAY ABOUT M-ME... B-BUT I JUST CAN'T DATE YOU...
I REALLY... REALLY... HAVE TROUBLE... WITH GUYS WITH S-SCARY FACES...! OH... RIGHT... YOU WANT MONEY, RIGHT? HERE, T-TAKE IT...!
SHAKE ガタ
SHAKE ガタ
HE WAS REJECTED DUE TO HIS APPEARANCE.

THE BENEFIT OF A T-REX

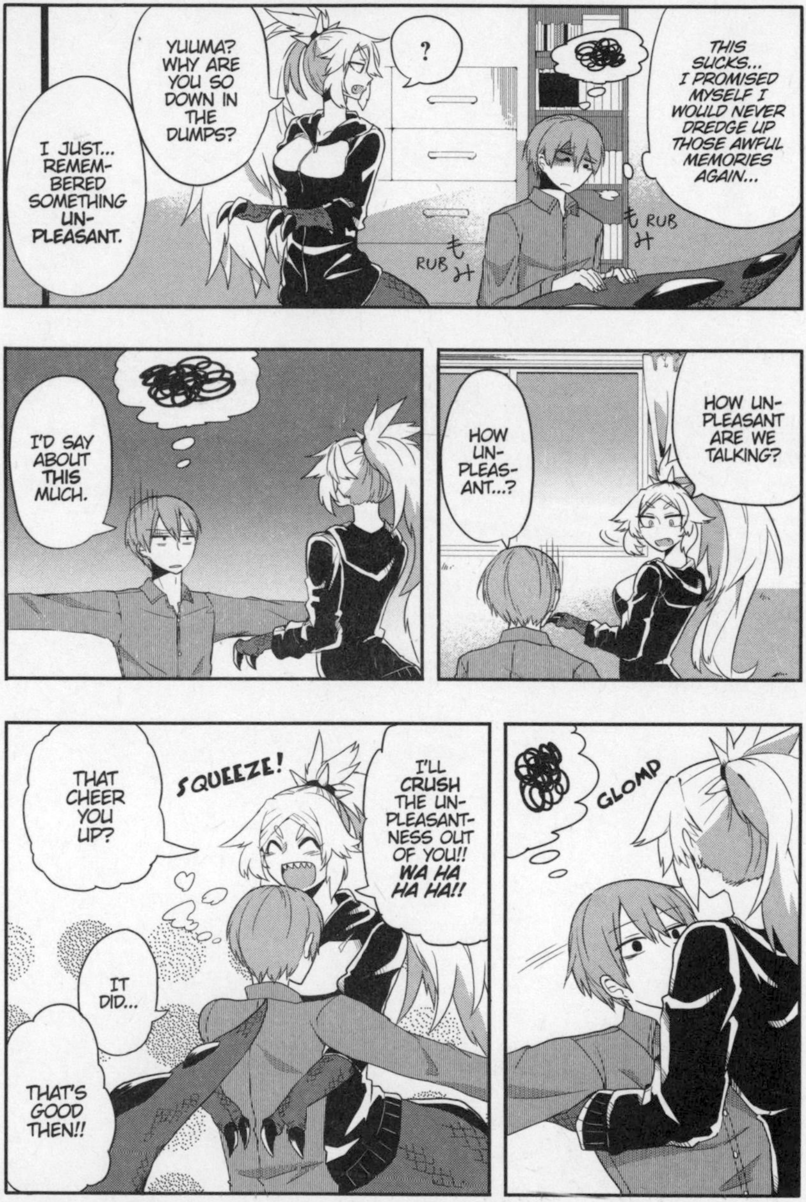
THIS SUCKS... I PROMISED MYSELF I WOULD NEVER DREDGE UP THOSE AWFUL MEMORIES AGAIN...
RUB
もみ
?
YUUMA? WHY ARE YOU SO DOWN IN THE DUMPS?
I JUST... REMEMBERED SOMETHING UNPLEASANT.
RUB
もみ
HOW UNPLEASANT ARE WE TALKING?
HOW UNPLEASANT...?
I'D SAY ABOUT THIS MUCH.
GLOMP
I'LL CRUSH THE UNPLEASANTNESS OUT OF YOU!! WA HA HA HA!!
SQUEEZE!
THAT CHEER YOU UP?
IT DID...
THAT'S GOOD THEN!!

My Girlfriend is a T-REX

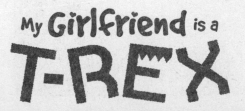

PAT   PAT

CHAPTER 13
MY CLEANING GIRLFRIEND

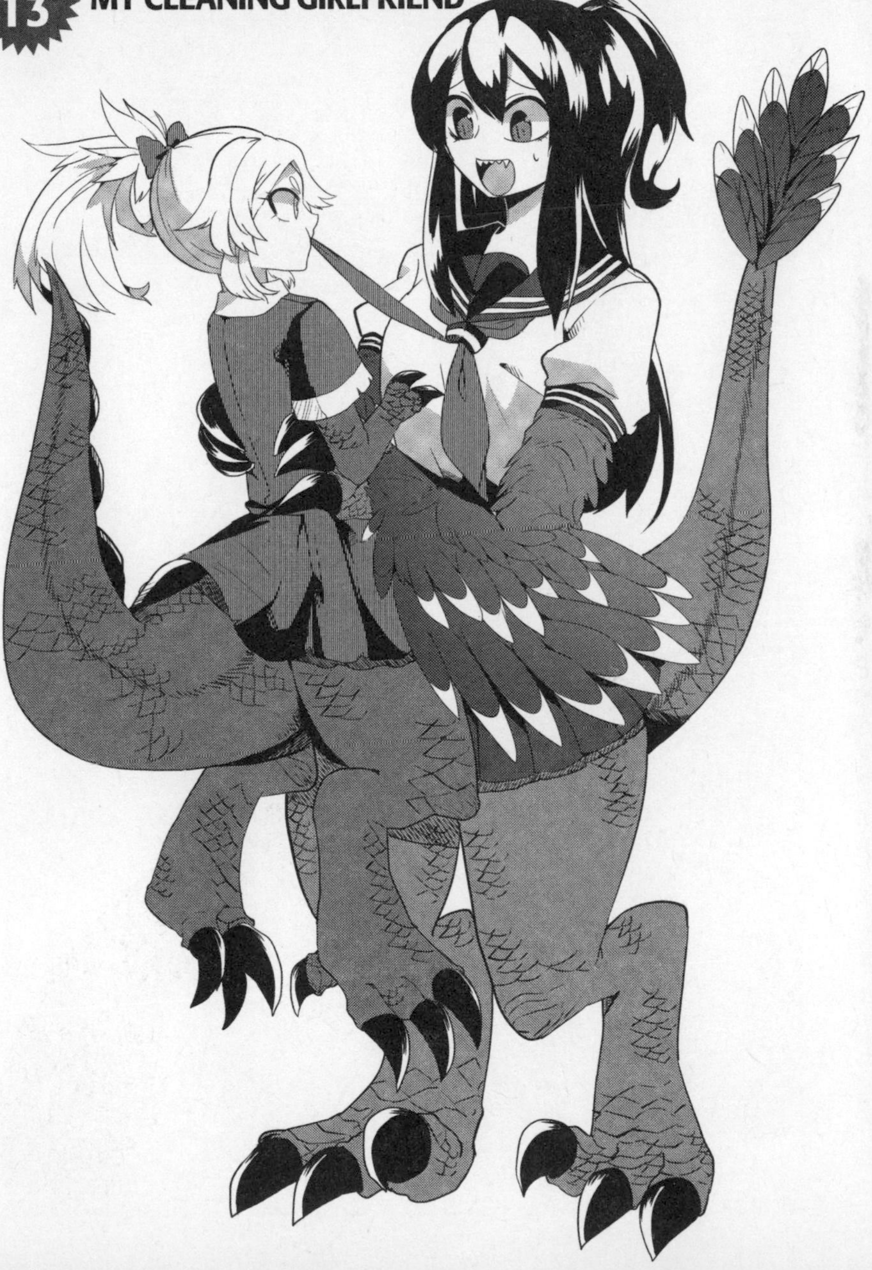

JUST A LITTLE BIT...

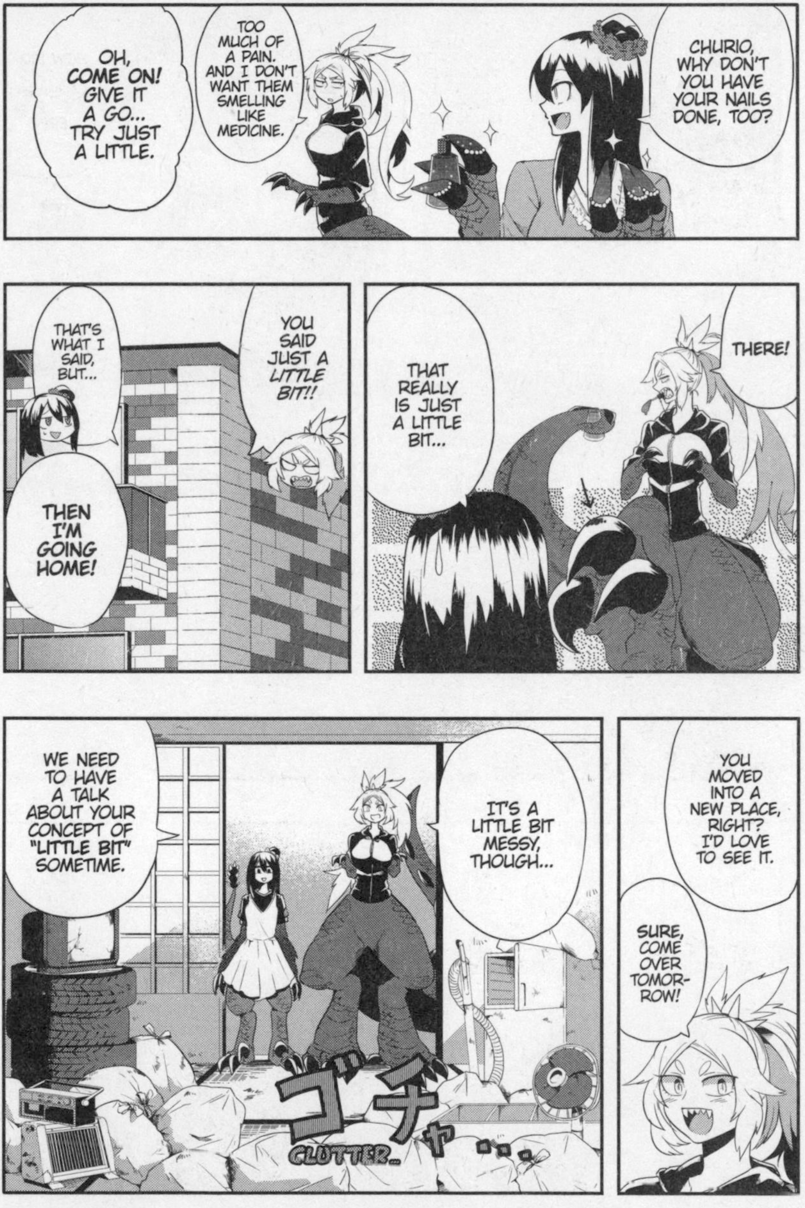
CHURIO, WHY DON'T YOU HAVE YOUR NAILS DONE, TOO?
TOO MUCH OF A PAIN. AND I DON'T WANT THEM SMELLING LIKE MEDICINE.
OH, COME ON! GIVE IT A GO... TRY JUST A LITTLE.
THERE!
THAT REALLY IS JUST A LITTLE BIT...
YOU SAID JUST A *LITTLE BIT*!!
THAT'S WHAT I SAID, BUT...
THEN I'M GOING HOME!
YOU MOVED INTO A NEW PLACE, RIGHT? I'D LOVE TO SEE IT.
SURE, COME OVER TOMORROW!
IT'S A LITTLE BIT MESSY, THOUGH...
WE NEED TO HAVE A TALK ABOUT YOUR CONCEPT OF "LITTLE BIT" SOMETIME.
CLUTTER...

EMERGENCY

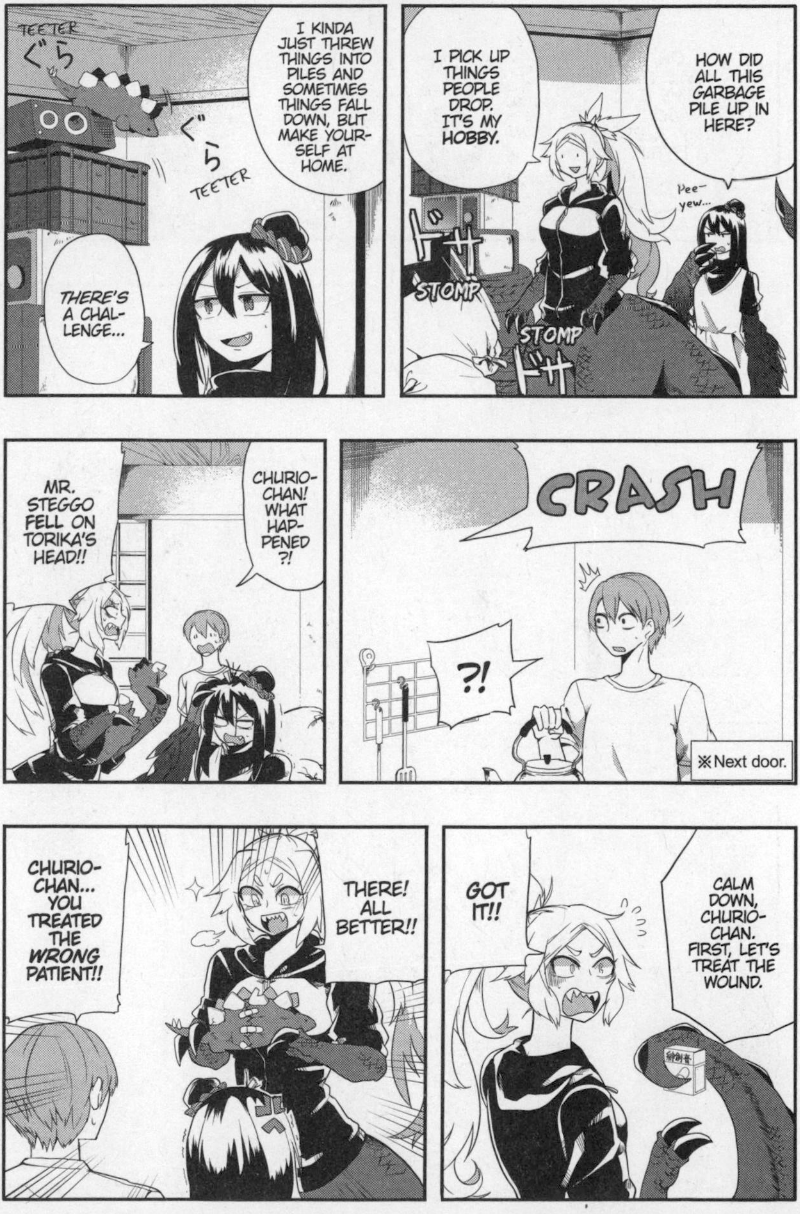
HOW DID ALL THIS GARBAGE PILE UP IN HERE?
I PICK UP THINGS PEOPLE DROP. IT'S MY HOBBY.
Pee-yew...
STOMP
STOMP
I KINDA JUST THREW THINGS INTO PILES AND SOMETIMES THINGS FALL DOWN, BUT MAKE YOUR-SELF AT HOME.
TEETER ぐら
ぐら TEETER
THERE'S A CHAL-LENGE...
CRASH
?!
※Next door.
CHURIO-CHAN! WHAT HAP-PENED?!
MR. STEGGO FELL ON TORIKA'S HEAD!!
CALM DOWN, CHURIO-CHAN. FIRST, LET'S TREAT THE WOUND.
GOT IT!!
THERE! ALL BETTER!!
CHURIO-CHAN... YOU TREATED THE WRONG PATIENT!!

EQUIVALENT VALUE

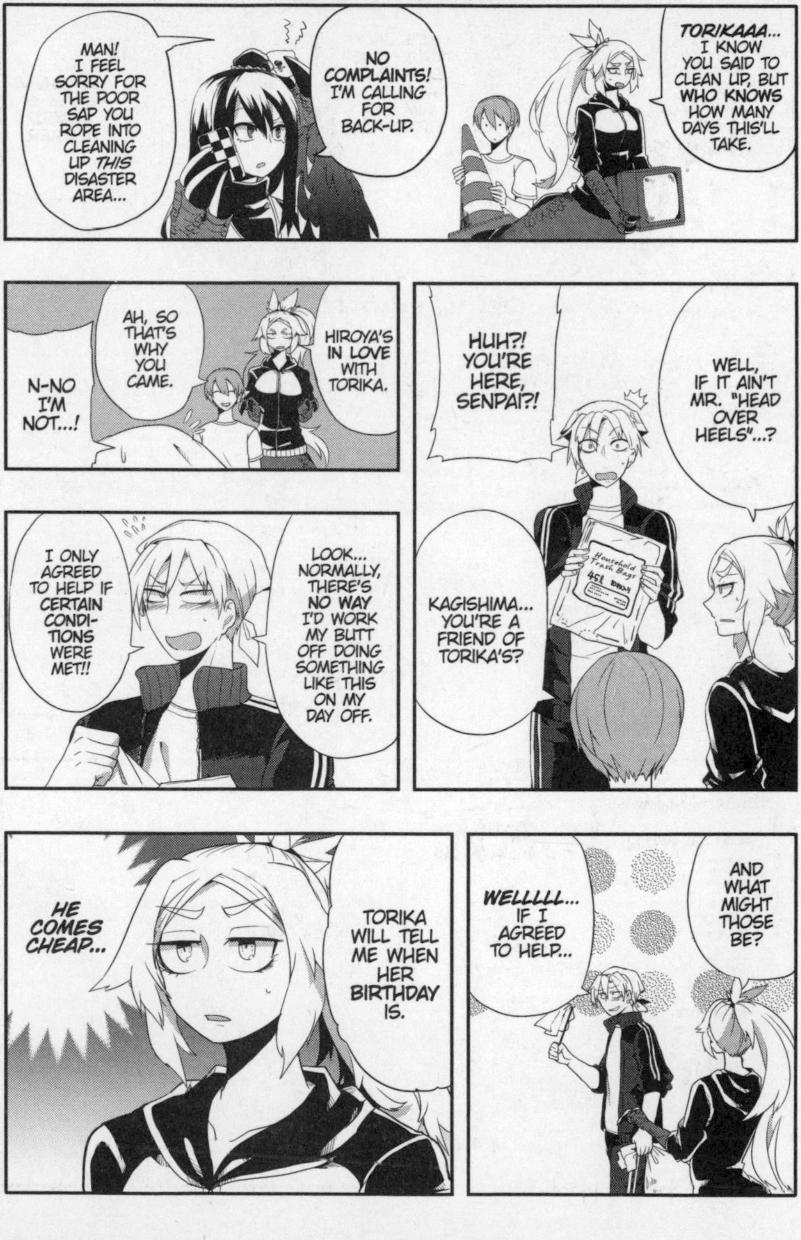

TORIKAAA... I KNOW YOU SAID TO CLEAN UP, BUT WHO KNOWS HOW MANY DAYS THIS'LL TAKE.
NO COMPLAINTS! I'M CALLING FOR BACK-UP.
MAN! I FEEL SORRY FOR THE POOR SAP YOU ROPE INTO CLEANING UP THIS DISASTER AREA...
WELL, IF IT AIN'T MR. "HEAD OVER HEELS"...?
HUH?! YOU'RE HERE, SENPAI?!
KAGISHIMA... YOU'RE A FRIEND OF TORIKA'S?
Household Trash Bags
45ℓ
HIROYA'S IN LOVE WITH TORIKA.
AH, SO THAT'S WHY YOU CAME.
N-NO I'M NOT...!
LOOK... NORMALLY, THERE'S NO WAY I'D WORK MY BUTT OFF DOING SOMETHING LIKE THIS ON MY DAY OFF.
I ONLY AGREED TO HELP IF CERTAIN CONDITIONS WERE MET!!
AND WHAT MIGHT THOSE BE?
WELLLLL... IF I AGREED TO HELP...
TORIKA WILL TELL ME WHEN HER BIRTHDAY IS.
HE COMES CHEAP...

DÉJÀ VU

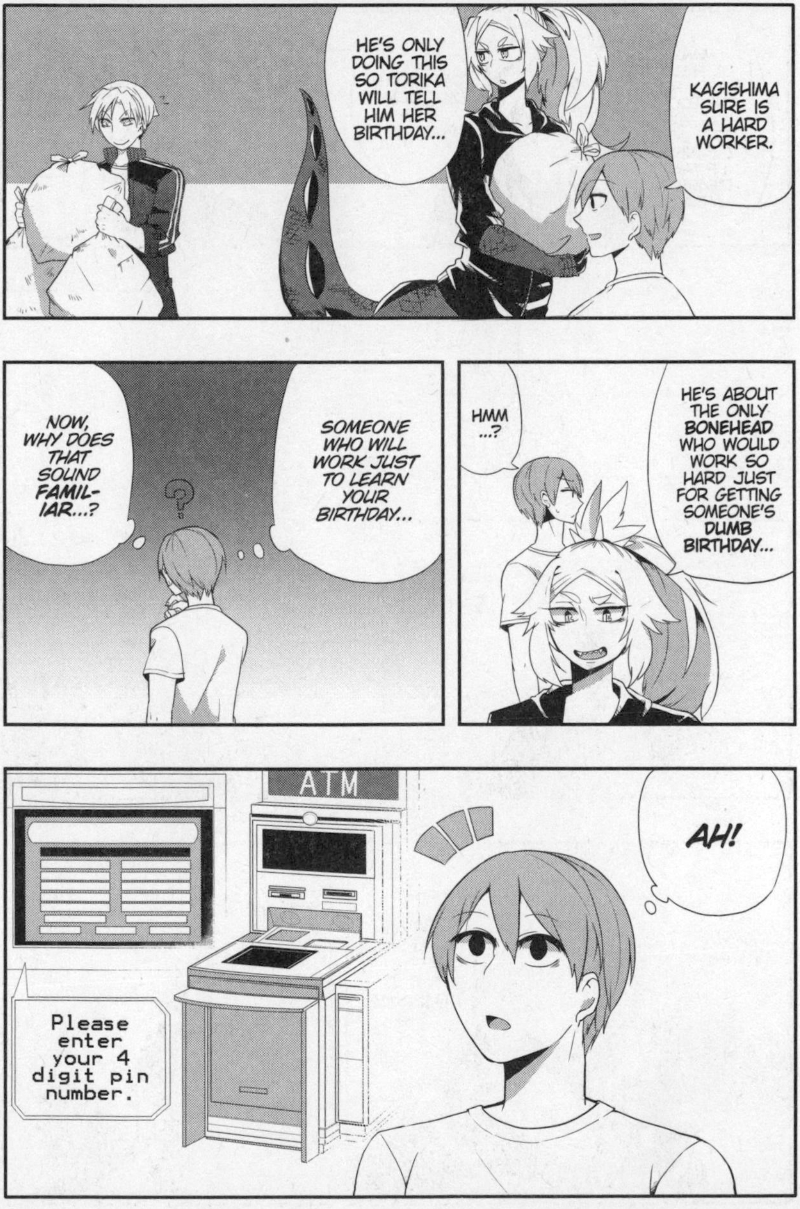
KAGISHIMA SURE IS A HARD WORKER.
HE'S ONLY DOING THIS SO TORIKA WILL TELL HIM HER BIRTHDAY...
HE'S ABOUT THE ONLY **BONEHEAD** WHO WOULD WORK SO HARD JUST FOR GETTING SOMEONE'S **DUMB** BIRTHDAY...
HMM ...?
SOMEONE WHO WILL WORK JUST TO LEARN YOUR BIRTHDAY...
*NOW, WHY DOES THAT SOUND **FAMILIAR...?***
AH!
ATM
Please enter your 4 digit pin number.

STRATEGY

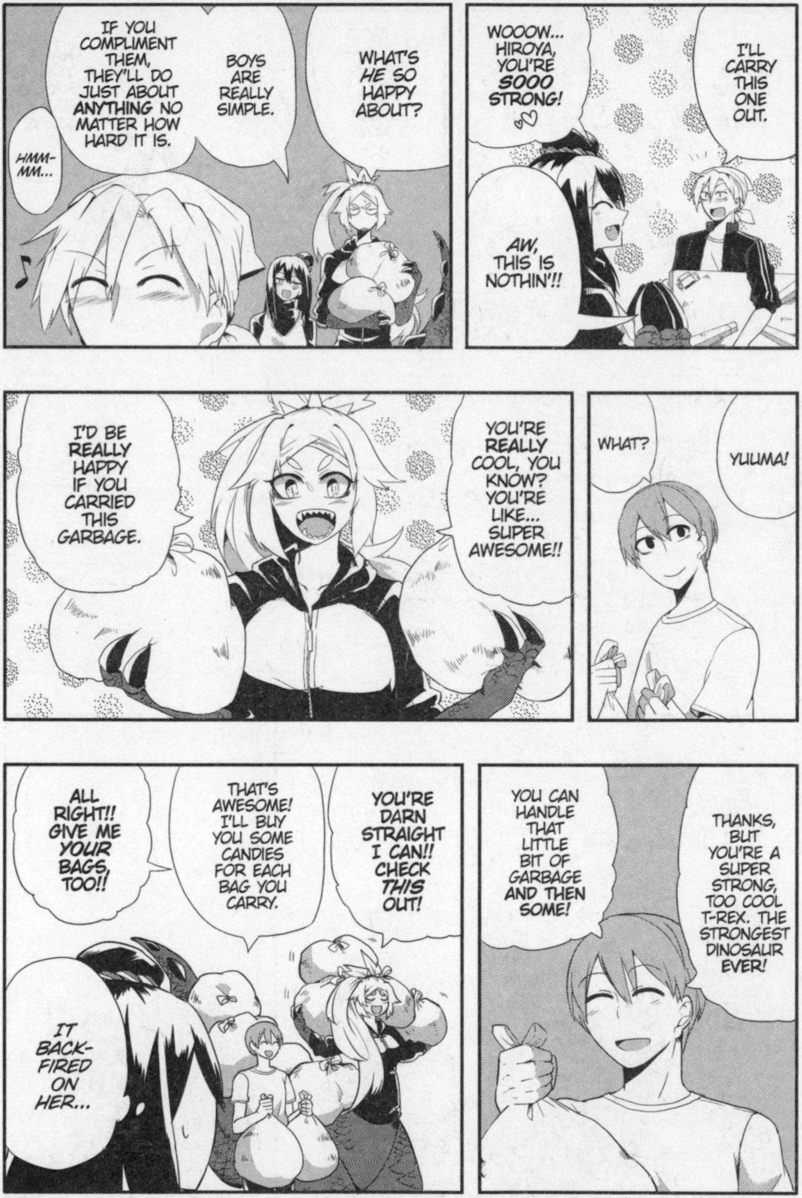
I'LL CARRY THIS ONE OUT.
WOOOW... HIROYA, YOU'RE *SOOO* STRONG!
AW, THIS IS NOTHIN'!!
WHAT'S *HE* SO HAPPY ABOUT?
BOYS ARE REALLY SIMPLE.
IF YOU COMPLIMENT THEM, THEY'LL DO JUST ABOUT ANYTHING NO MATTER HOW HARD IT IS.
HMMM-MM...
YUUMA!
WHAT?
YOU'RE REALLY COOL, YOU KNOW? YOU'RE LIKE... SUPER AWESOME!!
I'D BE REALLY HAPPY IF YOU CARRIED THIS GARBAGE.
THANKS, BUT YOU'RE A SUPER STRONG, TOO COOL T-REX. THE STRONGEST DINOSAUR EVER!
YOU CAN HANDLE THAT LITTLE BIT OF GARBAGE AND THEN SOME!
YOU'RE DARN STRAIGHT I CAN!! CHECK *THIS* OUT!
THAT'S AWESOME! I'LL BUY YOU SOME CANDIES FOR EACH BAG YOU CARRY.
ALL RIGHT!! GIVE ME *YOUR* BAGS, TOO!!
IT BACKFIRED ON HER...

A SPECIAL DAY

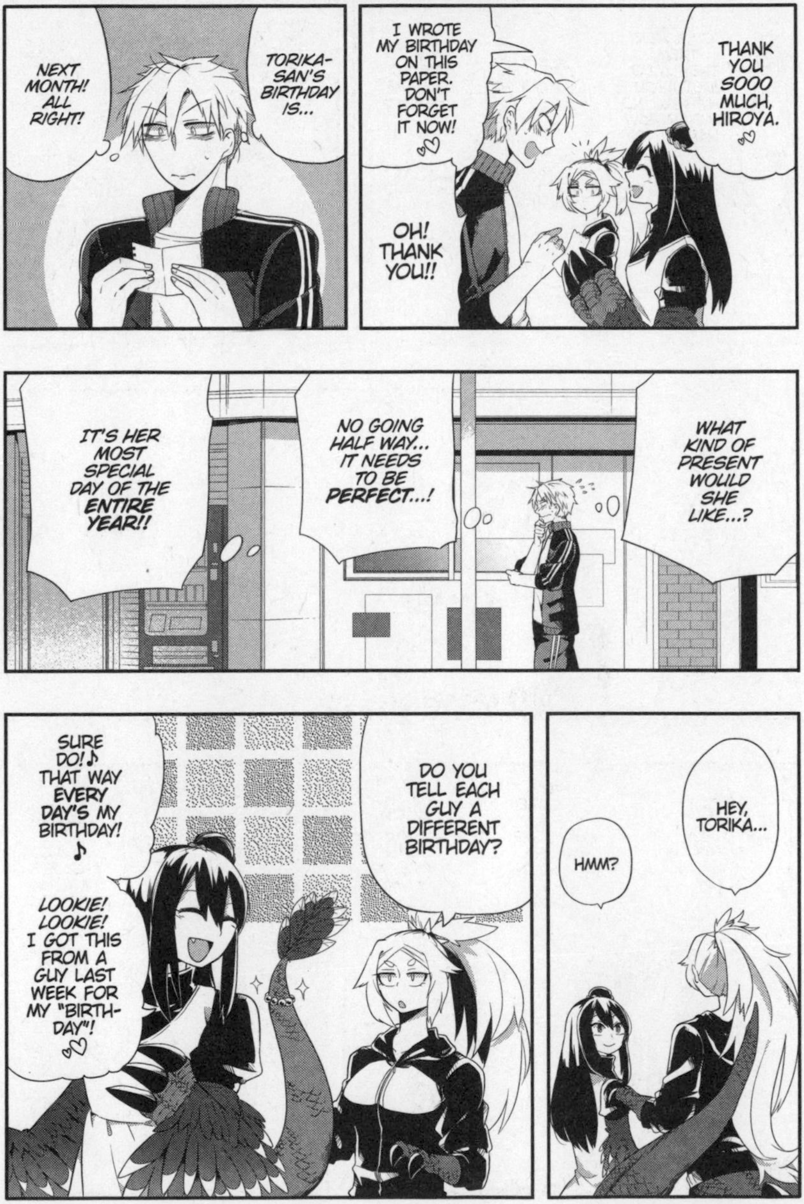
THANK YOU SOOO MUCH, HIROYA. ♡
I WROTE MY BIRTHDAY ON THIS PAPER. DON'T FORGET IT NOW! ♡
OH! THANK YOU!!
TORIKA-SAN'S BIRTHDAY IS...
NEXT MONTH! ALL RIGHT!
WHAT KIND OF PRESENT WOULD SHE LIKE...?
NO GOING HALF WAY... IT NEEDS TO BE PERFECT...!
IT'S HER MOST SPECIAL DAY OF THE ENTIRE YEAR!!
HEY, TORIKA...
HMM?
DO YOU TELL EACH GUY A DIFFERENT BIRTHDAY?
SURE DO! ♪ THAT WAY EVERY DAY'S MY BIRTHDAY! ♪
LOOKIE! LOOKIE! I GOT THIS FROM A GUY LAST WEEK FOR MY "BIRTH-DAY"! ♡

EARS TO THE WALL

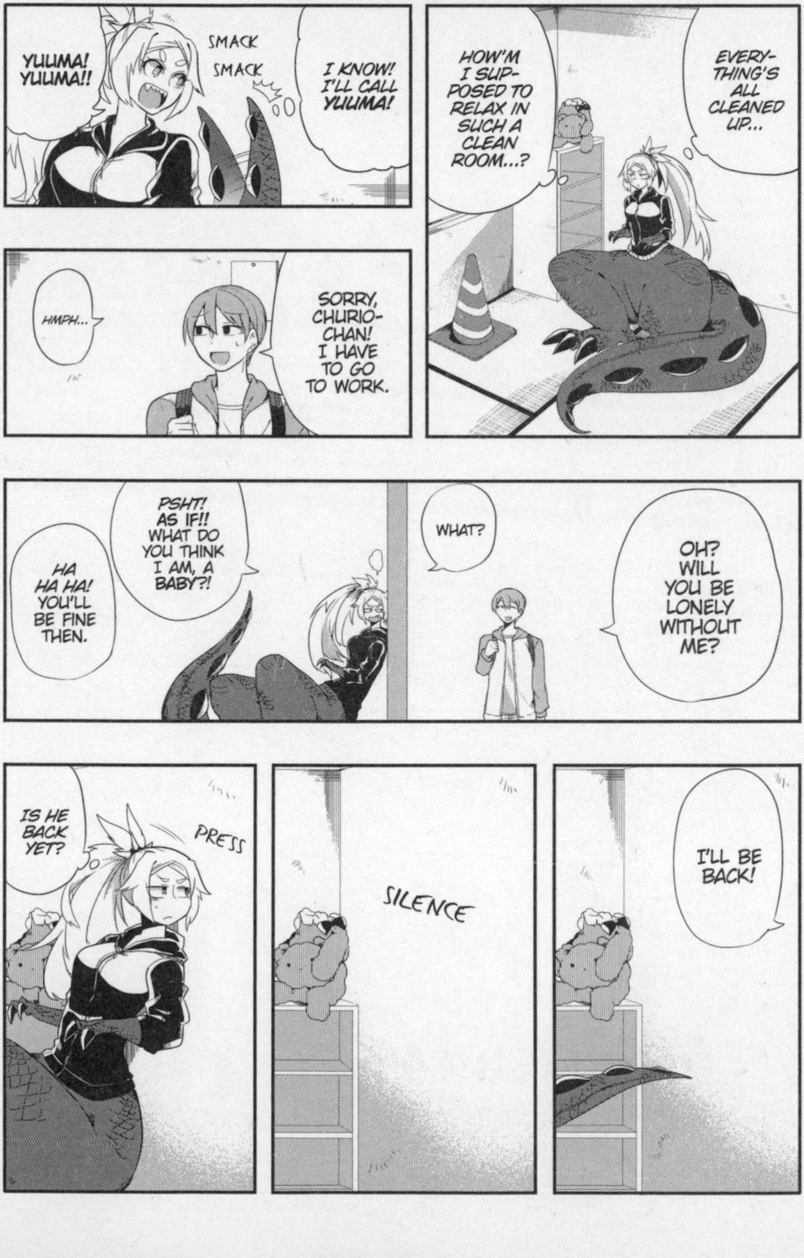
EVERY-THING'S ALL CLEANED UP...
HOW'M I SUP-POSED TO RELAX IN SUCH A CLEAN ROOM...?
I KNOW! I'LL CALL YUUMA!
SMACK
SMACK
YUUMA! YUUMA!!
SORRY, CHURIO-CHAN! I HAVE TO GO TO WORK.
HMPH...
OH? WILL YOU BE LONELY WITHOUT ME?
WHAT?
PSHT! AS IF!! WHAT DO YOU THINK I AM, A BABY?!
HA HA HA! YOU'LL BE FINE THEN.
I'LL BE BACK!
SILENCE
PRESS
IS HE BACK YET?

My Girlfriend is a T-REX

BONUS MANGA!

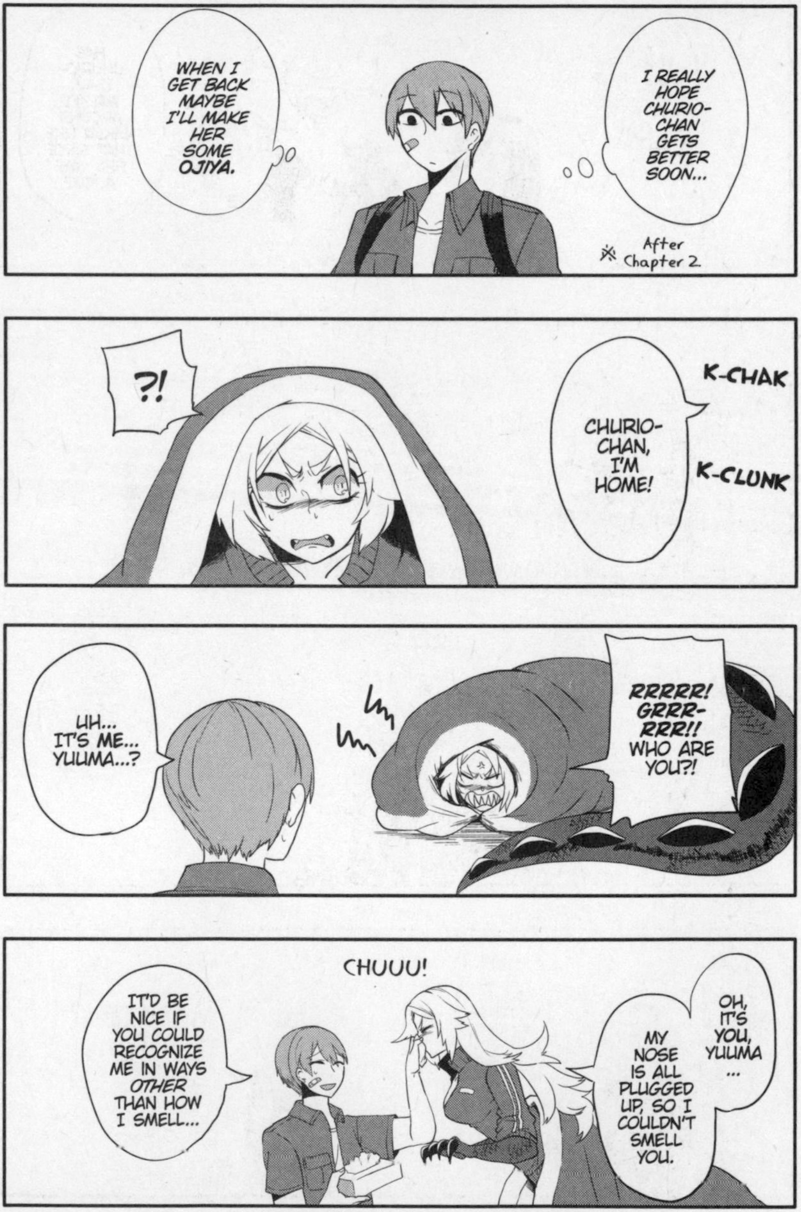
I REALLY HOPE CHURIO-CHAN GETS BETTER SOON...
WHEN I GET BACK MAYBE I'LL MAKE HER SOME OJIYA.
※ After Chapter 2.
K-CHAK
CHURIO-CHAN, I'M HOME!
K-CLUNK
?!
RRRRR! GRRR-RRR!! WHO ARE YOU?!
UH... IT'S ME... YUUMA...?
CHUUU!
OH, IT'S YOU, YUUMA...
MY NOSE IS ALL PLUGGED UP, SO I COULDN'T SMELL YOU.
IT'D BE NICE IF YOU COULD RECOGNIZE ME IN WAYS *OTHER* THAN HOW I SMELL...

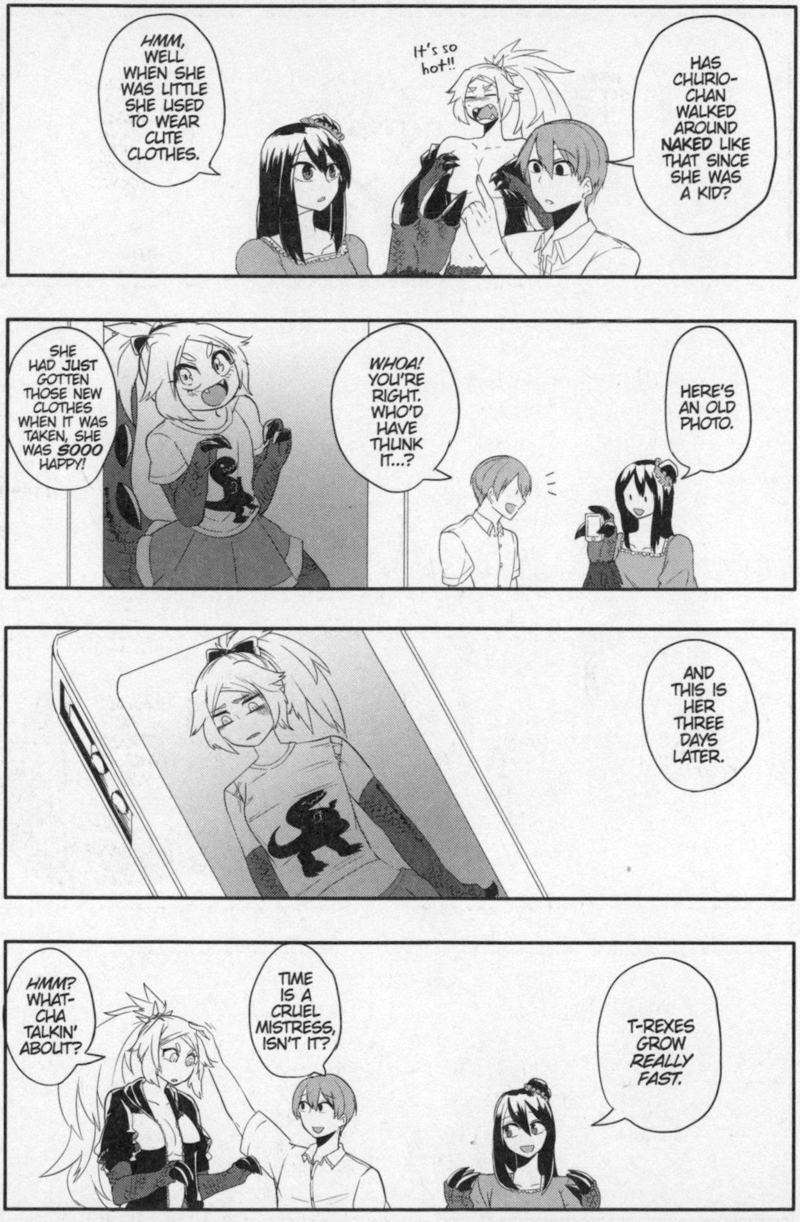
HAS CHURIO-CHAN WALKED AROUND NAKED LIKE THAT SINCE SHE WAS A KID?
It's so hot!!
HMM, WELL WHEN SHE WAS LITTLE SHE USED TO WEAR CUTE CLOTHES.
HERE'S AN OLD PHOTO.
WHOA! YOU'RE RIGHT. WHO'D HAVE THUNK IT...?
SHE HAD JUST GOTTEN THOSE NEW CLOTHES WHEN IT WAS TAKEN, SHE WAS *SOOO* HAPPY!
AND THIS IS HER THREE DAYS LATER.
T-REXES GROW *REALLY FAST.*
TIME IS A CRUEL MISTRESS, ISN'T IT?
HMM? WHAT-CHA TALKIN' ABOUT?

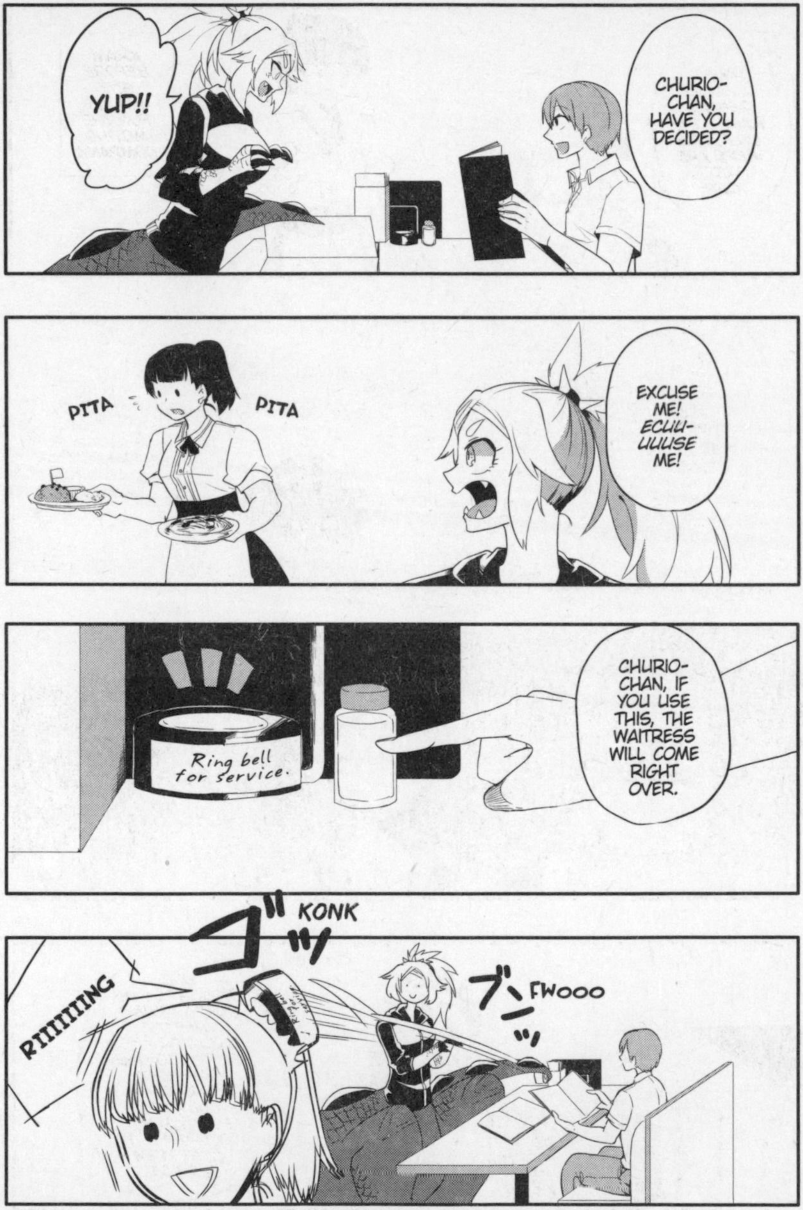
CHURIO-CHAN, HAVE YOU DECIDED?
YUP!!
EXCUSE ME! ECUU-UUUSE ME!
PITA
PITA
CHURIO-CHAN, IF YOU USE THIS, THE WAITRESS WILL COME RIGHT OVER.
Ring bell for service.
ブンッ
FWOOO
ゴッ
KONK
RIIIIIIING

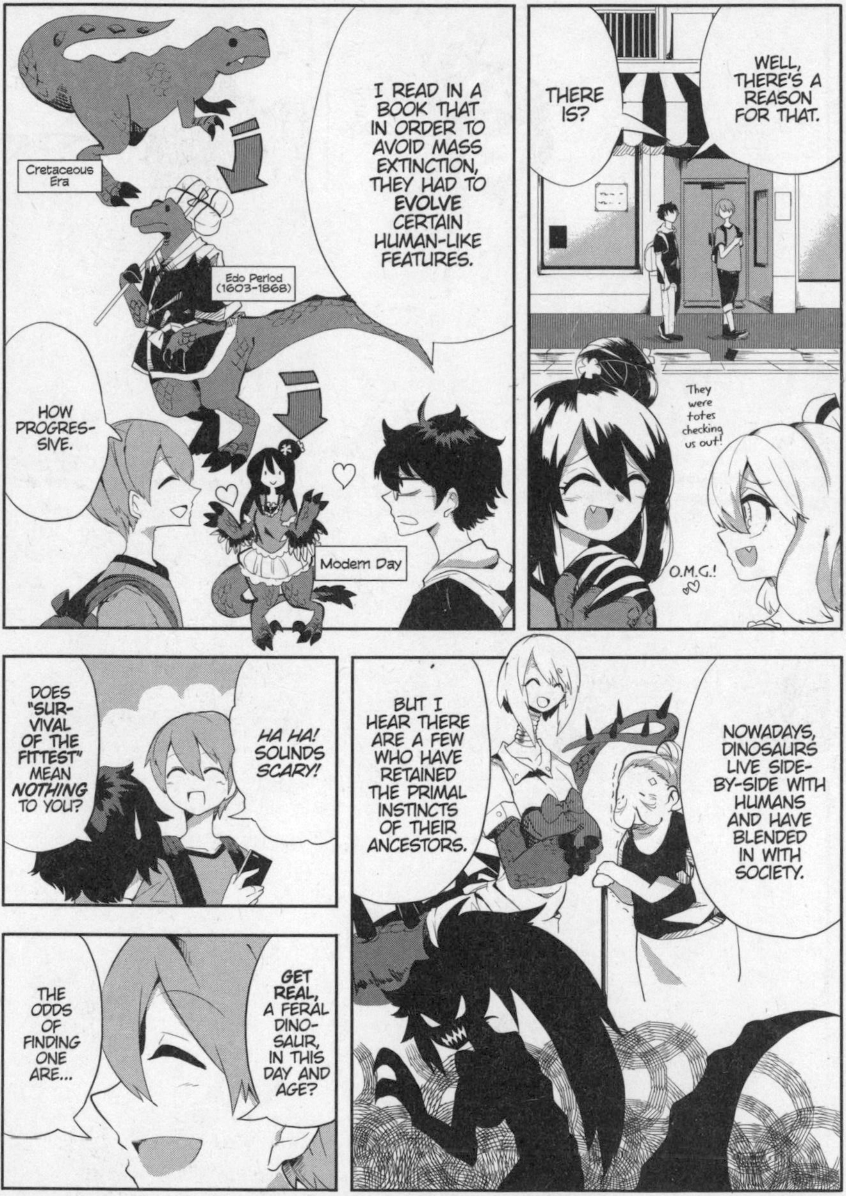
WELL, THERE'S A REASON FOR THAT.
THERE IS?
They were totes checking us out!
O.M.G.!
I READ IN A BOOK THAT IN ORDER TO AVOID MASS EXTINCTION, THEY HAD TO EVOLVE CERTAIN HUMAN-LIKE FEATURES.
Cretaceous Era
Edo Period (1603-1868)
HOW PROGRES-SIVE.
Modern Day
NOWADAYS, DINOSAURS LIVE SIDE-BY-SIDE WITH HUMANS AND HAVE BLENDED IN WITH SOCIETY.
BUT I HEAR THERE ARE A FEW WHO HAVE RETAINED THE PRIMAL INSTINCTS OF THEIR ANCESTORS.
HA HA! SOUNDS SCARY!
DOES "SUR-VIVAL OF THE FITTEST" MEAN *NOTHING* TO YOU?
GET REAL, A FERAL DINO-SAUR, IN THIS DAY AND AGE?
THE ODDS OF FINDING ONE ARE...

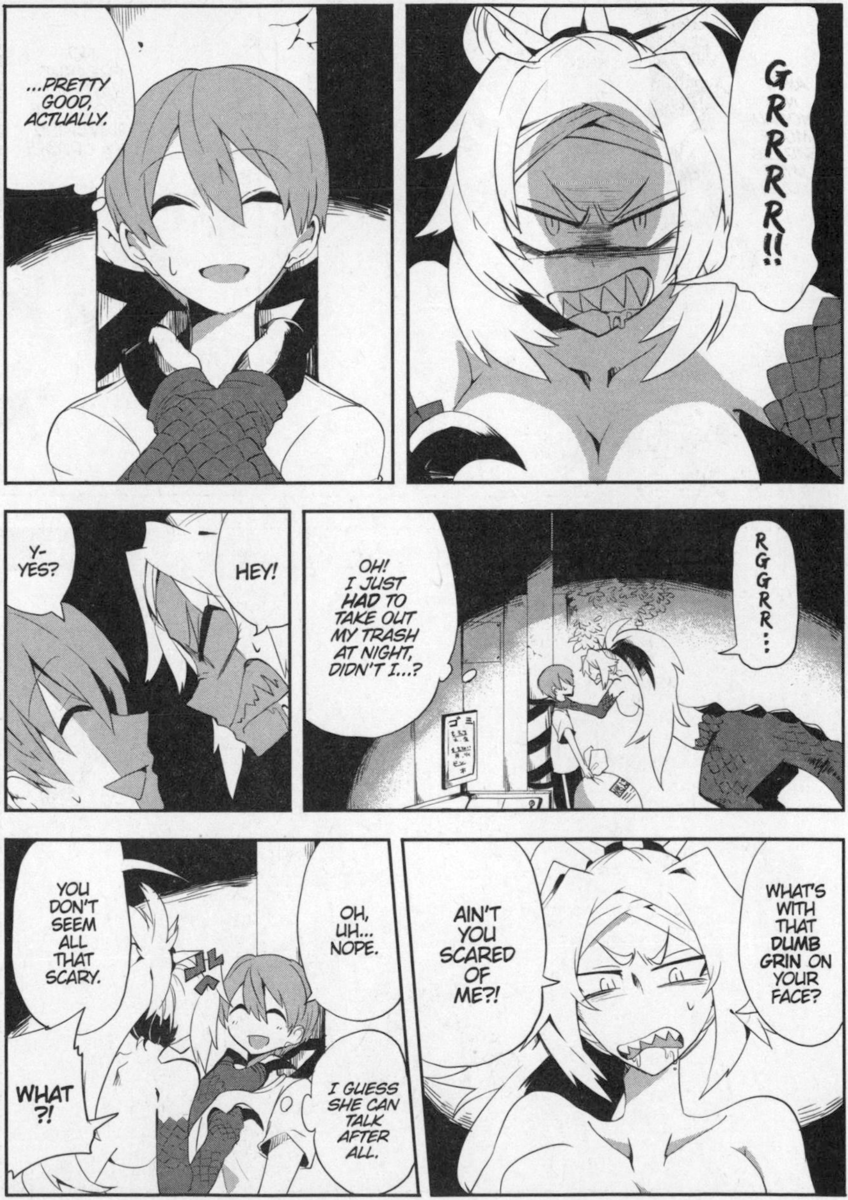
GRRRR!!
...PRETTY GOOD, ACTUALLY.
RGGRR...
OH! I JUST HAD TO TAKE OUT MY TRASH AT NIGHT, DIDN'T I...?
HEY!
Y-YES?
WHAT'S WITH THAT DUMB GRIN ON YOUR FACE?
AIN'T YOU SCARED OF ME?!
OH, UH... NOPE.
YOU DON'T SEEM ALL THAT SCARY.
I GUESS SHE CAN TALK AFTER ALL.
WHAT?!

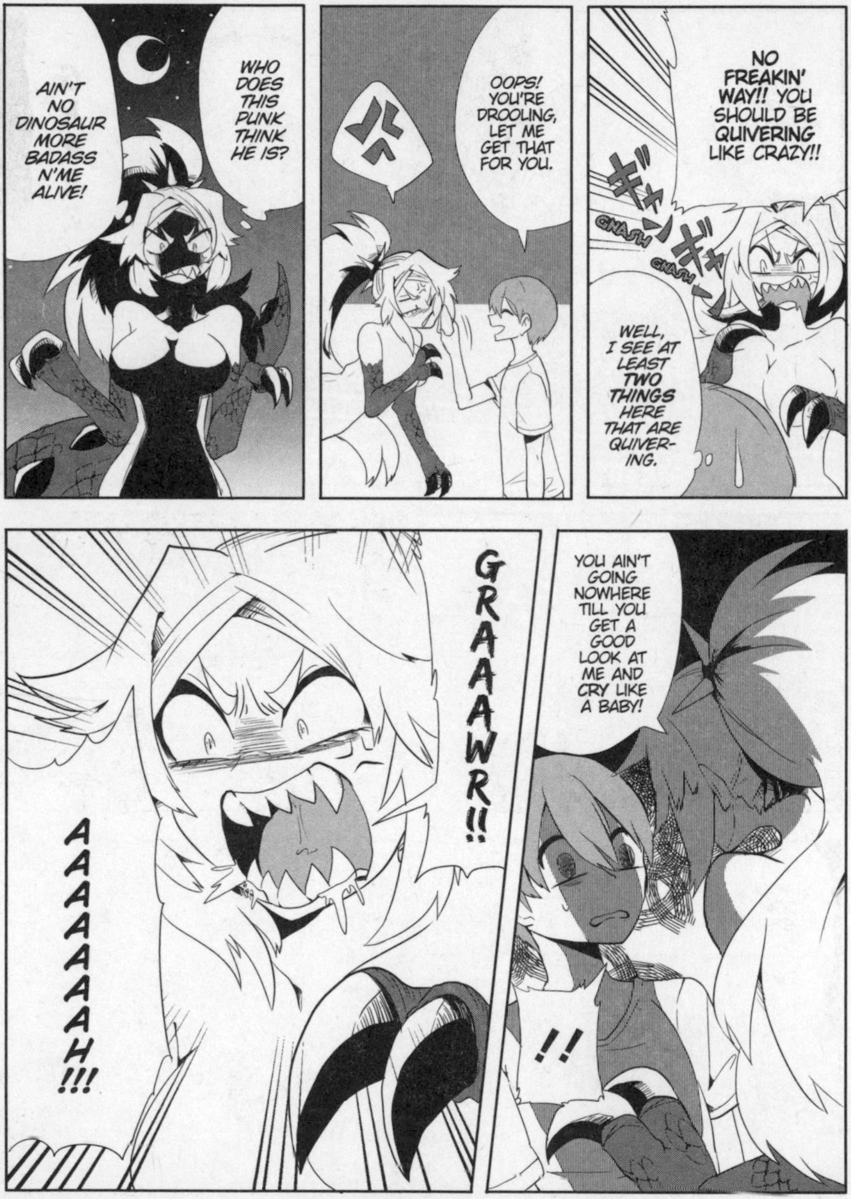
NO FREAKIN' WAY!! YOU SHOULD BE QUIVERING LIKE CRAZY!!
GNASH
GNASH
WELL, I SEE AT LEAST TWO THINGS HERE THAT ARE QUIVER-ING.
OOPS! YOU'RE DROOLING, LET ME GET THAT FOR YOU.
WHO DOES THIS PUNK THINK HE IS?
AIN'T NO DINOSAUR MORE BADASS N'ME ALIVE!
YOU AIN'T GOING NOWHERE TILL YOU GET A GOOD LOOK AT ME AND CRY LIKE A BABY!
!!
GRAAAAWR!!
AAAAAAAAAH!!!

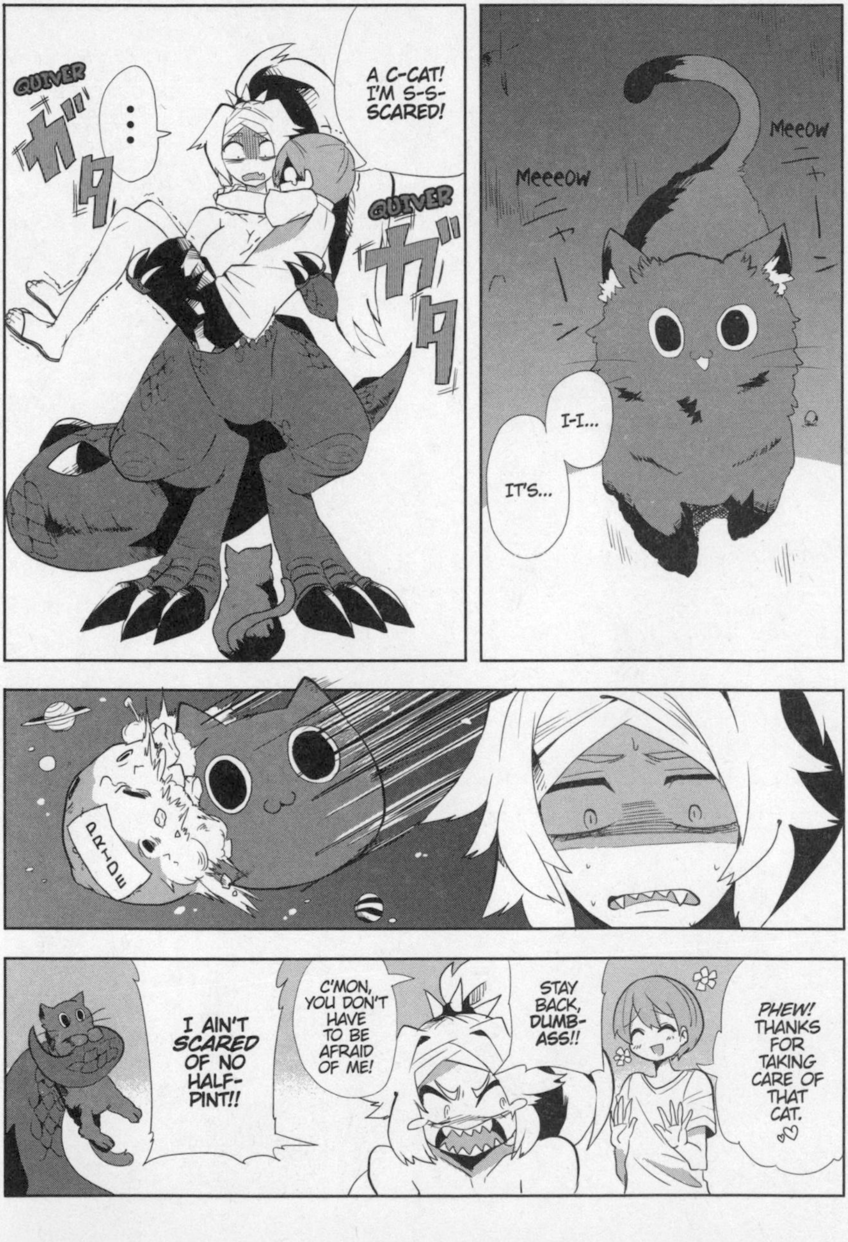
Meeow
Meeeow
I-I...
IT'S...
A C-CAT! I'M S-S-SCARED!
...
QUIVER
ガタ
QUIVER
ガタ
PRIDE
PHEW! THANKS FOR TAKING CARE OF THAT CAT.
STAY BACK, DUMBASS!!
C'MON, YOU DON'T HAVE TO BE AFRAID OF ME!
I AIN'T *SCARED* OF NO HALF-PINT!!

TYRANT OF THE CRETACEOUS ERA

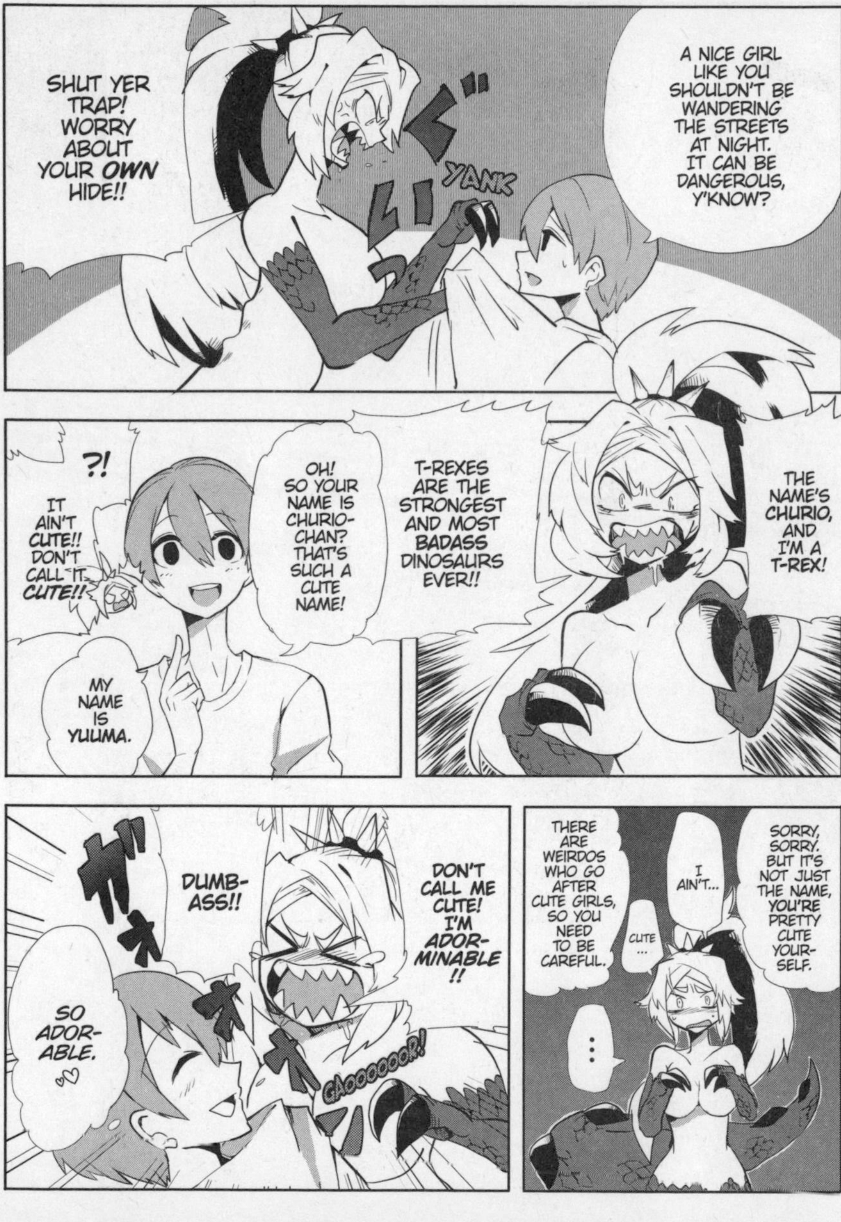
A NICE GIRL LIKE YOU SHOULDN'T BE WANDERING THE STREETS AT NIGHT. IT CAN BE DANGEROUS, Y'KNOW?
YANK
SHUT YER TRAP! WORRY ABOUT YOUR OWN HIDE!!
THE NAME'S CHURIO, AND I'M A T-REX!
T-REXES ARE THE STRONGEST AND MOST BADASS DINOSAURS EVER!!
OH! SO YOUR NAME IS CHURIO-CHAN? THAT'S SUCH A CUTE NAME!
?!
IT AIN'T CUTE!! DON'T CALL IT CUTE!!
MY NAME IS YUUMA.
SORRY, SORRY. BUT IT'S NOT JUST THE NAME, YOU'RE PRETTY CUTE YOURSELF.
I AIN'T...
THERE ARE WEIRDOS WHO GO AFTER CUTE GIRLS, SO YOU NEED TO BE CAREFUL.
CUTE ...
...
DON'T CALL ME CUTE! I'M ADORMINABLE!!
DUMB-ASS!!
SO ADORABLE.
GAOOOOOOR!

LIP SERVICE

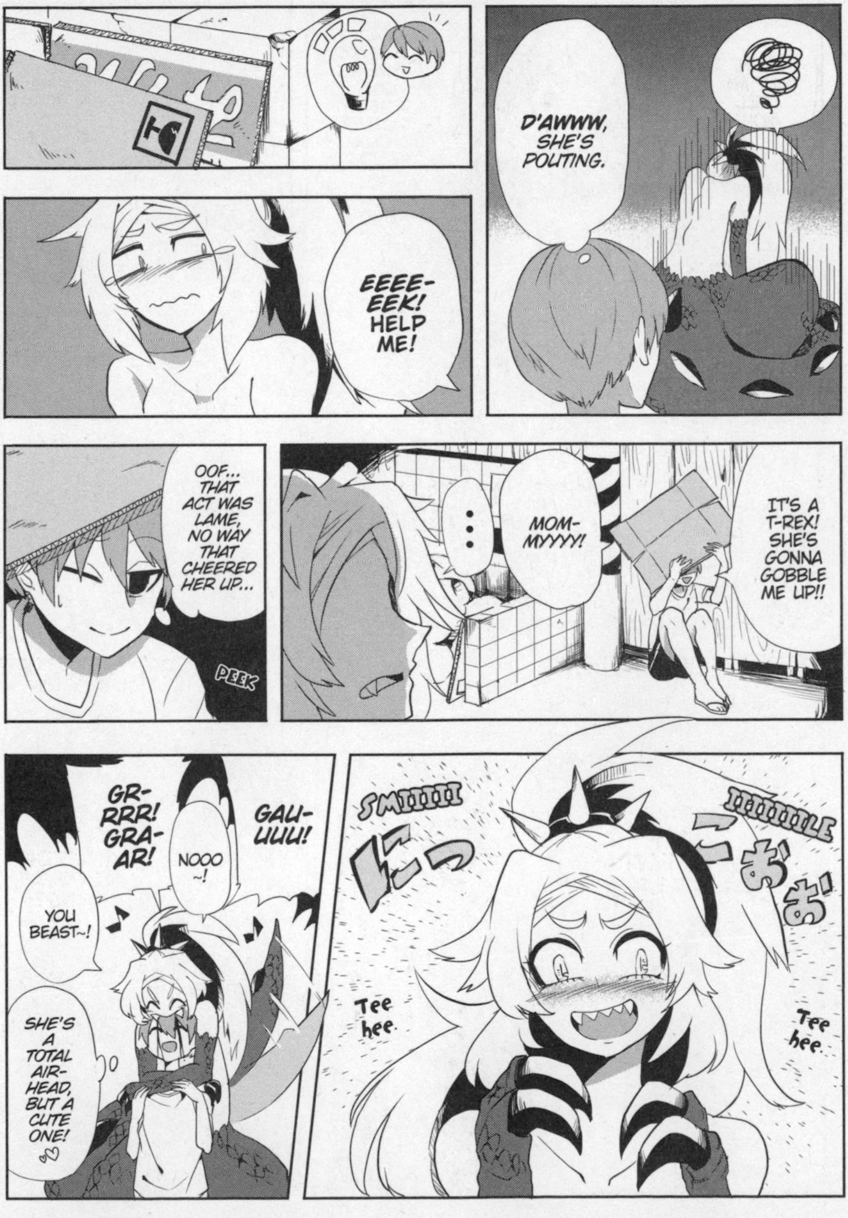
D'AWWW, SHE'S POUTING.
EEEE-EEK! HELP ME!
IT'S A T-REX! SHE'S GONNA GOBBLE ME UP!!
MOM-MYYYY!
...
OOF... THAT ACT WAS LAME, NO WAY THAT CHEERED HER UP...
PEEK
IIIIIIILE
こぉぉ
SMIIIII
にっ
Tee hee.
Tee hee.
GAU-UUU!
NOOO ~!
GR-RRR! GRA-AR!
YOU BEAST~!
SHE'S A TOTAL AIR-HEAD, BUT A CUTE ONE!

FIRST IMPRESSIONS

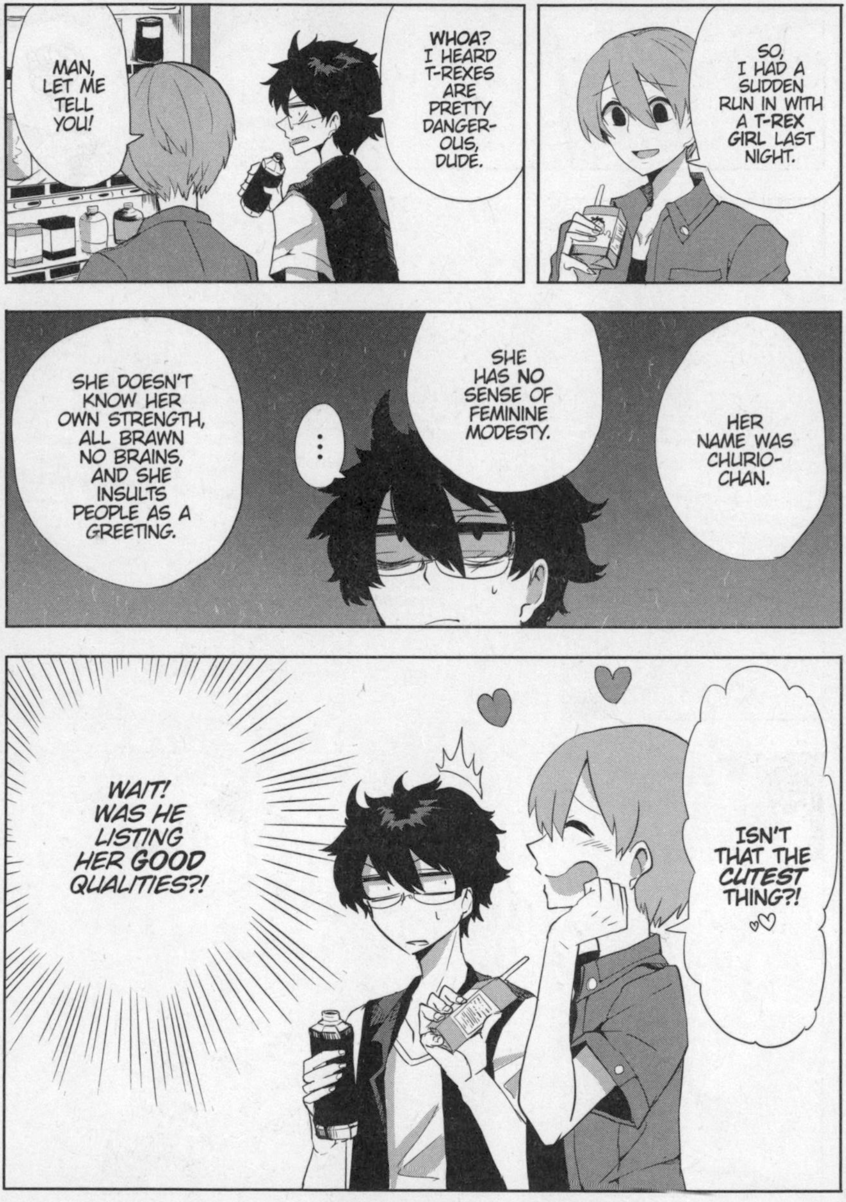
SO, I HAD A SUDDEN RUN IN WITH A T-REX GIRL LAST NIGHT.
WHOA? I HEARD T-REXES ARE PRETTY DANGER-OUS, DUDE.
MAN, LET ME TELL YOU!
HER NAME WAS CHURIO-CHAN.
SHE HAS NO SENSE OF FEMININE MODESTY.
...
SHE DOESN'T KNOW HER OWN STRENGTH, ALL BRAWN NO BRAINS, AND SHE INSULTS PEOPLE AS A GREETING.
ISN'T THAT THE CUTEST THING?! ♡♡
WAIT! WAS HE LISTING HER GOOD QUALITIES?!

HER COMMON SENSE

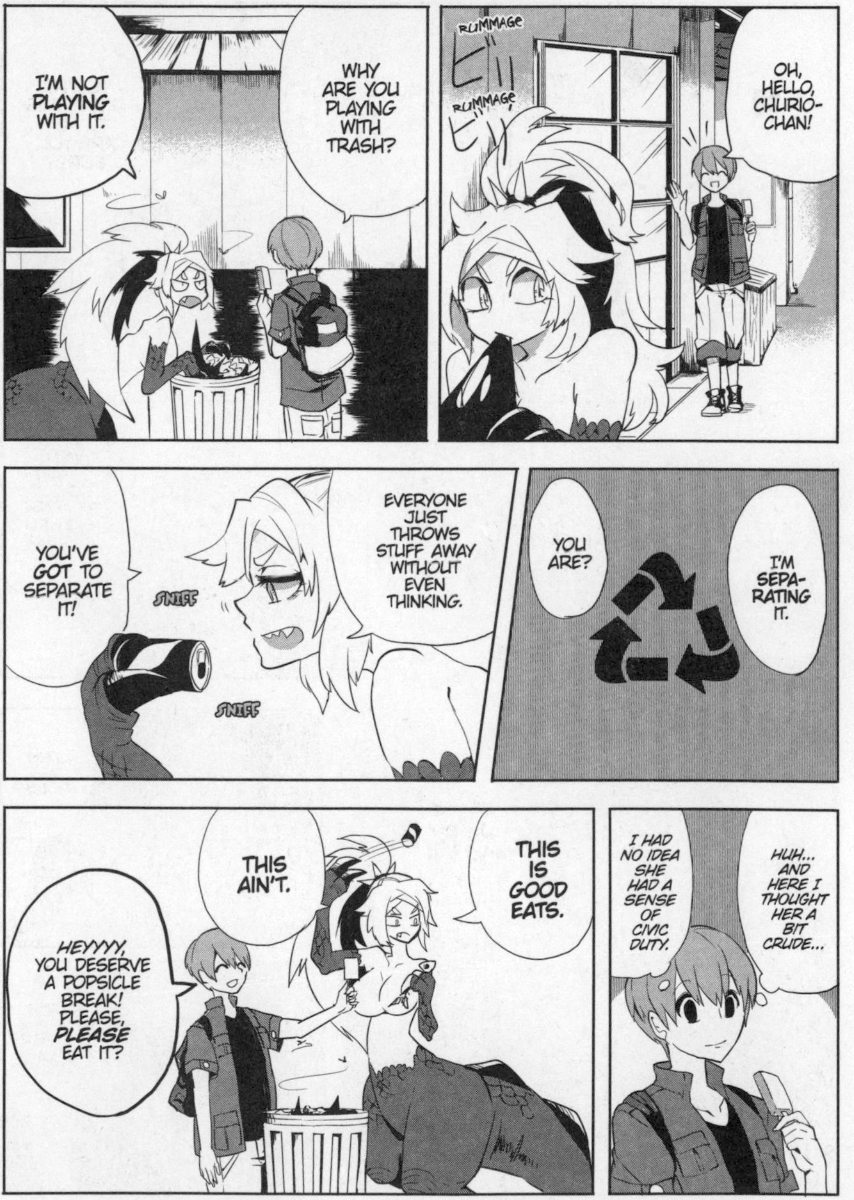
RUMMAGE
RUMMAGE
OH, HELLO, CHURIO-CHAN!
WHY ARE YOU PLAYING WITH TRASH?
I'M NOT PLAYING WITH IT.
I'M SEPA-RATING IT.
YOU ARE?
EVERYONE JUST THROWS STUFF AWAY WITHOUT EVEN THINKING.
SNIFF
YOU'VE GOT TO SEPARATE IT!
SNIFF
HUH... AND HERE I THOUGHT HER A BIT CRUDE...
I HAD NO IDEA SHE HAD A SENSE OF CIVIC DUTY.
THIS IS GOOD EATS.
THIS AIN'T.
HEYYYY, YOU DESERVE A POPSICLE BREAK! PLEASE, PLEASE EAT IT?

A T-REX'S GRATITUDE

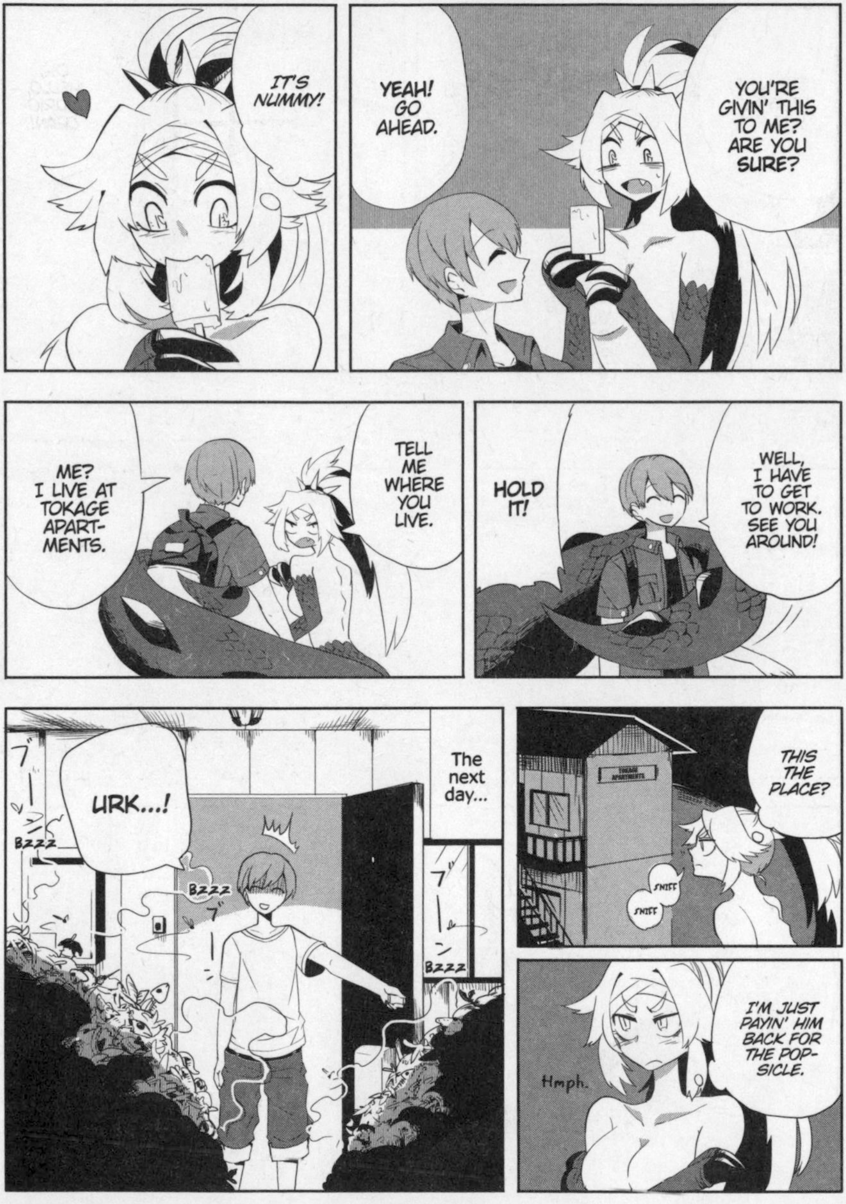

YOU'RE GIVIN' THIS TO ME? ARE YOU SURE?
YEAH! GO AHEAD.
IT'S NUMMY!
WELL, I HAVE TO GET TO WORK. SEE YOU AROUND!
HOLD IT!
TELL ME WHERE YOU LIVE.
ME? I LIVE AT TOKAGE APARTMENTS.
THIS THE PLACE?
SNIFF
SNIFF
I'M JUST PAYIN' HIM BACK FOR THE POP-SICLE.
Hmph.
The next day...
URK...!
BZZZ
BZZZ
BZZZ

RIP OFF

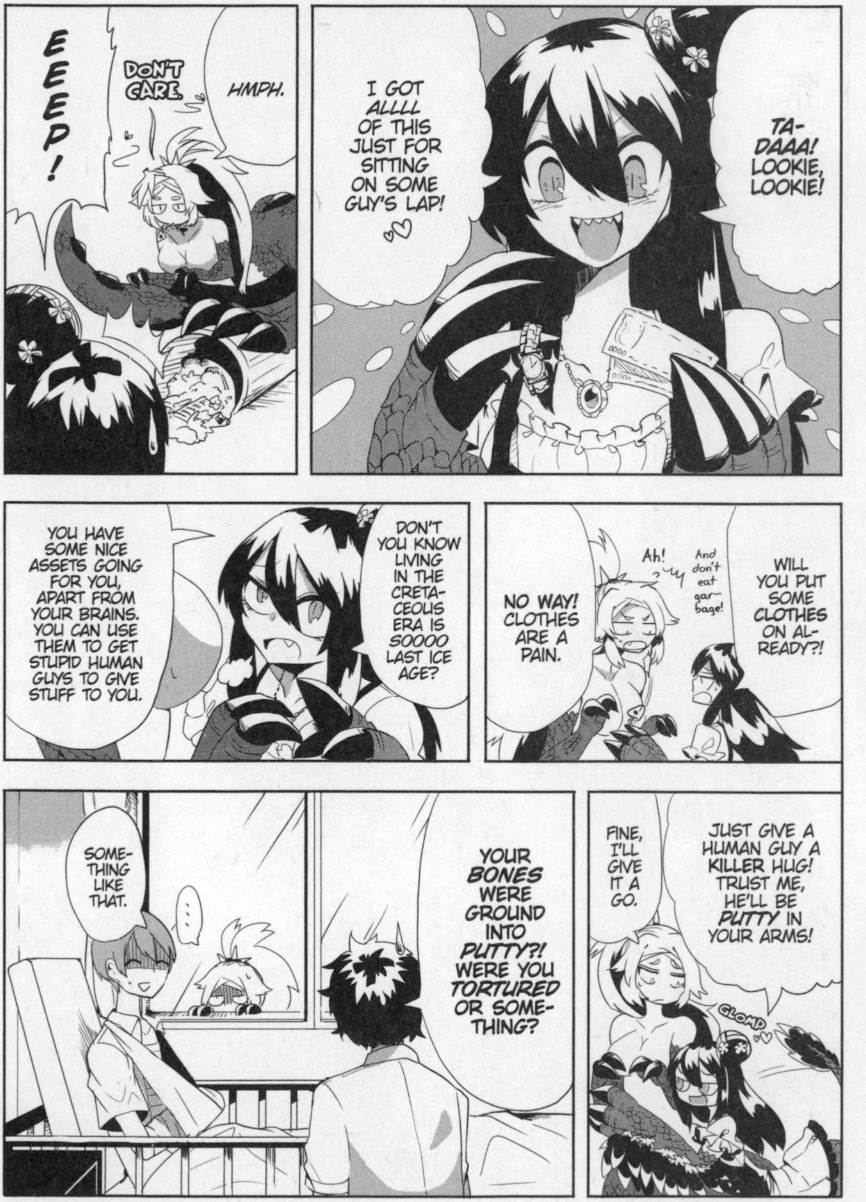
TA-DAAA! LOOKIE, LOOKIE!
I GOT ALLLL OF THIS JUST FOR SITTING ON SOME GUY'S LAP! ♡
HMPH.
DON'T CARE.
EEEP!
WILL YOU PUT SOME CLOTHES ON ALREADY?!
And don't eat garbage!
Ah!
NO WAY! CLOTHES ARE A PAIN.
DON'T YOU KNOW LIVING IN THE CRETACEOUS ERA IS SOOOO LAST ICE AGE?
YOU HAVE SOME NICE ASSETS GOING FOR YOU, APART FROM YOUR BRAINS. YOU CAN USE THEM TO GET STUPID HUMAN GUYS TO GIVE STUFF TO YOU.
JUST GIVE A HUMAN GUY A KILLER HUG! TRUST ME, HE'LL BE PUTTY IN YOUR ARMS!
FINE, I'LL GIVE IT A GO.
GLOMP ♡
YOUR BONES WERE GROUND INTO PUTTY?! WERE YOU TORTURED OR SOMETHING?
SOMETHING LIKE THAT.
...

PRESENT 1

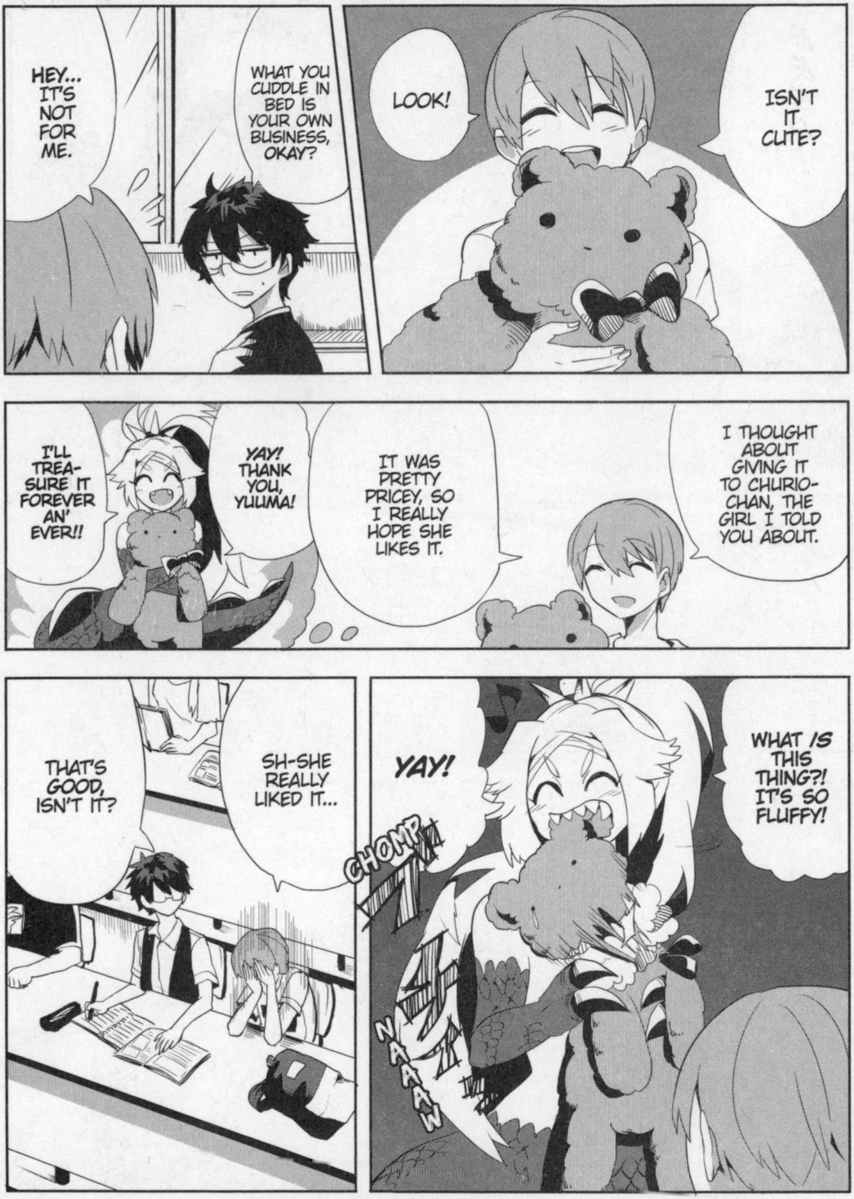
ISN'T IT CUTE?
LOOK!
WHAT YOU CUDDLE IN BED IS YOUR OWN BUSINESS, OKAY?
HEY... IT'S NOT FOR ME.
I THOUGHT ABOUT GIVING IT TO CHURIO-CHAN, THE GIRL I TOLD YOU ABOUT.
IT WAS PRETTY PRICEY, SO I REALLY HOPE SHE LIKES IT.
YAY! THANK YOU, YUUMA!
I'LL TREASURE IT FOREVER AN' EVER!!
WHAT IS THIS THING?! IT'S SO FLUFFY!
YAY!
CHOMP
NAAAAW
SH-SHE REALLY LIKED IT...
THAT'S GOOD, ISN'T IT?

PRESENT 2

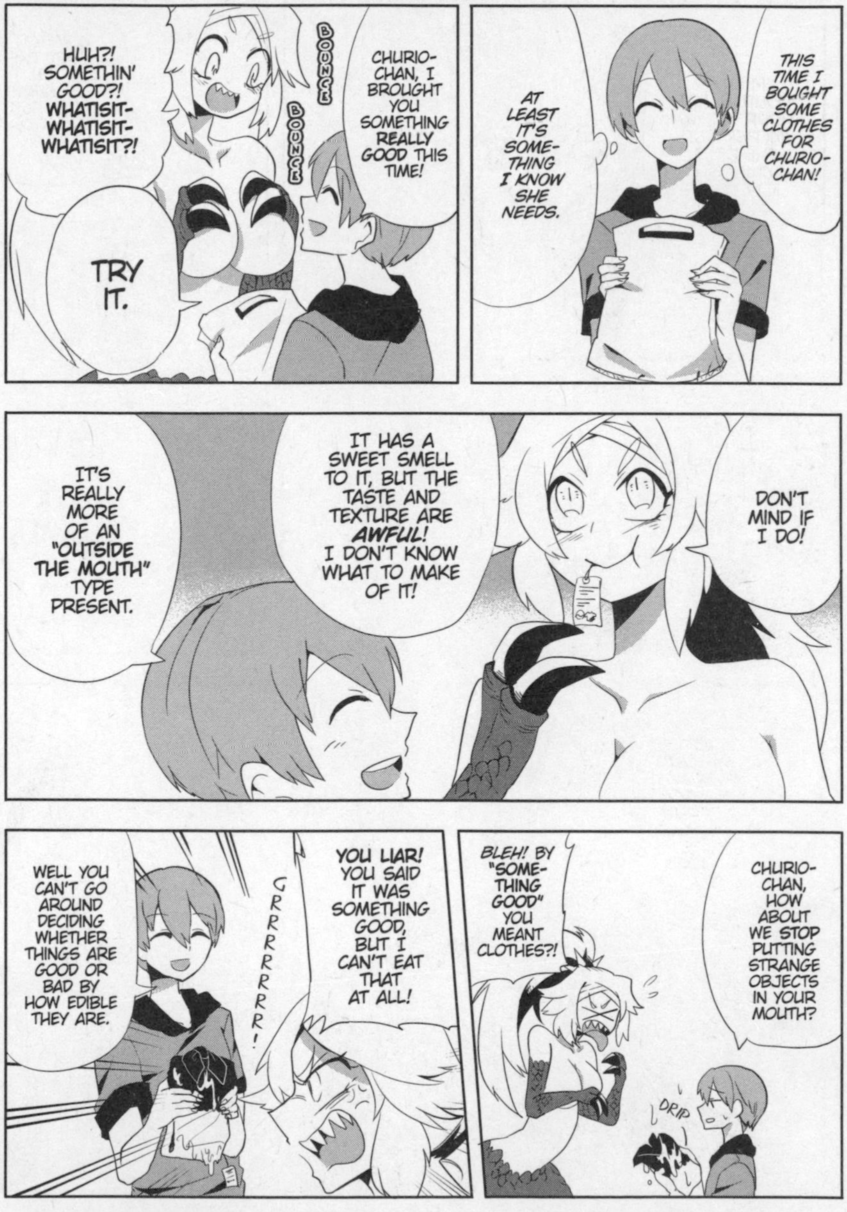
THIS TIME I BOUGHT SOME CLOTHES FOR CHURIO-CHAN!
AT LEAST IT'S SOMETHING I KNOW SHE NEEDS.
CHURIO-CHAN, I BROUGHT YOU SOMETHING REALLY GOOD THIS TIME!
BOUNCE
BOUNCE
HUH?! SOMETHIN' GOOD?! WHATISIT-WHATISIT-WHATISIT?!
TRY IT.
DON'T MIND IF I DO!
IT HAS A SWEET SMELL TO IT, BUT THE TASTE AND TEXTURE ARE AWFUL! I DON'T KNOW WHAT TO MAKE OF IT!
IT'S REALLY MORE OF AN "OUTSIDE THE MOUTH" TYPE PRESENT.
CHURIO-CHAN, HOW ABOUT WE STOP PUTTING STRANGE OBJECTS IN YOUR MOUTH?
BLEH! BY "SOMETHING GOOD" YOU MEANT CLOTHES?!
DRIP
YOU LIAR! YOU SAID IT WAS SOMETHING GOOD, BUT I CAN'T EAT THAT AT ALL!
GRRRRRRR!
WELL YOU CAN'T GO AROUND DECIDING WHETHER THINGS ARE GOOD OR BAD BY HOW EDIBLE THEY ARE.

PRESENT 3

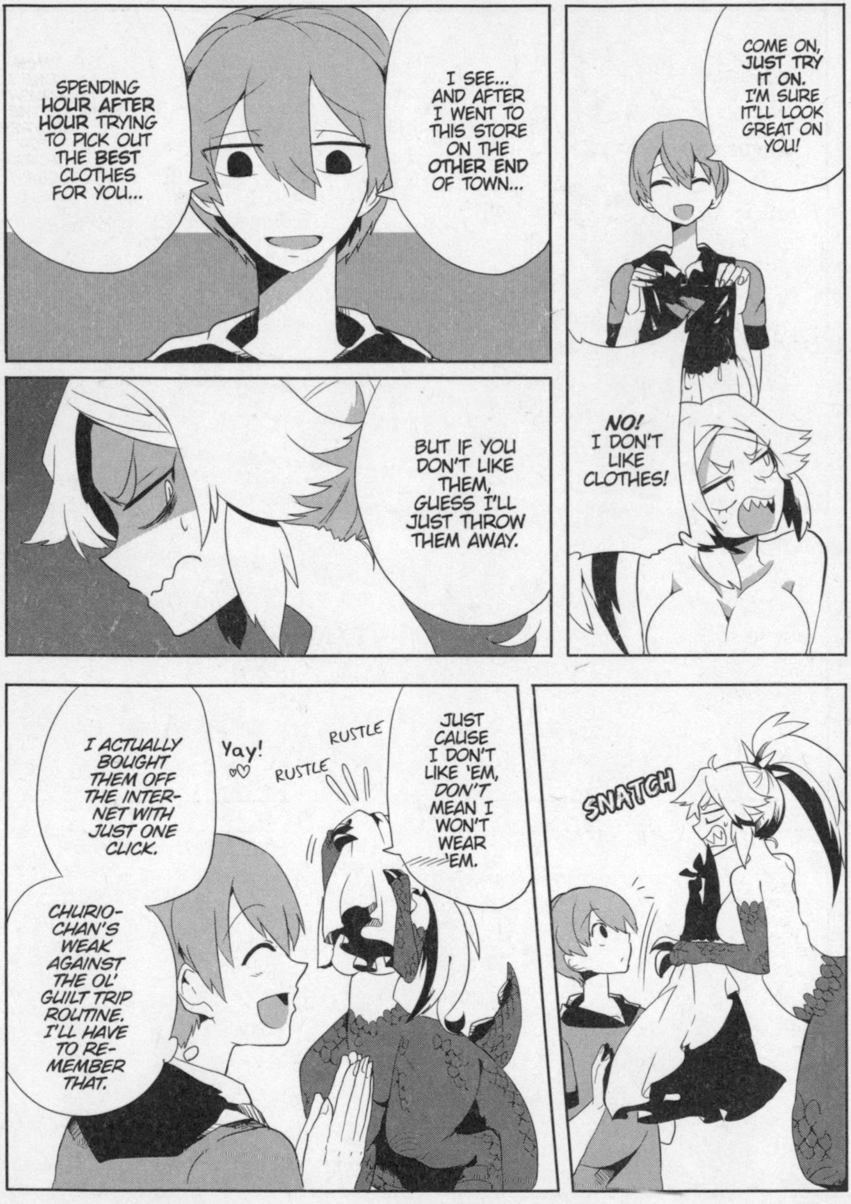
COME ON, JUST TRY IT ON. I'M SURE IT'LL LOOK GREAT ON YOU!
NO! I DON'T LIKE CLOTHES!
I SEE... AND AFTER I WENT TO THIS STORE ON THE OTHER END OF TOWN...
SPENDING HOUR AFTER HOUR TRYING TO PICK OUT THE BEST CLOTHES FOR YOU...
BUT IF YOU DON'T LIKE THEM, GUESS I'LL JUST THROW THEM AWAY.
SNATCH
JUST CAUSE I DON'T LIKE 'EM, DON'T MEAN I WON'T WEAR 'EM.
RUSTLE
RUSTLE
Yay!
I ACTUALLY BOUGHT THEM OFF THE INTER-NET WITH JUST ONE CLICK.
CHURIO-CHAN'S WEAK AGAINST THE OL' GUILT TRIP ROUTINE. I'LL HAVE TO RE-MEMBER THAT.

BOLD NEW WORLD

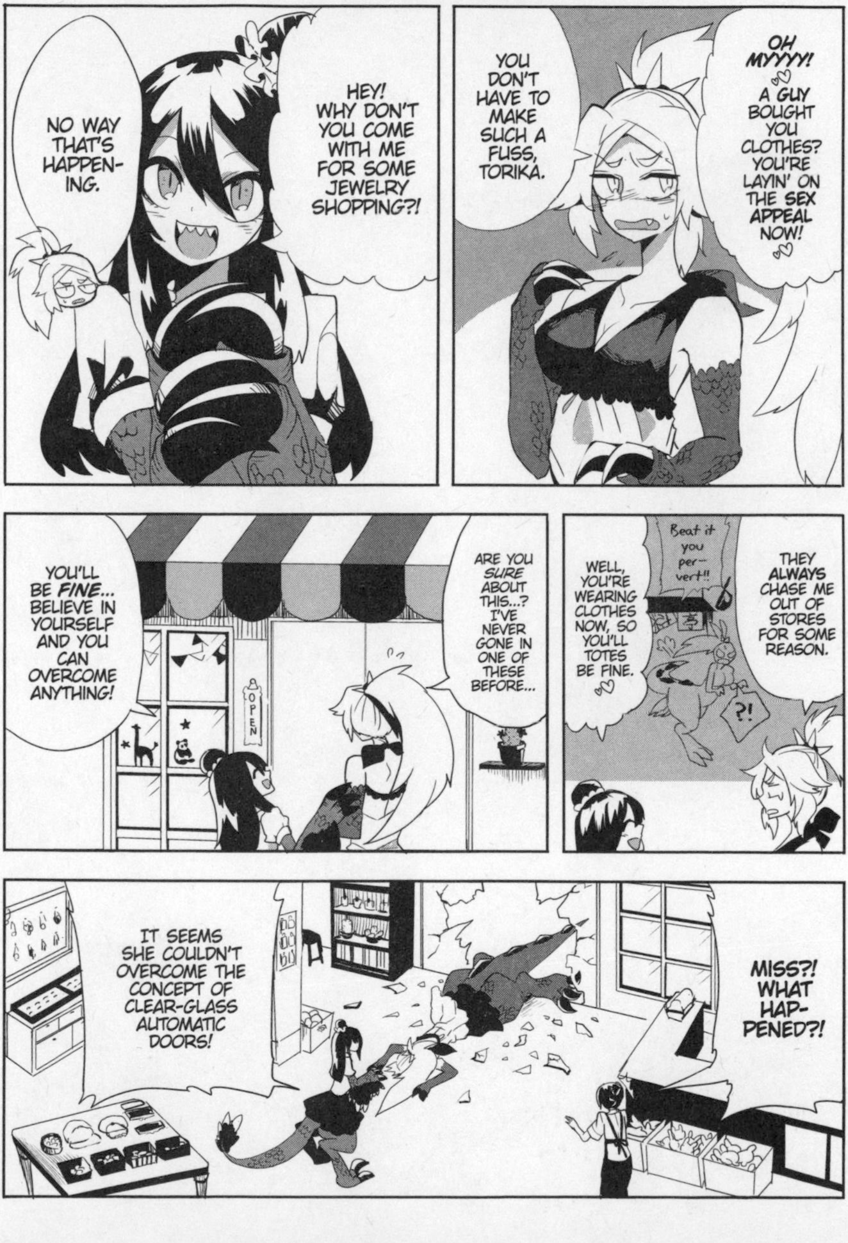

OH MYYYY! A GUY BOUGHT YOU CLOTHES? YOU'RE LAYIN' ON THE SEX APPEAL NOW!
YOU DON'T HAVE TO MAKE SUCH A FUSS, TORIKA.
HEY! WHY DON'T YOU COME WITH ME FOR SOME JEWELRY SHOPPING?!
NO WAY THAT'S HAPPEN-ING.
THEY ALWAYS CHASE ME OUT OF STORES FOR SOME REASON.
Beat it you per-vert!!
?!
WELL, YOU'RE WEARING CLOTHES NOW, SO YOU'LL TOTES BE FINE.
ARE YOU SURE ABOUT THIS...? I'VE NEVER GONE IN ONE OF THESE BEFORE...
OPEN
YOU'LL BE FINE... BELIEVE IN YOURSELF AND YOU CAN OVERCOME ANYTHING!
MISS?! WHAT HAP-PENED?!
IT SEEMS SHE COULDN'T OVERCOME THE CONCEPT OF CLEAR-GLASS AUTOMATIC DOORS!

My Girlfriend is a

T-REX

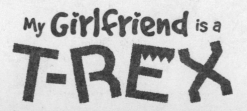

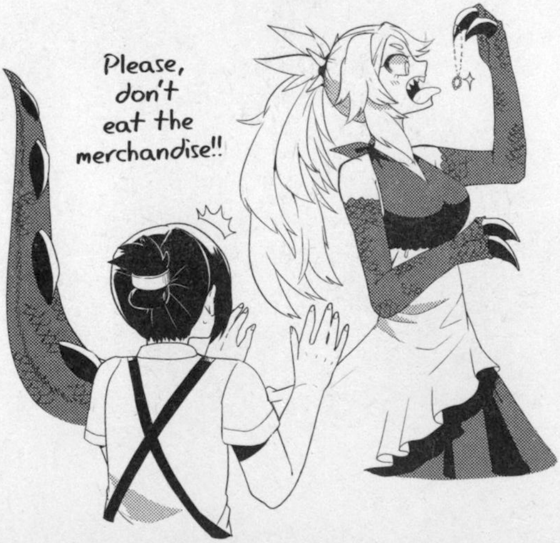
Please, don't eat the merchandise!!

CHAPTER 2

MY RAINY-DAY GIRLFRIEND

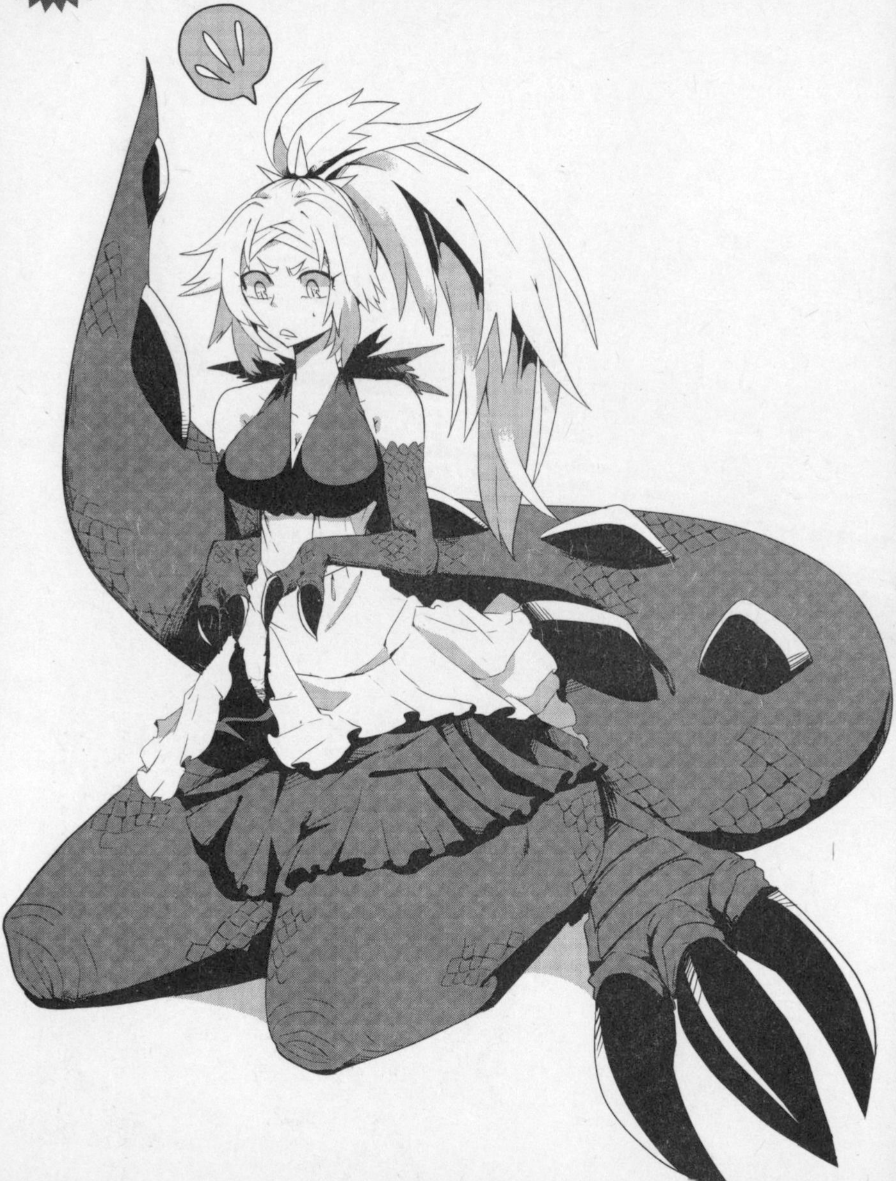

THE TYRANT'S COMPASSION

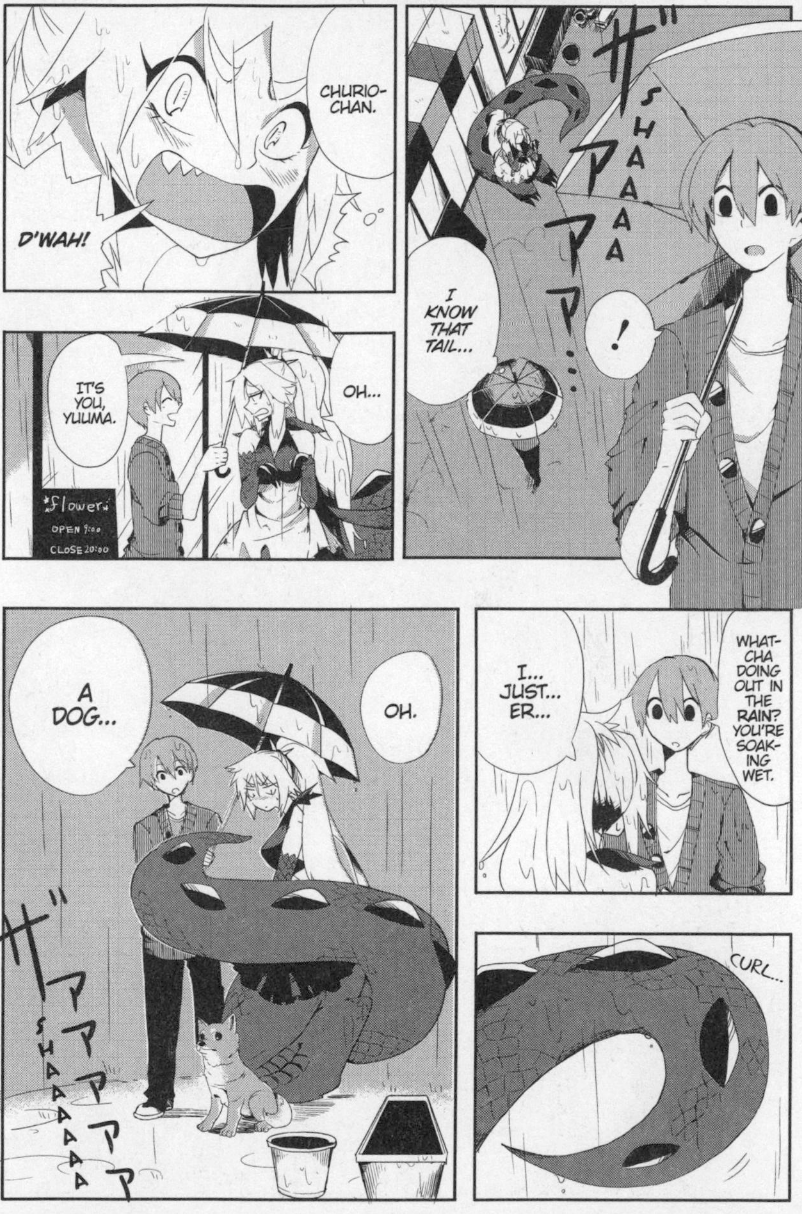
ザアアア
SHAAAAA
I KNOW THAT TAIL...
!
CHURIO-CHAN.
D'WAH!
OH...
IT'S YOU, YUUMA.
flower
OPEN 9:00
CLOSE 20:00
WHATCHA DOING OUT IN THE RAIN? YOU'RE SOAKING WET.
I... JUST... ER...
CURL...
OH.
A DOG...
ザアアアア
SHAAAAAA

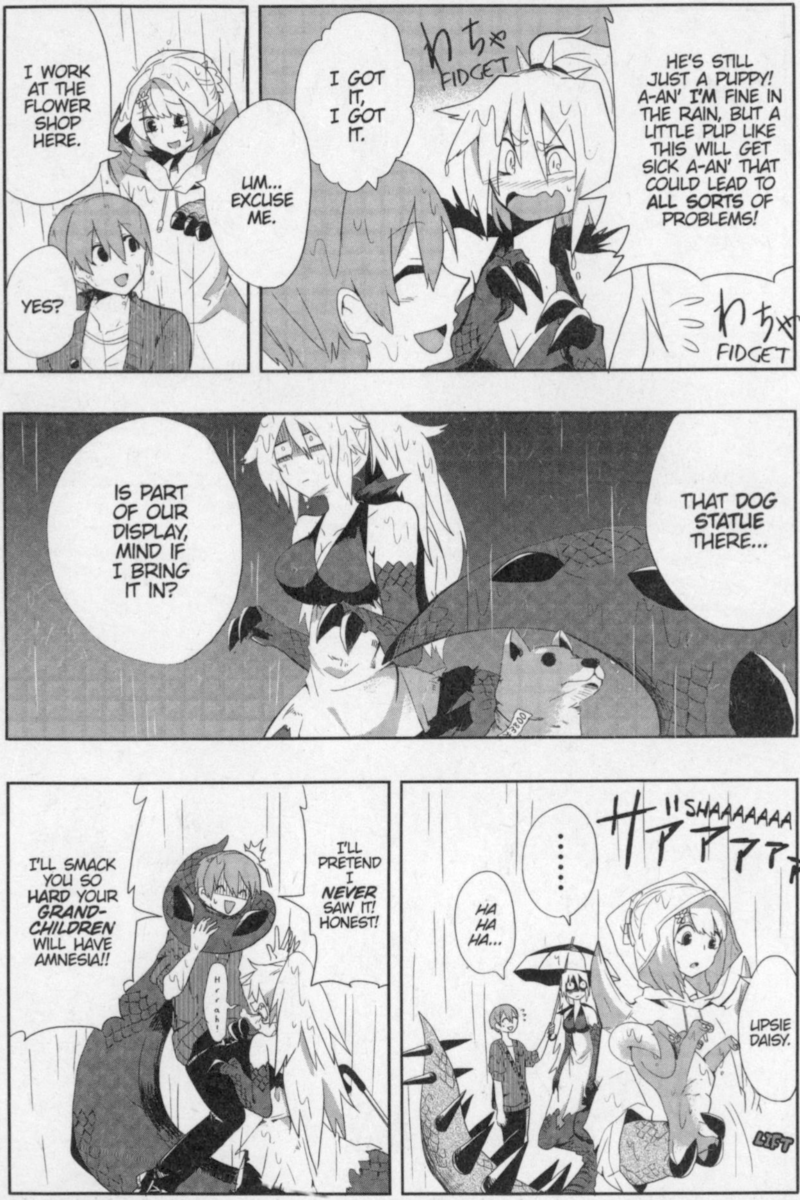
わちゃ FIDGET
HE'S STILL JUST A PUPPY! A-AN' I'M FINE IN THE RAIN, BUT A LITTLE PUP LIKE THIS WILL GET SICK A-AN' THAT COULD LEAD TO ALL SORTS OF PROBLEMS!
I GOT IT, I GOT IT.
わちゃ FIDGET
UM... EXCUSE ME.
YES?
I WORK AT THE FLOWER SHOP HERE.
THAT DOG STATUE THERE...
IS PART OF OUR DISPLAY, MIND IF I BRING IT IN?
サァァァァ SHAAAAAAA
......
HA HA HA...
UPSIE DAISY.
LIFT
I'LL PRETEND I NEVER SAW IT! HONEST!
I'LL SMACK YOU SO HARD YOUR GRAND-CHILDREN WILL HAVE AMNESIA!!
Hrrah!

EARLY DISCOVERY

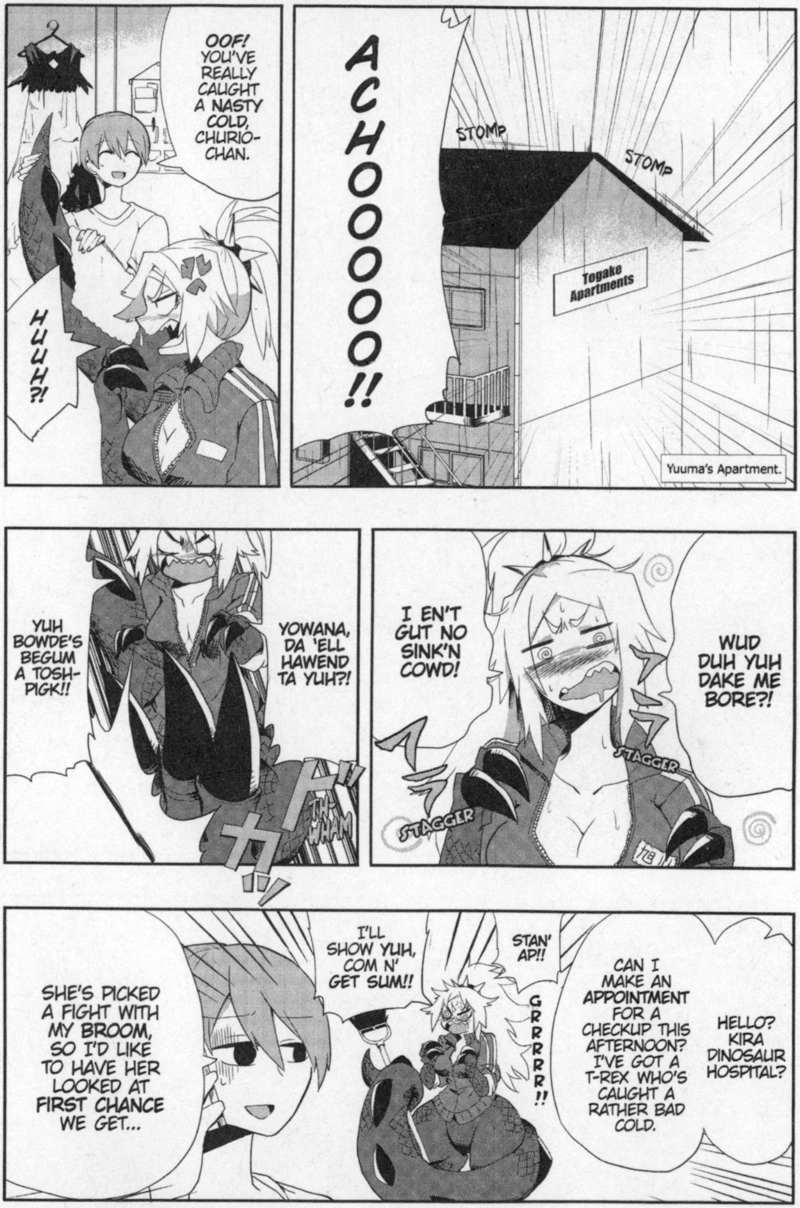
ACHOOOOOOO!!
STOMP
STOMP
Togake Apartments
Yuuma's Apartment.
OOF! YOU'VE REALLY CAUGHT A NASTY COLD, CHURIO-CHAN.
HUUH?!
WUD DUH YUH DAKE ME BORE?!
I EN'T GUT NO SINK'N COWD!
STAGGER
STAGGER
YOWANA, DA 'ELL HAWEND TA YUH?!
YUH BOWDE'S BEGUM A TOSH-PIGK!!
TH-WHAM
HELLO? KIRA DINOSAUR HOSPITAL?
CAN I MAKE AN APPOINTMENT FOR A CHECKUP THIS AFTERNOON? I'VE GOT A T-REX WHO'S CAUGHT A RATHER BAD COLD.
STAN' AP!!
GRRRRR!!
I'LL SHOW YUH, COM N' GET SUM!!
SHE'S PICKED A FIGHT WITH MY BROOM, SO I'D LIKE TO HAVE HER LOOKED AT FIRST CHANCE WE GET...

SHOTS

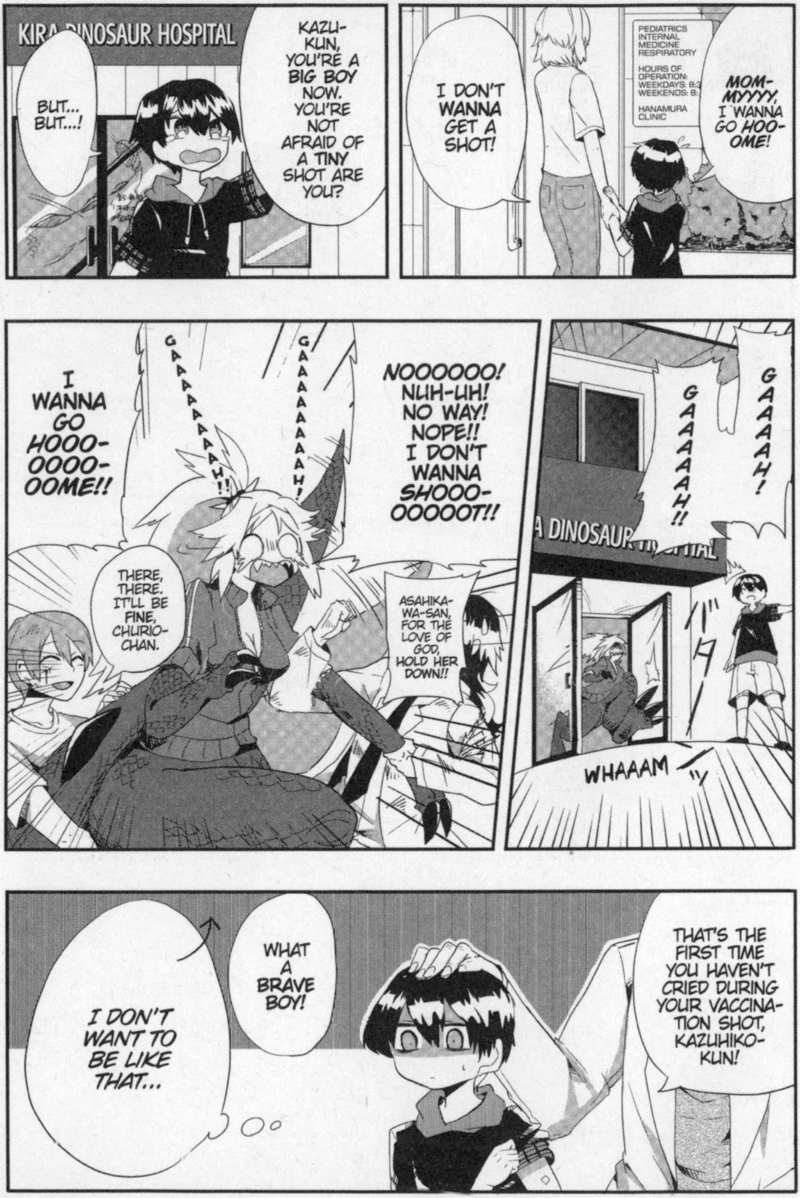
PEDIATRICS
INTERNAL MEDICINE
RESPIRATORY
HOURS OF OPERATION:
WEEKDAYS: 8:3
WEEKENDS: 8:
HANAMURA CLINIC
MOM-MYYYY, I WANNA GO HOO-OME!
I DON'T WANNA GET A SHOT!
KIRA DINOSAUR HOSPITAL
KAZU-KUN, YOU'RE A BIG BOY NOW. YOU'RE NOT AFRAID OF A TINY SHOT ARE YOU?
BUT... BUT...!
GAAAAAH!
GAAAAAAH!!
A DINOSAUR HOSPITAL
WHAAAM
NOOOOOO! NUH-UH! NO WAY! NOPE!! I DON'T WANNA SHOOO-OOOOOT!!
GAAAAAAAAAAH!
GAAAAAAAAAH!!
I WANNA GO HOOO-OOOO-OOME!!
ASAHIKA-WA-SAN, FOR THE LOVE OF GOD, HOLD HER DOWN!!
THERE, THERE. IT'LL BE FINE, CHURIO-CHAN.
THAT'S THE FIRST TIME YOU HAVEN'T CRIED DURING YOUR VACCINA-TION SHOT, KAZUHIKO-KUN!
WHAT A BRAVE BOY!
I DON'T WANT TO BE LIKE THAT...

INJECTION TIME

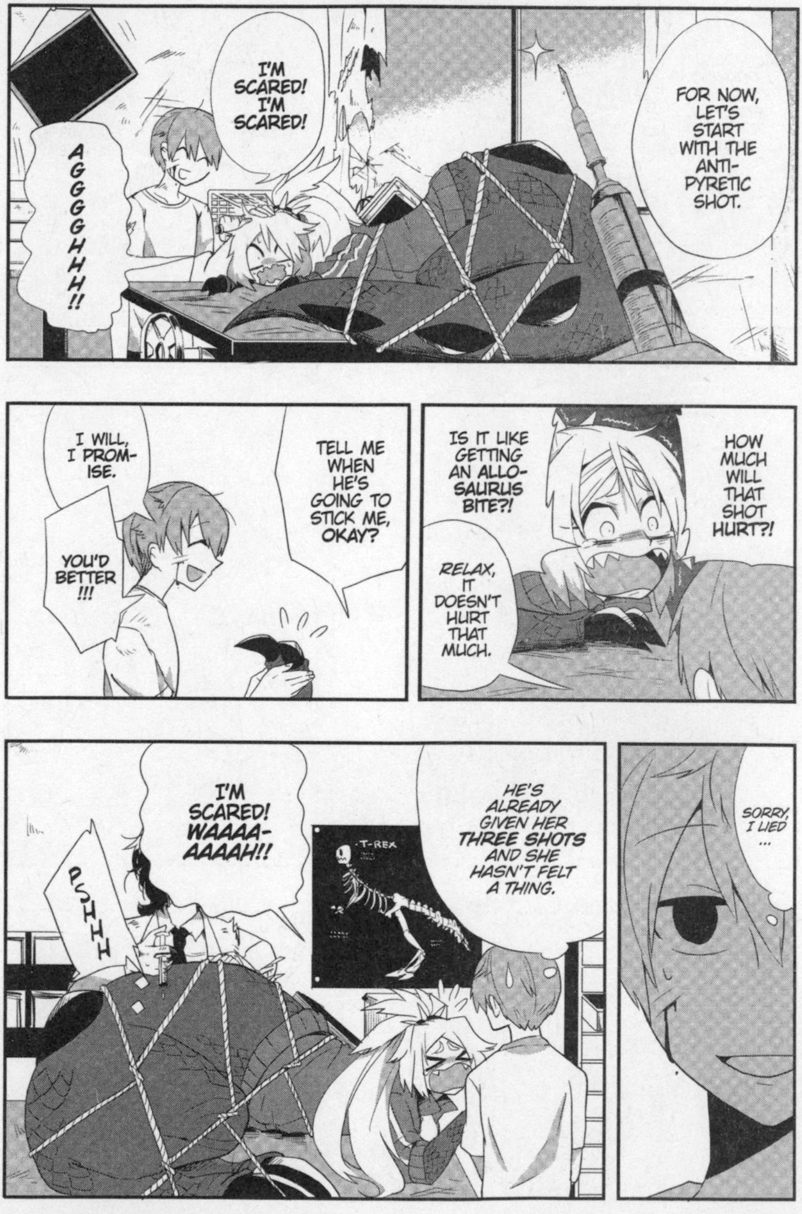
FOR NOW, LET'S START WITH THE ANTI-PYRETIC SHOT.
I'M SCARED! I'M SCARED!
AGGGGHHH!!
HOW MUCH WILL THAT SHOT HURT?!
IS IT LIKE GETTING AN ALLO-SAURUS BITE?!
RELAX, IT DOESN'T HURT THAT MUCH.
TELL ME WHEN HE'S GOING TO STICK ME, OKAY?
I WILL, I PROMISE.
YOU'D BETTER!!!
SORRY, I LIED ...
HE'S ALREADY GIVEN HER THREE SHOTS AND SHE HASN'T FELT A THING.
I'M SCARED! WAAAA-AAAAH!!
T-REX
PSHHH

PROMISES ARE ABSOLUTE

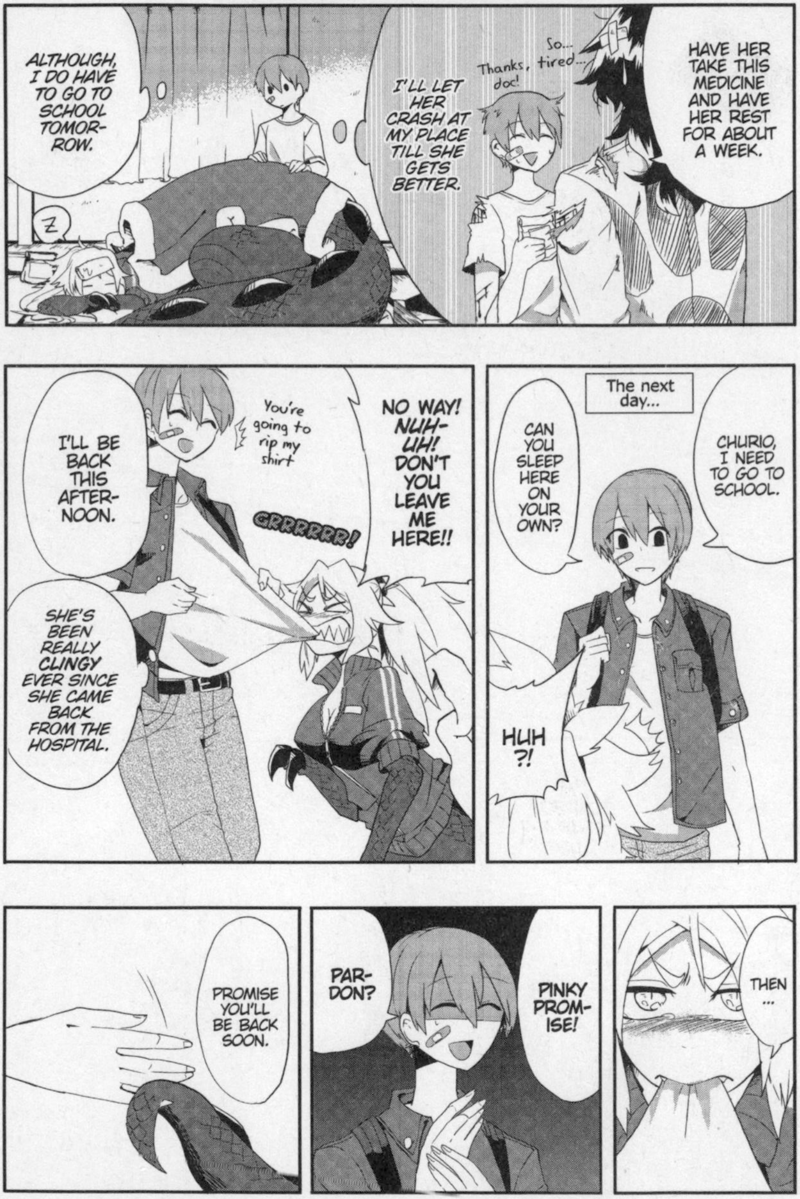
HAVE HER TAKE THIS MEDICINE AND HAVE HER REST FOR ABOUT A WEEK.
So... tired...
Thanks, doc!
I'LL LET HER CRASH AT MY PLACE TILL SHE GETS BETTER.
ALTHOUGH, I DO HAVE TO GO TO SCHOOL TOMORROW.
Z
The next day...
CHURIO, I NEED TO GO TO SCHOOL.
CAN YOU SLEEP HERE ON YOUR OWN?
HUH?!
NO WAY! NUH-UH! DON'T YOU LEAVE ME HERE!!
You're going to rip my shirt
GRRRRRR!
I'LL BE BACK THIS AFTERNOON.
SHE'S BEEN REALLY CLINGY EVER SINCE SHE CAME BACK FROM THE HOSPITAL.
THEN...
PINKY PROMISE!
PARDON?
PROMISE YOU'LL BE BACK SOON.

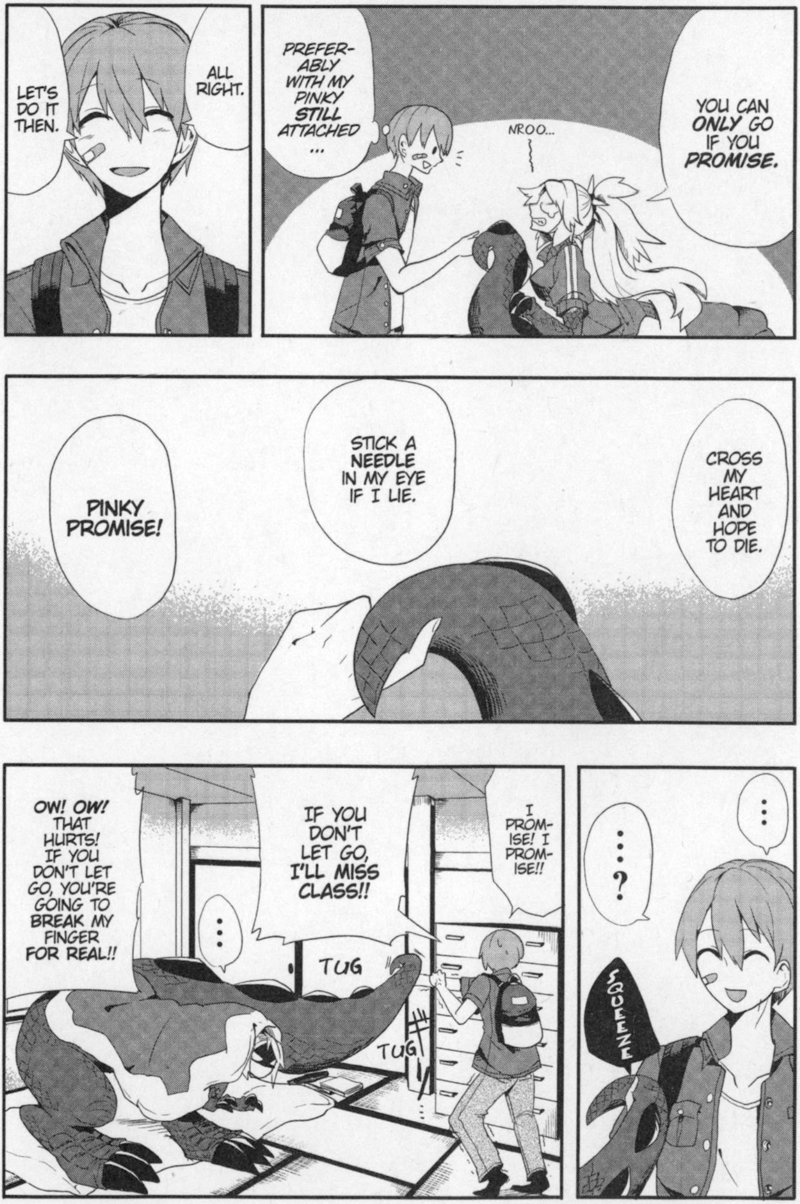
YOU CAN ONLY GO IF YOU PROMISE.
NROO...
PREFERABLY WITH MY PINKY STILL ATTACHED...
ALL RIGHT.
LET'S DO IT THEN.
CROSS MY HEART AND HOPE TO DIE.
STICK A NEEDLE IN MY EYE IF I LIE.
PINKY PROMISE!
...
...?
SQUEEZE
I PROMISE! I PROMISE!!
IF YOU DON'T LET GO, I'LL MISS CLASS!!
OW! OW! THAT HURTS! IF YOU DON'T LET GO, YOU'RE GOING TO BREAK MY FINGER FOR REAL!!
...
TUG
TUG

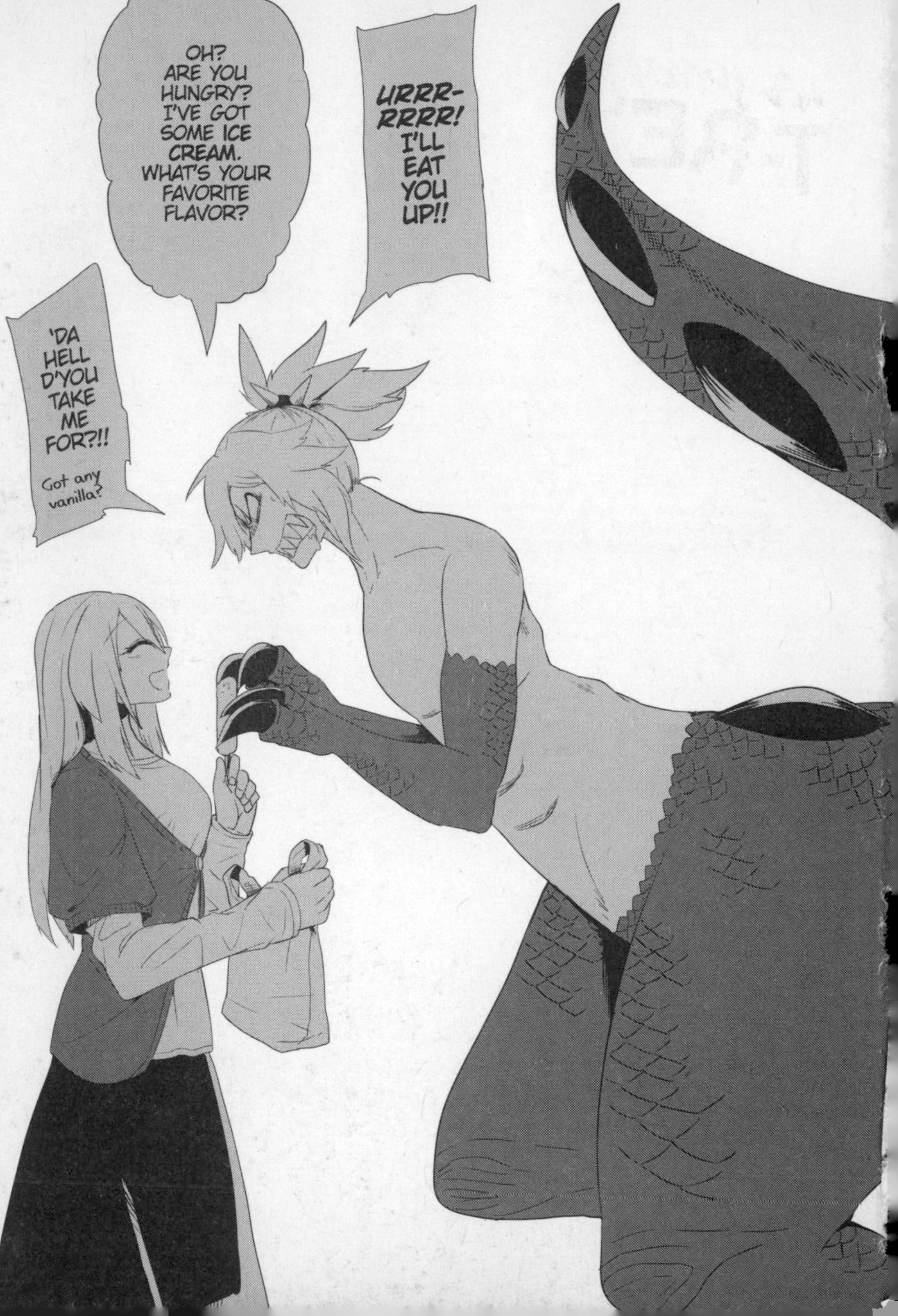
URRRR-RRRR! I'LL EAT YOU UP!!
OH? ARE YOU HUNGRY? I'VE GOT SOME ICE CREAM. WHAT'S YOUR FAVORITE FLAVOR?
'DA HELL D'YOU TAKE ME FOR?!!
Got any vanilla?

AFTERWORD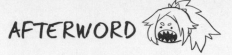

This is my very first manga!! I'm so happy, my heart is racing and I still can't believe it all! I am so thrilled that you guys enjoyed reading *My Girlfriend is a T-Rex!*

I've been a huge fan of monster girls, so before I knew it...it was like I became addicted to them! You can be sure that I'll be drawing up some more stuff of the everyday lives of strange girls!
Hope to see you all in volume 2!

To my managers who supported me,

To all the people at genepixiv,

To Mayumi Tsuge-chan who helped me out,

To all of you who kept cheering me on,

And to everyone who read this manga...

Thank you all so much!

さん ぞう
三 三

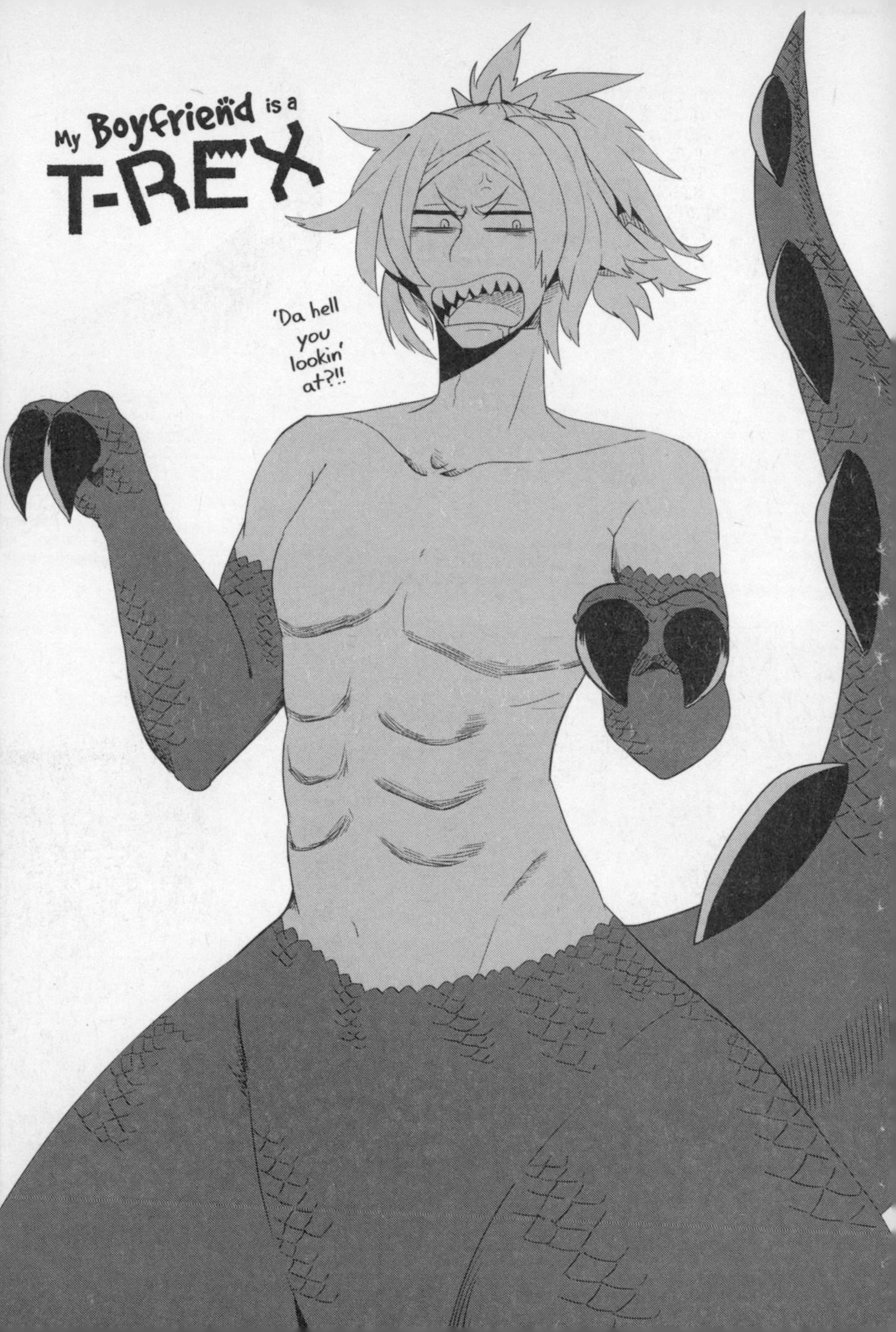
My Boyfriend is a T-REX
'Da hell you lookin' at?!!

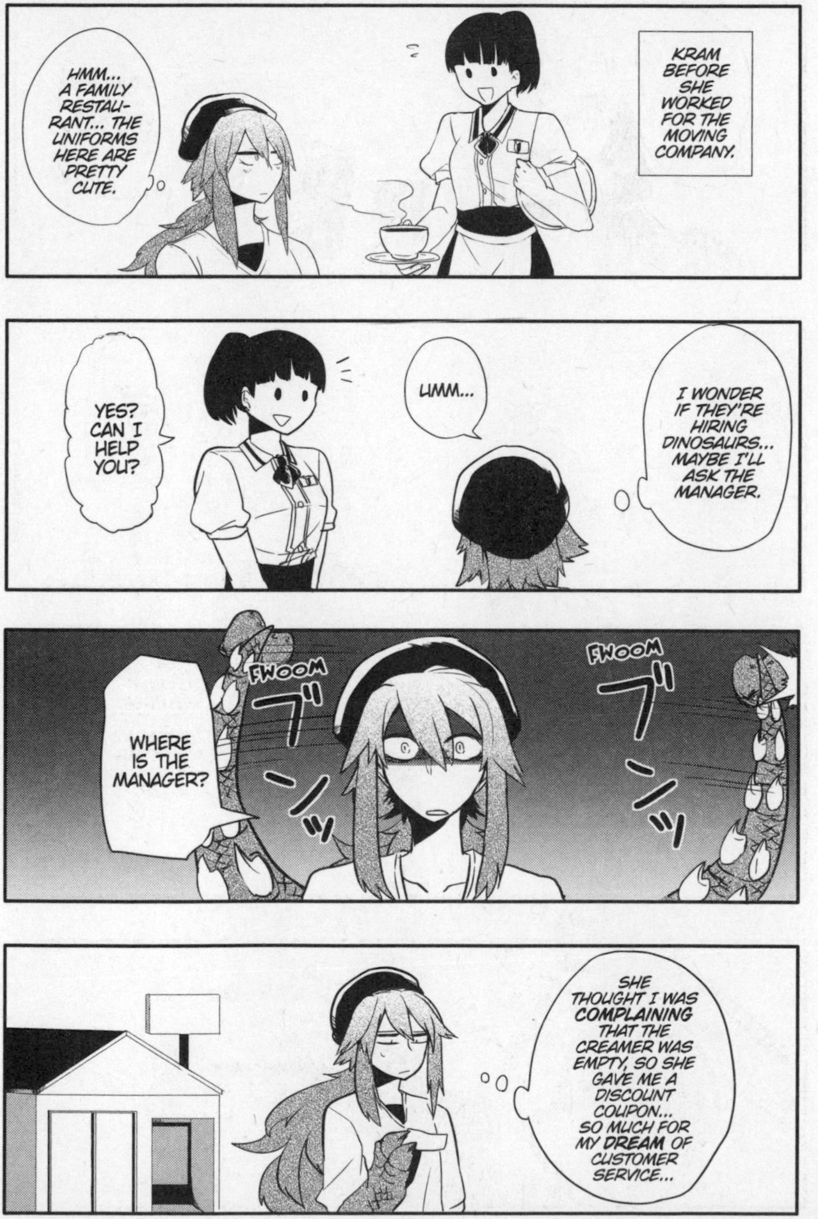
KRAM BEFORE SHE WORKED FOR THE MOVING COMPANY.
HMM... A FAMILY RESTAU-RANT... THE UNIFORMS HERE ARE PRETTY CUTE.
I WONDER IF THEY'RE HIRING DINOSAURS... MAYBE I'LL ASK THE MANAGER.
UMM...
YES? CAN I HELP YOU?
FWOOM
ブンッ
FWOOM
ブンッ
WHERE IS THE MANAGER?
SHE THOUGHT I WAS **COMPLAINING** THAT THE CREAMER WAS EMPTY, SO SHE GAVE ME A DISCOUNT COUPON... SO MUCH FOR MY **DREAM** OF CUSTOMER SERVICE...